D1438829

BURNS—BY HIMSELF

BURNS—BY HIMSELF

*The Poet-ploughman's Life in his own words—pieced
together from his diaries, letters & poems—with
comments by his Brothers & his Sister & a
few other contemporaries*

*arbitrarily arranged
to form a continuous story
with 68 illustrations*

by

KEITH HENDERSON

METHUEN—PUBLISHERS—LONDON

36 Essex Street, Strand, W.C.2

First published in 1938

PRINTED IN GREAT BRITAIN

W. and R.,

Since you, my dearest sister and brother, have agreed that this modest labour of love should be dedicated (whatever that may mean) to the land of our

FOREFATHERS,

it only now remains to make a list of those who have so kindly given me their help in various ways. The list begins, of course, with

HELEN.

After her it goes on alphabetically and ever gratefully thus

MR. IAIN CAMPBELL, *Spean Bridge*; MRS. CATHERINE CARSWELL, *Glasgow*; MISS HELEN CRUICKSHANK, *Edinburgh*; MR. STANLEY CURSITER, *Edinburgh*; MR. ROBERT DINWIDDIE, *Dumfries*; COLONEL T. C. DUNLOP, *Sauchrie*; MR. NEIL M. GUNN, *Dingwall*; MISS ANNIE JOHNSTON, *Isle of Barra*; REV. A. MACKINTOSH, *Roy Bridge*; R. R. MONSIGNOR MACKINTOSH, *Roy Bridge*; MR. HASWELL MILLER, *Edinburgh*; MISS EUNICE MURRAY, *Cardross*; MRS. RYAN, *Roy Bridge*; MAJOR I. H. MACKAY SCOBIE, *Edinburgh*

INTRODUCTION

ROBERT BURNS is one of the great figures. There are books about him by the hundred. Read Catherine Carswell, brilliant as ever; or romantic John Lindsey; or Hecht, cool and accurate; or the indispensable Chambers-Wallace in four volumes complete; those for a start. His eager biographers have explained Burns, exposed him, excused him, sanctified him, psychoanalysed him. He has been medically examined. But if only—if only he had written an autobiography.

Did he never think of that? He did once make a beginning in a letter. There are few details, unfortunately. In other letters, however, and scattered about in the poems and diaries, there are other details, plenty. He was never tired of telling about himself. And, I thought suddenly—why not get him to tell the whole of his own story in his own words? At the worst, the idea (or am I mistaken?) is new. At the best, it might be something much more, a conception of the man as he saw or thought he saw himself.

For the assistance of readers beyond Scotland, I have ventured, though regretfully, to simplify some of the spelling, but not more than a word here and there, such as ' sunny ' for ' sinny ', ' full ' for ' fu ' (which can sound like something else), ' country ' for ' kintra '. Even in his own day, most Highlanders and a good few Lowlanders were bothered by the queer spelling.

When at twenty-seven he found himself, a ploughman, standing correctly enough dressed under the chandeliers of Edinburgh, he was facing not only his admirers but also his critics. The latter were not tactful. This is the sort of thing that appeared in the Press:

' One bar indeed his birth and education have opposed to his fame, the language in which most of these poems are written. Even in Scotland the provincial dialect he has used is now read with a difficulty which greatly damps the pleasure of the reader; in England it cannot be read at all without such constant reference to a glossary as nearly to destroy the pleasure.'

As a result of the Union (of which he disapproved) persons of refinement north of the Border were growing more and more anxious to acquire the latest London accent. This seems remarkably silly to us now. But the fact remains that at any time and in any language an unfamiliar dialect *written down phonetically* is troublesome.

If the purist be further disturbed at the shortening of long prose periods and at finding favourite passages taken out of order, I plead my main purpose and a desire to make all meanings plain. My own brief explanatory and connecting sentences appear but rarely and then always within square brackets. Not a word of what Burns wrote has been changed, not a word has been added, with the harmless exception of an ' and ' or a ' but ' now and then.

In the margins, I had hoped to include numbered references to the Henley-Henderson edition of the Poems, and to the Fergusson edition of the Life and Works. This, however, I agreed with the publishers, might have given the book a somewhat Biblical appearance, which was far from my thoughts.

But enough of technicalities. You are now going to hear the authentic voice of this oddly affectionate ' Robin ' as he called himself, ' that impudent staring fellow ' as a superior contemporary called him. The only other speakers who will occasionally be allowed to put in a few comments are his second brother Gilbert, his youngest brother William, his youngest sister Isbal, and one or two selected friends and acquaintances. Well, that, I think, must be all for the present. And here is Mr. Burns.

KEITH HENDERSON *Glen Nevis, Inverness-shire*

CONTENTS

I

POVERTY AND OBSCURITY

I have not the most distant pretensions to being what the guardians of escutchions call a Gentleman. I am not R. B. Esqre. I am simply Mr. Robert Burns at your service. I was bred to the Plough. When I matriculate in the Herald's Office, I intend that my supporters shall be two Sloths, my crest a Slow-worm and my motto 'Deil tak the foremost'.

My forefathers rented land of the noble Keiths [the hereditary Earls Marischall of Scotland] and had the honour to share their fate with them [in 1715, my grandfather being at that time gardener to the Earl Marischall at Inverugie Castle].

Loyal and disloyal I take to be merely *relative* terms; but those who dare welcome Ruin for what they sincerely believe to be the cause of their king and country are honourable men.

Though my Fathers had not illustrious honours and vast properties to hazard in the contest; though they left their humble cottages only to add so many units more to the unnoted croud that followed their Leaders; yet what they could they did and what they had they lost.

I

I mention this because it threw my father on the world at large.

I have met few to equal him, a tender father, a generous friend. But ungainly integrity and headlong ungovernable irrascibility are disqualifying. Consequently I was born [at Alloway in Ayrshire, 25th January 1759] a very poor man's son.

My father was advanced in life when he married. I was the eldest of seven children.

['One very stormy morning,' says Gilbert, 'when Robert was nine or 'ten days old, a little before daylight, a part of the gable fell out, and the rest 'appeared so shattered that my mother, with Robert, had to be carried 'through the storm to a neighbour's house, where they remained a week 'until our own dwelling was adjusted.

'The house (built with clay) consisted of a kitchen in one end and a 'room in the other with a fireplace and chimney. And my father had con- 'structed a concealed bed in the kitchen with a small closet at the end.

' When altogether cast over, outside and in, with lime, it had a neat comfort-
' able appearance, such as no family of the same rank, even in the present
' improved style of living, would think themselves ill lodged in.']

Honest folk of creditable stock are not always so wretched as one would
think. Indeed they're mostly wonderfully contented, their faithful wives
their dearest comfort and young ones ranting through the house or at play
by the fire-side, wonderfully well contented—while old Baudrons [the cat]
sits there washing her face with her loof.

> Blythe hae I been on yon hill
> As the lambs before me;
> Careless ilka thought and free
> As the breeze flew o'er me.

[A note in the handwriting of ' the tender father, the generous friend'
reads—' I have a family of four sons and three douthers, all with me in the
' farm-way. My eldest son is named Robert; the second Gilbert; the third
' William. My eldest douther is named Agnes; my youngest is named
' Isbal.']

For the first six or seven years of my life my father was gardener to a
worthy gentleman of small estate in the neighbourhood of Ayr. Had my
father continued in that situation, I must have been marched off to be one
of the little underlings about a farm-house; but it was his dearest wish and
prayer to have it in his power to keep his children under his own eye.

[' In 1765', says Gilbert, ' we learned with a Mr. Murdoch' (at a small
school a mile away, the teacher himself being only 18) ' to read tolerably
' well and to write a little.']

I have just now drawn a thumb-stall on my finger, which I unfortunately
gashed in mending my pen.

I want someone to laugh with me, someone to be grave with me, someone to please me and at times no doubt to admire my acuteness and penetration. For these reasons I am determined to make these pages my confidant.

I think a lock and key security at least equal to the bosom of any friend whatever.

This faithful account of my life, my own private story—and it is truth, every word of it—will shew what character of a man I am. My amours, my rambles and my poems shall be occasionally inserted. I shall every leisure hour take up my pen and gossip away whatever comes first, zig here, zag there, happy-go-lucky.

Alas ! not infrequently, when my heart is in a wandring humour, I live past scenes over again. My bosom achs with tender recollections. I hear a spinning wheel thrum. My mother sings a favorite lullaby to a Gaelic air. And there lonely in the ingle sit I in my little early way eying the smoke-reek that fills the auld clay biggin. The elfine lamp of my glimmerous understanding shines. I hear the restless rats squeak about the rafters. The red peat gleams. The gale rustles and whistles . . .

> November chill blaws loud wi' angry sugh.
>   The shortning winter-day is near a close.
>   The toil-worn Cotter * frae his labour goes—   [*My father]
> This night his weekly moil is at an end,
>   Collects his spades, his mattocks and his hoes,
> Hoping the morn in ease and rest to spend
> And weary o'er the moor his course does hameward bend.
>
> At length his lonely cot appears in view
>   Beneath the shelter of an aged tree.
> Th' expectant wee-things, toddlin, stacher through
>   To meet their dad wi' flichterin' noise and glee.
>   His wee-bit ingle blinkin' bonilie
> His clean hearth-stane, his thrifty wifie's smile
>   The lisping infant prattling on his knee,
> Does a' his weary kiaugh and care beguile.

My mother, listening the doors and windows rattle, is darning stockings, spectacles on nose, or with her needle and sheers she makes old clothes look almost as well as new. My father mixes all with admonition. We younkers are warned: 'Mind your duty duly morn and night, lest in 'temptation's path ye gang astray. Implore His counsel.'

And now supper—porridge, with milk from our only cow that beyond the wall snugly chews her cud.

> The chearful supper done, wi' serious face
>   They round the ingle form a circle wide.
> The sire turns o'er wi' patriarchal grace
>   The big ha' Bible, ance *his* father's pride.
> His bonnet rev'rently is laid aside.
> He wales a portion with judicious care
> And 'Let us worship God,' he says with solemn air.

My father [in 1766 when I was seven years of age] now ventured, with the assistance of his generous master, on a small farm [called Mount Oliphant, about two miles from Alloway].

['Mr. Murdoch our teacher', this is Gilbert again, 'once came to spend the night with us at Mount 'Oliphant. He brought us two presents, a small com- 'pendium of English Grammar and the trajedy of Titus 'Andronius. By way of passing the evening he began 'to read the play aloud. We were all attention, till 'presently the whole party was dissolved in tears. A female in the play (I 'have but a confused recollection of it) had her hands chopt off. At 'this, in an agony of distress, we with one voice desired he would read 'no more. My father said it would be needless to leave the play with us. 'Robert said that if it was left he would burn it.']

Though I cost Mr. Murdoch the schoolmaster some thrashings, I made an excellent English scholar and against the years of ten or eleven, I was absolutely a critic in substantives, verbs, and particles.

['Something extraordinary will come from that boy,' Isbal once heard her father say.]

['Nothing', continues Gilbert, 'could be more retired than our general

' manner of living at Mount Oliphant. We rarely saw anybody but the
' members of our own family. There were no boys of our own age in the
' neighbourhood. My father was for some time almost the only companion
' we had. He conversed familiarly on all subjects with us as if we had been
' men and was at great pains, as we accompanied him in the labours of the
' farm, to lead the conversation to such subjects as might increase our
' knowledge or confirm our virtuous habits.

' Robert at the age of thirteen assisted in thrashing the corn. All the
' members of the family exerted themselves to the utmost of their strength—
' and rather beyond it.']

> . . . wi' weary legs,
> Rattlin the corn out owre the rigs.

[' My father came into difficulties which were increased ', Gilbert explains
further, ' by the loss of several of his cattle from accidents or disease.

' To the buffetings of misfortune we could only oppose hard labour and
' the most rigid economy. We lived very sparingly. We had no hired
' farm-servants, male or female.

' The anguish of mind Robert and I felt under these straits was very great
' at our tender years. To think of our father growing old (for he was now
' above fifty), broken down with the long fatigues of his life, with a wife and
' five other children (besides our two selves) produced in our minds sensa-
' tions of the deepest distress and I doubt not but this hard labour and sorrow
' were in a great measure the cause of that depression of spirits with which my
' brother was so often afflicted through his whole life afterwards. At this time
' he was almost constantly afflicted in the evenings with a dull headache.'

' Robert was about fourteen, when my father sent him to Ayr ' (whither
Mr. Murdoch had been transferred) ' to revise his English Grammar. He
' had been there only one week when he was obliged to return to assist in
' the harvest. When the harvest was over he went back to school, where
' he remained two weeks more. This completes the account of Robert's
' school education, excepting one summer quarter some time afterwards, that
' he attended the parish school at Kirkoswald.']

[A boy called John Tennant also attended Mr. Murdoch's school at Ayr.

'Robert and I were favourite pupils of Mr. Murdoch,' he writes. 'Mr.
'Murdoch used to take us alternately to live with him, allowing us a share
'of his bed. He was so anxious to advance his favourite pupils that while
'we were lying with him, he was always taking opportunities of com-

7

' municating knowledge. The intellectual gifts of Robert even at this time
' greatly impressed me, his fellow-scholar.']

[John Murdoch himself writes thus—' I was about eighteen then.
' Robert and his younger brother Gilbert had been grounded a little in
' English before they were put under my care. They both made a rapid
' progress in reading and a tolerable progress in writing. They were
' generally at the upper end of the class.
' Gilbert always appeared to me to possess a more lively imagination
' and to be more of the wit than Robert. Robert's countenance was generally
' grave.
' I attempted to teach them a little church-music. Here they were left far
' behind by all the rest of the school. Robert's ear in particular was remark-
' ably dull and his voice untunable. It was long before I could get them to
' distinguish one tune from another.
' In 1773 Robert came to board and lodge with me (at Ayr) for the
' purpose of revising his English grammar &c. that he might be better
' qualified to instruct his brothers and sisters at home. He was now with
' me day and night, in school, at all meals and in all my walks, a very apt
' pupil and consequently an agreeable companion. I did not ' (after his
return to the farm) ' lose sight of him, but was a frequent visitant at his
' father's house, when I had my half-holiday. Robert always had a hundred
' questions to ask me. Mrs. Burnes too was of the party as much as possible.
' At all times and in all companies she listened to her husband with a more
' marked attention than to anybody else. When under the necessity of being
' absent while he was speaking, she seemed to regret as a real loss that she had
' missed what the good man said. And I can by no means wonder that she
' so highly esteemed him. I have always considered William Burnes as by
' far the best of the human race that ever I had the pleasure of being acquainted
' with.
' He was a kind and affectionate father. He took care to find fault but
' seldom and therefore when he did rebuke, his look of disapprobation was
' felt, a reproof severely so ; and a stripe from the tawz not only gave heart-
' felt pain, but produced a loud lamentation and brought forth a flood of
' tears.']

[But Mrs. Burns used to declare that ' Mr. Burns never gave what might

' be called a *beating* to any of his children but once, when he punished his
' eldest daughter Agnes for showing obstinacy while he was teaching her to
' read.']

[John Murdoch never saw him really angry but twice; the one time it
was ' for not reaping as he desired ' and the other time it was with a man
' for using smutty inuendoes '.]

[' My father', says Isbal, ' was a thin sinewy figure, about five feet eight
' or nine inches in height, somewhat bent with toil, with a dark swarthy
' complexion and thin haffet-locks. My mother was about the ordinary
' height, a well-made sonsy figure, with a beautiful red and white complexion,
' red hair, dark eyes and eyebrows and a fine square forehead. With all her
' good qualities—and they were many—her temper was at times irascible.']

My mother [Robert now resumes] in her girlish years lived a while with
an old grand-uncle. The good old man was long blind ere he died. His
most voluptuous enjoyment was to sit and cry while my mother would sing.
And I remember a grand-aunt. She used to sing a song by the name of
' Liggeram cosh, my bonie wee lass ', to the tune of a well-known reel, ' The
Quaker's Wife '. An old Highland gentleman, a deep antiquarian, has
told me that the air is a Gaelic air.
[The Gaelic was still spoken in south Ayr-shire till the beginning of the
18th century.]
In these my boyish days I owed much to an old maid, Betty Davidson,
my mother's cousin [' who often ' Isbal says, ' stayed with us at Alloway and
' at Mount Oliphant. She was most assiduous in spinning, carding and
' doing all kinds of good offices that were in her power. She was of a
' mirthful temperament and therefore a great favourite with us children.']
She, Betty Davidson, had, I suppose, the largest collection in the county
of tales and songs concerning devils, ghosts, fairies, witches, warlocks,
spunkies, elf-candles, dead-lights, wraiths, apparitions, cantraips, giants,
inchanted towers and dragons, bogles by the eerie side of an old thorn in
a dreary glen, brownies summoned by cock-crowing to an ample cog of
substantial brose, kelpies haunting the ford in the starless night. All this
had so strong an effect on my imagination, that to this hour in my nocturnal

rambles I sometimes keep a sharp look-out in suspicious places. And though nobody can be more sceptical in such matters than I, yet it often takes an effort of philosophy to shake off these idle terrors.

Warlocks and witches
Ye midnight bitches!

Poverty and Obscurity

My grannie often told me that the Devil (or in her more classical phrase SPUNKIE) rode on Will-o'-wisp, here awa there awa through the mosses and moors. And I've heard her say that he likes straying in lonely glens or where old ruined castles nod to the moon. When twilight summoned her to her prayers, douce, reverend, honest woman, she often heard Spunkie rustling through the boortrees [the elder bushes].

> In days when daisies deck the ground
>   And blackbirds whistle clear,
> With honest joy our hearts will bound
>   To see the coming year.

When I think on the lightsome days I spent, adrift after some wayward pursuit, arranging wild-flowers in fantastical nosegays, tracing the grass-hopper to his haunt by his chirping song, watching the frisks of the little minnows in the sunny pool, or hunting after the intrigues of wanton butterflies . . .

> The trout within yon wimpling burn
>   Glides swift, a silver dart,
> And safe beneath the shady thorn
>   Defies the angler's art.
> My life was once that careless stream,
>   That wanton trout was I.

Such the pleasures I enjoyed. O enviable early days, how ill exchanged for riper times! How happy have I been. And since so little of that scantling portion of time called the Life of Man is sacred to happiness, we must *catch the moments as they fly.*

> Like schoolboys at th' expected warning
>   We frisk away,
> Cold-pausing Caution's lessons scorning,
>   To joy and play.
> We wander there, we wander here,
> We eye the rose upon the brier,

Unmindful that the thorn is near
Among the leaves:
And though the puny wound appear
Short while it grieves.

The earliest song I remember to have got by heart was ' O Willy, weel I mind'. Betty Davidson sung it to me and I picked up every word at first hearing. And there was another song ' Oh saw ye my Peggy, high kilted was she', a song familiar from the cradle to every Scottish ear.

At these years I was a good deal noted for a retentive memory, a stubborn, sturdy something in my disposition and an enthusiastic idiot piety. I say idiot piety because I was then but a child.

I remember, and 'tis *almost* the earliest thing I do remember, when I was quite a boy, one day in church being enraged at seeing a young creature, one of the maids at the big house, rise from the mouth of a pew to give way to that bloated son of wealth her Master, an ugly, stupid, purse-proud monster, who waddled surlily past her. The girl was very pretty.

The first two books I ever read in private and which gave me more pleasure than any other two books I have ever read since, were a Life of Hannibal [borrowed from the blacksmith] and a History of Sir William Wallace.

Hannibal gave my young ideas such a turn that I used to strut in raptures up and down after the recruiting drum and bagpipe and wish myself tall enough to be a soldier.

The bonniest lad that e'er I saw,
Bonie laddie, Highland laddie,
Wore a plaid and was full braw,
Bonie Highland laddie.
On his head a bonnet blue . . .

A sodger laddie! Drum and bagpipe! Bold, soldier-featured boys, they strode along. Thus early in life I reckoned on a recruiting drum as my Forlorn Hope.

For glory is the sodger's prize,
The sodger's wealth is honour.

And as for that History of Sir William Wallace, it poured a Scottish prejudice in my veins, which will boil along them till the flood-gates of life shut in eternal rest. I remember in particular a fine summer Sunday, the only day in the week in my power, I walked half a dozen miles to the Leglen Wood [one of Wallace's retreats] with as much devout enthusiasm as ever pilgrim did, to explore every den and dell where I could suppose my heroic countryman to have sheltered. I recollect that my heart glowed with a wish to be able to make a song on him for poor old Scotland's sake.

My dear native soil, long may thy hardy sons be blest with health and peace.

> . . . Independent, unconquered and free
> Her bright course of glory for ever shall run
> For brave Caledonia *immortal* must be.

How readily we get into prattle upon a subject dear to our hearts !

Bred and educated in the principles of reason and common-sense, I made shift to unravel Euclid's Elements of Geometry by my father's fireside in the winter evenings of the first season that I held the Plough.

During my ploughboy days our vicinity to Ayr was of great advantage to me. My social disposition was without bounds or limits. I formed many connections with younkers who possessed superior advantages and who were shortly to appear on that stage where I, alas, was destined to drudge behind the scenes. At these green years the young noblesse and gentry have no just sense of the immense distance between them and their ragged play-fellows. It takes a few dashes into the world to give the young Great Man that proper, decent, unnoticing disregard for the poor insignificant, stupid devils the peasantry around him.

My Superiors never insulted the clouterly appearance of my ploughboy carcase, the two extremes of which were often exposed to the inclemencies of all the seasons. They would give me stray volumes of books. And ONE helped me to a little French.

Parting with these my young friends and benefactors was often to me a sore affliction. When *they* were all striking off with eager hope, I saw myself alone,

> The thresher's weary flinging-tree *   [*Flail]
> The lee-lang day had tired me . . .

But although the twig will easily take a bent, it will as easily return to its former state—and the merry ploughboy cheers his team again.

In my fifteenth autumn ['At fifteen', writes Gilbert, 'Robert was the 'principal labourer on the farm'] my partner in the labors of Harvest—in accordance with our country custom—was a bewitching creature [Nellie Kilpatrick], who just counted an autumn less. She was a bonie, sweet, sonsie lass. In short she altogether unwittingly initiated me in a certain delicious Passion, which in spite of acid disappointment I hold to be the first of human joys, our dearest pleasure here below. I never expressly told her that I loved her. Indeed I did not well know myself why I liked so much to loiter behind with her when returning in the evening from our labors; why the tones of her voice made my heart-strings thrill like an

Eolian harp; and particularly why my pulse beat such a furious ratann when I looked and fingered over her hand to pick out the nettle-stings and thistles. She sung sweetly. And 'twas her favourite reel to which I first attempted giving rhyme.

'O once I lov'd a bonie lass' is indeed very puerile and silly, but I am always pleased with it as it recalls to my mind those happy days. I was a few months more than my sixteenth year.

These are the fifth, sixth and seventh stanzas. I remember I composed them in a wild enthusiasm of passion, and to this hour I never recollect it but my heart melts and my blood sallies at the remembrance.

> She dresses ay sae clean and neat
>   Both decent and genteel,
> And then there's something in her gait
>   Gars * onie dress look weel.   [*Makes]

> A gaudy dress and gentle air
>   May slightly touch the heart,
> But it's innocence and modesty
>   That polishes the dart.

> 'Tis this in Nelly pleases me,
>   'Tis this enchants my soul,
> For absolutely in my breast
>   She reigns without controul.

I was not so presumptive as to imagine that I could make verses like *printed* ones, composed by men who had Greek and Latin; but my girl sung a song which was said to be composed by a small country laird's son on one of his father's maids, with whom he was in love. And I saw no reason why I might not rhyme as well as he, for he had no more scholarship (his father living on the moors) than I had.

Thus with me began Love and Poesy.

> I mind it weel in early date
> When I was beardless young and blate
>   And first could thresh the barn
> Or haud a yokin at the pleugh—
> And tho' forfoughten * sair eneugh   [*Exhausted]
>   Yet unco proud to learn—
> When first amang the yellow corn
>   A man I reckoned was.

My father struggled on. His spirit was soon irritated, but not easily broken. ['He always treated superiors with a becoming respect,' writes John Murdoch, the schoolmaster, ' but he never gave the smallest encourage-

'ment to aristocratical arrogance.'] There was a freedom in our lease in two years more, and to weather these two years we retrenched expenses.

I had early felt some stirrings of Ambition, the blind gropins of a Cyclops round the walls of his cave. But I saw that my father's situation entailed on me perpetual labor.

How unequal the distribution of the good things of this life. The struggle for bread, the dread of poverty, these are matters of which those self-important beings whose intrinsic worthlessness is concealed under the advantages of their rank, have not nor care to have any idea. *They* look indifferently on, make a passing remark and proceed to the next novel occurrence. But the poor and needy, alas, for them what bitter toil and straining. Their nerves, sinews, health, time, nay even a good part of their very thoughts are sold for months and years. They are anxious drudges, weary slaves to the Important Few, who look down on the poor devils with their stupidity and rascality, their impertinent wives and clouterly brats as the lordly bull does on the little dirty ant-hill.

Our gentry care little for delvers, ditchers, and such. They only wonder some folks do not starve. Our Laird rises when he likes. His flunkies answer at the bell. On the Court Day his Factor gets in the rents. And the poor tenant bodies must endure that Factor's abuse. He'll threaten, curse them, and swear he'll apprehend them [for debt] while they, huffed and cuffed and ' disrespeckit ' must stand hearing it all with humble aspect—and fear and tremble lest the Magistracy (thrice-honored and never-enough-to-be-praised) should wind them as a spaniel winds the unsuspecting covey, and hunt them down with the perseverance of a bloodhound.

My father's farm had proved a ruinous bargain : and thus—to clench the curse, [for well he knew the uncertainty of ever emerging from a Debtors' Jail], we too fell into the hands of the Factor. My indignation yet boils at the recollection of the scoundrel's insolent threatening epistles which used to set us all in tears.

The Many, the Swinish Multitude *with their clouterly brats*, are but beasts and like beasts must be goaded in the backside. Poor devils. No wonder that the greater part of men grasp at riches as if poverty were but another word for damnation.

That there *is* an incomprehensible Great Being is, I think, self-evident.

18

But, from the imperfection, nay positive *injustice* in the administration of the world, there must surely be a retributive scene of existence elsewhere.

If, I thought to myself, there be a life beyond the grave, which I trust there is, a glorious world where titles and honours are the disregarded reveries of an idle dream, a world where our hearts will no longer be wounded by the scorn of the proud whom accident has placed above us, then ' how welcome '— [this is from a poem ' The Ruined Farmer ' written at the age of sixteen]— ' how welcome to me were the grave '.

> The prosperous man is asleep
> Nor hears how the whirlwinds sweep.
> But Misery and I must watch . . .
>
> No comfort, no comfort have I.
> How welcome to me were the grave.

My father's spirit was not easily broken, but he was advanced in life and unfit for labour. He could only fight for existance in this miserable manner in the very jaws of a Debtors' Jail.

I could do nothing, though I was a dexterous ploughman for my years. Gilbert the next eldest to me could drive the plough very well too and help me thrash. We must steel our hearts against evils of which we had already had a pretty decent share and with manly fortitude [at the ages of fifteen and sixteen] support what could not be remedied.

We had withstood poverty, oppression and contempt many a hard-labored day already.

> Think ye that sic as you and I
> Wha drudge and drive thro' wet and dry
>   Wi' never ceasing toil,
> Think ye we are less blest than they
> Wha scarcely tent * as in the way   [*Heed]
>   As hardly worth their while ?

I was at this period unacquainted with the ways of the world and perhaps the most awkward being in the parish.

My knowledge of ancient story was gathered from Salmon's and Guthrie's Geographical Grammars; my knowledge of modern manners and of literature and criticism I got from the Spectator. These, with Pope's works, some plays of Shakespear, Tull and Dickson on Agriculture, The Pantheon, Locke's Essay on the Human Understanding, Stackhouse's History of the Bible, Justice's British Gardener's Directory, Boyle's Lectures, Allan Ramsay's works, Taylor's Scripture Doctrine of Original Sin, a Select Collection of English Songs and Hervey's Meditations had been the extent of my reading.

The Collection of Songs was my vade mecum. I pored over them, driving my cart or walking to labor, song by song, verse by verse, unmindful of tomorrow. And in the evening

> I'd sit down o'er my scanty meal
> Be't water-brose or muslin-kale
> Wi' cheerful face.

Poverty and Obscurity

In my seventeenth year, to give my manners a brush, I went to a country dancing-school.

My father had an unaccountable antipathy against these meetings; and many a solitary hour have I *stole* out after the laborious vocations of the day.

The princely may survey our rustic dance with scorn, but are their hearts as light as ours? We danced till the piper-lads were weary—hornpipes, jigs, strathspeys, and reels, threesome reels and foursome reels. We were the hairum-scairum ram-stam boys! Well! Laughing is no bad way of spending one's precious hours and precious breath. Hornpipes, jigs, strathspeys, reels . . .

> Up in the morning's no for me
> Up in the morning early,
> When all the hills are covered in snaw
> I'm sure it's winter fairly.

My father, as I have mentioned, had an unaccountable antipathy against these meetings; and my going was—what to this hour I repent—in absolute defiance of his commands.

From that instance of rebellion he took a kind of dislike to me. But my strong appetite for sociability, my native hilarity and bookish knowledge made me generally a welcome guest.

How happy have I been with friends most dear.

> Meet me on the Warloch knowe,
> Daintie Davie, daintie Davie,
> There I'll spend the day wi' you,
> My ain dear dainty Davie.

[This is David Sillar, a year younger than our Robert and also keen on poetry. Davie's father's farm was only two miles from Lochlea.]

> When purple morning starts the hare
> To steal upon her early fare,
> Then thro' the dews I will repair
> To meet my faithful Davie.

We might be poor, but for all the joys that gold brings, I didna care a single flea. Blythe was the blink of Robie's eye! O enviable days sporting about the lady-thorn with Jamie Candlish or going to see Jamie Smith—

Jamie, I swear by sun and moon—(This is James Smith, son of a Mauchline Merchant, a much-valued trusty Trojan on whose friendship I count myself possessed of a life-rent lease.)

> Jamie, I swear by sun and moon
> And every star that blinks aboon . . .

I was extremely happy with Jamie Smith. Yet happiness is shy and comes not when sought. We ought to be *economists* in happiness. I hated nought but to be sad.

But the nights are long in winter now. I sit thinking on friends most dear and the thought of them gives me many a heart-ach.

I got your letter, winsome Willie [This is William Simpson, also of Mauchline] . . .

> I got your letter, winsome Willie;
> Wi' gratefu' heart I thank you brawlie;
> Tho' I maun say't, I wad be silly
>   And unco vain
> Should I believe, my coaxin Billie,
>   Your flatterin strain.
>
> But whether summer kindly warms
>   Wi' life and light
> Or winter howls in gusty storms
>   The lang dark night. . . .
>
> While Terra Firma on her axis
>   Diurnal turns,
> Count on a friend in faith and practice
>   In Robert Burns.

The applause—perhaps the partiality—of friendship had awakened my vanity so far as to make me think anything of mine, the little creations of my fancy, worth showing round as some kind of *counterpoise* to the fatigues of a laborious life.

My heart meanwhile was compleatly tinder and was eternally lighted up by some goddess or other. I was sometimes crowned with success, sometimes mortified with defeat. At the plough, scythe or reap-hook I feared no competitor and set want at defiance, though I never cared farther for my

labors than while I was in actual exercise. I spent the evening in the way
after my own heart.

> Then up wi' it a', my ploughman lad,
>   And hey my merry ploughman.
> Of all the trades that I do ken
>   Commend me to the ploughman.
>
> The ploughman, he's a bonie lad
>   His mind is ever true, jo,
> His garters knit below his knee
>   His bonnet it is blue, jo.
>
> I hae been east, I hae been west,
>   I hae been at St. Johnston *;   [*Perth]
> The bonniest sight that e'er I saw
>   Was the ploughman laddie dancin.
>
> Snaw-white stockings on his legs
>   And siller buckles glancin,
> A guid blue bonnet on his head
>   And Oh but he was handsome !

A country lad rarely carries on an amour without an assisting confident.
I possessed a curiosity, zeal and intrepid dexterity in these matters which
recommended me a proper Second. And I dare say I felt as much pleasure
at being in the secret of half the amours of the parish as ever did Premier at
knowing the intrigues of half the courts of Europe.

> Gin a body meet a body
>   Comin thro' the rye.
> Gin a body kiss a body
>   Need a body cry ?
>
> Gin a body meet a body
>   Comin thro' the glen,
> Gin a body kiss a body
>   Need the world ken ?

The very goosefeather in my hand is with difficulty restrained from giving
a couple of paragraphs on the amours of my compeers, love-sick youths and
sighing girls, the humble inmates of farm-house or cottage.

The grave baptize these things by the name of follies. To the sons and daughters of labor and poverty they are matters of the most serious nature. To them the ardent hope, the stolen interview, the tender farewell, are the greatest and most delicious part of their enjoyments.

Meanwhile I was learning to observe.

[*Observations in church*]
Here some are thinkin' on their sins
    And some upon their claes,
Ane curses feet that fyl'd his shins
    Another sits and prays.
On this hand sits a chosen swatch *   [*Group]
    Wi' screw'd-up, grace-proud faces,
On that a set o' chaps at watch,
    Thrang † winkin on the lasses.   [†Busy]

[*Further observations in church*]
On seeing a louse on a lady's bonnet
O Jenny, dinna toss your head
And set your beauties all abroad.
    Ye little ken !
Oh would some Power the giftie gie us
To see ourselves as ithers see us . . .

[*And on another occasion*]
Ye high exalted virtuous dames
    Tied up in godly laces,
Before ye gie poor Frailty names
    Suppose a change of cases :
A dear-lov'd lad—convenience snug—
    A treach'rous inclination—
But let me whisper i' your lug
    Ye're aiblins ‡ nae temptation !   [‡ Maybe]

Another circumstance in my life which made very considerable alterations in my mind and manners was—I spent my seventeenth summer a good distance from home at a noted school [at Kirkoswald] to learn Mensuration, Surveying, Dialling &c. in which I made a pretty good progress.

24

But [Kirkoswald being on a smuggling coast] I made greater progress in the knowledge of mankind. The contraband trade was at that time very successful. Scenes of swaggering riot and roaring dissipation were as yet new to me, but I was no enemy to social life.

> Wi' quaffing and laughing
> They ranted and they sang,
> Wi' humping and thumping
> The vera girdle rang.
>
> See the smoking bowl before us !
> Mark our jovial ragged ring !
> Round and round take up the chorus
> And in raptures let us sing—

(Tune—Soldier's Joy)
> I am a son of Mars who have been in many wars
> And show my cuts and scars wherever I come.
> This here was for a wench and that other in a trench
> When welcoming the French at the sound of the drum.
> Lal de daudle, &c.

I learned to look unconcernedly on a large tavern-bill and mix without fear in a drunken squabble, but I kept clear of vicious habits. I was seventeen.

One of my earliest pieces, composed during this year, begins:

> I dreamed I lay where flowers were springing
> Gaily in the sunny beam,
> Listening to the wild birds singing
> By the falling crystal stream;
> Straight the sky grew black and daring,
> Through the woods the whirlwinds rave,
> Tree with aged arms were warring . . .

I went on with a high hand in my Geometry. I am not lazy.

But, stepping out to the garden one charming noon to take the sun's altitude, I met an Angel [Peggy Thomson].

25

Burns—by Himself

It was vain to think of doing any more good at school.

> The time flew by wi' tentless heed
>   Till, 'tween the late and early,
> Wi' sma' persuasion she agreed
>   To see me thro' the barley.
>
> I ken't her heart was a' my ain
>   I lov'd her most sincerely,
> I kiss'd her oure and oure again
>   Amang the rigs o' barley.

The remaining week [at Kirkoswald] I did nothing but steal out to meet her.

The following song to her was composed that August:

> Now westlin winds and slaught'ring guns
>   Bring autumn's pleasant weather,
> And the muircock springs on whirring wings
>   Amang the blooming heather.
> Now waving crops with yellow tops
>   Delight the weary farmer,
> And the moon shines bright when I rove at night
>   To muse upon my charmer.
>
> O Peggy dear, the evening's clear,
>   Thick flies the skimming swallow;
> The sky is blue, the fields in view
>   All fading-green and yellow;
> Come let us stray our gladsome way
>   And view the charms of nature,
> The rustling corn, the fruited thorn
>   And ilka happy creature.
>
> We'll gently walk and sweetly talk
>   While the silent moon shines clearly,
> I'll clasp thy waist and, fondly prest,
>   Swear how I love thee dearly.
> Not vernal show'rs to budding flow'rs
>   Not autumn to the farmer
> So dear can be as thou to me,
>   My fair, my lovely charmer.

The last two nights of my stay, had sleep been a mortal sin, I was innocent. But fond lovers' parting is sweet, painful pleasure.

I returned home very considerably improved.

There is certainly some connection between love and music and poetry. For my own part I never had the least thought of turning poet till I got in love. And *then* . . .

> When youthful love, warm-blushing, strong
> Keen-shivering shot my veins along . . .

rhyme and song were the spontaneous language of my heart.

If anything on earth deserves the name of rapture, it is the feelings of green eighteen in the company of the mistress of his affection.

Burns—by Himself

A country lad is my degree
And few there be that ken me
But what care I how few they be?

Yet those stirrings of ambition . . . I was, I think, about eighteen or
nineteen when nothing less would serve me than courting the Trajic
Muse. I sketched the outlines of a trajedy forsooth! In those days I
never *wrote down* anything; so, except a speech or two, the whole has
escaped my memory. The following however, which I most distinctly
remember . . .

Poverty and Obscurity

Still my heart melts at human wretchedness.
Ye poor, despised, abandoned vagabonds,
Oh ! but for friends and interposing Heaven,
I had been driven forth, like you, forlorn.
With talents passing most of my compeers . . .

Having now [in 1777] reached the freedom in his lease, my father
entered on another farm [called Lochlea] about ten miles farther in the
country.

Upon a summer Sunday morn
When nature's face is fair
I walked forth to view the corn
And snuff the caller air.

The rising sun owre Galton muirs
Wi' glorious light was glintin
The hares were hirplin down the furs
The lav'rocks they were chantin.

For four years we lived at Lochlea ; and then a lawsuit began between
my father and his landlord.

My life flowed on till about my twentieth year, when for some six or
eight months another Peggy [a local servant girl] was my deity.
[' Though when quite young ', observes clever Gilbert, ' Robert was
' bashful and awkward in his intercourse with women, yet when he
' approached manhood, his attachment to their society became very strong.
' The symptoms of his passion, the agitation of his mind exceeded any-
' thing of the kind I ever knew.']

She's stately like yon youthful ash
That grows the cowslip braes between
And drinks the stream with vigour fresh . . .

Her hair is like the curling mist
That climbs the mountain-sides at e'en
When flow'r-reviving rains are past . . .

Her teeth are like the nightly snow
 When pale the morning rises keen
While hid the murm'ring streamlets flow . . .

  I think young men [these are some jottings in a note-book]—I think young men may be divided into two classes, those who, goaded on by the love of money, wish to make a figure in the world [of fashion] and those who, with a happy sweetness of temper, generally steal through life in poverty and obscurity.

  I was quite indolent about those great concerns that set the bustling and busy agog; but never did a heart pant more ardently than mine to be *distinguished.*

TO DAVIE*—ACE OF HEARTS   [*David Sillar]

It's hardly in a body's power
To keep at times frae being sour
 To see how things are shared,
How best o' chiels † are whyles in want . . .   [†Chaps]

But Davie lad, ne'er fash your head—
 Tho' we hae little gear,
We're fit to win our daily bread
 As lang's we're hale and fier.

The last of it, the worst, is only but to beg—to lie in barns. But Lord be thanked (I often said to myself) I *can* plough.

We labour soon, we labour
 late
 To feed the titled knave
And a' the comfort we're to
 get
 Is that ayont the grave.

July 29th. Lochlee.   *To Willie Niven.*

As for my being in your country, I don't know when it will happen.
Such is our hurry that a pleasure jaunt is what I dare not ask. But I
have three acres of pretty good flax this season. Perhaps in the course of
marketing it I may come your way.   R. B.

My reading at about this period was enlarged with the very important
addition of Thomson's and Shenstone's Works and a collection of Letters
of Queen Anne's reign. This last helped me much in composition and
I engaged several of my schoolfellows to keep up a literary correspondence
with me. Why, I said to myself, may not a son of poverty with an intelligent mind and independent spirit make an agreeable, intimate and entertaining correspondent ? I kept copies of any of my own letters that pleased
me. And a comparison between them and the composition of most of
my correspondents flattered my vanity. Every post brought me many
letters.

> Ye sprightly youths, quite flushed with hope and spirit
> Who think to storm the world by dint of *merit* ! . . .

Meanwhile, though I had resumed the plough [wages £7 a year], I
was ambitious as ever of shining in Conversation Parties, on Sundays,
between sermons, funerals, &c.

Nov. 3rd. Lochlee.

The hurried season of autumn is over. . . .

I am beginning to think ambition renders human life one uphill gallop
from the cradle to the grave. It is improbable that I shall ever acquire
riches and I am therefore endeavouring to gather a philosophical contempt of enjoyments so hard to be gained and so easily lost. I will just
be grateful for my daily bread.

I am still so happy as to have now and then a sweetheart or two, but
with as little view of *Matrimony* as ever.

[Gilbert's comment is that ' whenever Robert selected any one out of
' the sovereignty of his good pleasure to whom he should pay his particular
' attention, she was instantly invested with sufficient charms out of the

' plentiful stores of his imagination.   One generally reigned paramount in
' his affections but he was frequently encountering other attractions, which
' formed so many under-plots in the drama of his love.   These connections
' were governed by the strictest rules of virtue and modesty from which
' he never deviated till he reached his twenty-third year.']

Nov. 11th.

THE BATCHELORS' CLUB

We, the following lads, namely Robert Burness, Gilbert Burness [and
five others] have resolved to unite ourselves into a Club under such rules
that while we shall forget our cares, we may not transgress the bounds of
innocence and decorum.   Every man proper for a member of this society
must have a frank, honest open heart above anything dirty or mean—
and must be a professed lover of one or more of the female sex.   No haughty
person who looks upon himself as superior, and whose only will is to
heap up money, shall be admitted.

After agreeing to these regulations we held our first meeting at Tar-
bolton upon the evening of the 11th November 1780, commonly called
Hallowe'en and after choosing Robert Burness president for the night,
we proceeded to debate on this question:—

' Suppose a young man, bred a farmer but without any fortune,
has it in his power to marry either of two women, the one a girl of
large fortune but neither handsome in person nor agreeable in conversation, but who can manage the household affairs of a farm well
enough; the other of them a girl in every way agreeable in person,
conversation and behaviour but without fortune—which of them shall
he choose ? '

Finding ourselves very happy in our society, we resolved to continue
to meet once a month.

Later on we chose six other members [including David Sillar].   The
Club being thus increased, we resolved to meet on the race-night the
July following and have a dance in honour of our society.   Accordingly
we did meet, each one with a partner, and spent the evening with such

merriment and good-humour that every brother will long remember it
with delight.

[The following are among the other questions subsequently debated.]
' Whether do we derive more happiness from love or friendship ? '
' Whether between friends who have no reason to doubt each other,
there should be any reserve ? '

[David Sillar, ' Daintie Davie ', a year younger than Robert, talks of
how ' his appearance had such a magical influence on my curiosity as
' made me particularly solicitous of his acquaintance. *He wore the only*
' *tied hair in the parish*; and his plaid, which was of the colour called
' fillemot [*feuille morte*] he wrapped in a particular manner round his
' shoulders. I was introduced to him by Gilbert.
' His social disposition easily procured him acquaintance. But a
' certain satirical seasoning, while it set the rustic circle in a roar, was not
' unaccompanied by suspicious fear. I recollect hearing his neighbours
' observe that he had a great deal to say for himself and that they *suspected*
' *his principles*.
' Some book he always carried and read when not otherwise employed.
' He and I frequently met on Sundays at church. Between sermons,
' instead of going with our friends or lassies to the inn, we often took a
' walk in the fields. In these walks I have frequently been struck by his
' facility in addressing the fair sex ; and it was generally a death-blow to
' our conversation, however agreeable.']

[But Isabella Steven of Little Hill, a farm which marched with Lochlea,
was superior. She disliked being called Tibbie. She would not listen.
So she is put into rhyme.]

> Yestreen I met you on the moor
> Ye spak na but gaed by like stoure.*   [*Dust]
> Ye geek at me because I'm poor
>   But fient a hair care I.

> When comin hame on Sunday last
> Upon the road as I cam past
> Ye snufft and gave your head a cast
>   But trowth, I care't na by.

And Tibbie lass, take my advice
Your daddie's gear maks you sae nice,
The Deil-a-ane * wad spier your price   [*No one]
    Were ye as poor as I !

It is natural for a young fellow to like the acquaintance of the females and customary for him to keep them company when occasion serves.

I was becoming more and more aware that nothing on earth this side of eternity would give me greater transport than the married life [perhaps along with another farmer's daughter, whose real name, Alison Begbie, is changed for rhythmic and other reasons to ' Mary Morison '].

O Mary, at thy window be !
    It is the wished, the trysted hour.
Those smiles and glances let me see
    That make the miser's treasure poor.
    How blythely wad I bide the stoure
A weary slave frae sun to sun
    Could I the rich reward secure
The lovely Mary Morison.

Yestreen, when to the trembling string
    The dance gaed through the lighted ha',
To thee my fancy took its wing;
    I sat, but neither heard or saw,
    Tho' this was fair and that was braw
And you the toast of a' the town
    I sigh'd and said among them a':—
Ye are na Mary Morison.

This poem is one of my juvenile works.   I do not think it remarkable. [Isbal says ' My brother went frequently of an evening to visit Alison ' and as he did not as a rule return till a late hour, his father at length became ' alarmed at the irregularity of his habits.']

In the cheerful bloom of spring or the pensive mildness of autumn, the grandeur of summer or the hoary majesty of winter, the poet feels a charm unknown to the rest of the species.

Poverty and Obscurity

The sight of a fine flower or the company of a fine woman (by far the finest part of God's works below) have sensations for the poetic heart that the Herd are strangers to.

> Let others love the city
>   And gaudy show at sunny noon.
> Give me the lonely valley
>   The dewy eve and rising moon.
>
> Fair beaming and streaming
>   Her silver light the boughs amang
> While falling recalling,
>   The amorous thrush concludes his song.

Lochlea.   *To ' Mary Morison '.*

I hope you will forgive me when I tell you that I love you and that there is nothing on earth I so ardently wish for as one day to see you mine. You are the first woman to whom I ever made such a declaration.

Some men may go a-wooing as they go to the horse-market, to chuse one who is stout and firm. I disdain their dirty, puny ideas. I dont envy them their happiness who have such notions. For my part I propose quite other pleasures with my dear partner and I look to the divine Disposer of Events that he may bless my endeavours in bettering the unkindly circumstances of my fortune.

It would oblidge me much if you would send me a line or two when convenient.   R. B.

> As I gaed up by yon gate-end
>   When day was waxin weary,
> Wha did I meet come down the street
>   But pretty Peg my dearie . . .
>
> *Wilt* thou be my dearie ?
>   O wilt thou let me cheer thee ?
> I swear and vow that only thou
>   Shall ever be my dearie. . . .

O lay thy loof in mine, lass,
  In mine, lass, in mine, lass,
And swear on thy white hand, lass,
  That thou wilt be my ain.

I will not attempt to describe what I felt on receiving her letter in answer.

I was so shocked with the contents of it that I could scarcely collect my thoughts. I read it over and over again. It was in the politest language of refusal.

[Dr. John MacKenzie, after his first visit to Lochlea, 'found Gilbert 'frank, modest, well informed and communicative. But Robert seemed

'distant, suspicious and without any wish to interest or please. He kept
'himself very silent in a dark corner of the room.']

> The wanton coot the water skims,
>   Among the reeds the ducklings cry.
> The stately swan majestic swims
>   And everything is blest but I.
> And when the lark, 'tween light and dark
>   Blythe wakens by the daisy's side
> And mounts and sings on flittering wings
>   A woe-worn ghost I homeward glide.

June 12th. Lochlee.   *To Willie Niven.*

I am entirely got rid of all connections with the tender sex.

How long I shall continue so Heaven only knows, but be that as it
may, I shall never be involved as I was again.   R. B.

['Robert', says a female cousin who occasionally helped on the farm,
was always anxious to cheer and assist the younger labourers. He was
'especially attentive to a small boy usually known as "Wee Davoc"
'whom he used to carry home from the field on his shoulders.']

My passions, when once they were lighted up raged like so many
devils till they got vent in rhyme. But then conning over my verses like
a spell soothed all into quiet.

> Here's to thy health, my bonie lass,
>   Guid night and joy be wi' thee,
> O dinna think, my pretty pink,
>   But I can live without thee.
> I vow and swear I dinna care
>   How lang ye look about ye.
> Thou'rt ay sae free informing me
>   Thou hast nae mind to marry
> I'll be as free informing thee
>   Nae time hae I to tarry.

4   37

To the hopeful youth listed under the gaudy banners of Ambition, a love-disappointment, as such, is an easy business ; nay perhaps he hugs himself on his escape.

> O why the deuce should I repine
> And be an ill foreboder ?
> I'm twenty-three and five feet nine:
> I'll go and be a sodger.

My twentythird year was to me important. I had reckoned on the recruiting drum as my forlorn hope since early days. But [instead of joining the Army] I joined with a flax dresser in a neighbouring town, Irvine, to learn his trade.

This however (the flax-dressing) turned out a sadly unlucky affair. My partner was a scoundrel of the first water, who made money by the mystery of thieving ; and, to finish the whole, while we were giving a welcoming carousal to the New Year, our shop, by the drunken careless-ness of my partner's wife, took fire and was burnt to ashes. This left me not worth sixpence.

> Prone to enjoy each pleasure riches give
> Yet haply wanting wherewithal to live.

I was obliged to give up business.

Here (at Irvine) my body was attacked by fainting fits [Gilbert says ' palpitation of the heart and a threatening of suffocation in his bed in the ' night-time.']—fainting fits and other alarming symptoms of a pleurisy or some such dangerous disorder (which indeed still threatens me), as well as a hypochondria or confirmed melancholy—though I am a good deal inclined to think with those who maintain that what are called nervous affections are in fact diseases of the mind.

In this wretched state, the recollection of which always makes me shudder, I cannot reason, I cannot think, except in lucid intervals, in one of which I composed a ' Prayer under the pressure of violent anguish ', beginning

> O Thou Great Being, what Thou art
> Surpasses me to know . . .

and another beginning

O Thou Unknown Almighty Cause
Of all my hope and fear . . .

Dec. 27th. Irvin.   *Copy of a letter to my Father.*

Honored Sir—I have purposely delayed writing in the hope that I
would have the pleasure of seeing you on Newyearday.

My health is much about what it was.   The weakness of my nerves has
so debilitated my mind that I dare not look forward.   Sometimes indeed,
when for an hour my spirits are a little lightened, I glimmer into futurity
and am quite transported at the thought that ere long, perhaps very soon,
I shall bid an eternal adieu to this weary life.   I am heartily tired of it.

As for this world, I despair of ever making a figure in it.   I foresee
that poverty and obscurity await me and I am in some measure prepared
to meet them.

Present my dutiful respects to my Mother.

Wishing you all a merry Newyearday, I am, honored Sir, your dutiful
son   Robert.

My oat meal is nearly out, but I am going to borrow till I get more.

For three months I was in a distressed state of body and mind scarcely
to be envied, my hypochondriac complaint being irritated to such a degree
that I was in a kind of fever.

The principal thing which gave my mind a turn was—I formed a
bosom-friendship with a wild, bold, generous young fellow Richard
Brown.   He was the son of a plain mechanic; but a Great Man in the
neighbourhood had taken him under his patronage and given him a
genteel education with a view to bettering his situation in life.   The Patron
however dieing just as he was ready to launch forth into the world, the
poor fellow in despair went to sea.

I loved him.   I admired him to a degree of enthusiasm.   I strove to
imitate him.   In some measure I succeeded.   His knowledge of the
world was vastly superior to mine.   And I was all attention to learn.
He was the only man I ever saw who was a greater fool than myself when
WOMAN was the presiding star, but he spoke of a certain fashionable failing

39

with levity, which hitherto I had regarded with horror. Here his friendship did me a mischief.

After this (since the fire at the flax shop had left me not worth sixpence), my horny fist assumed the plough again.

Poverty and obscurity . . . and meanwhile, O Thou in whom we live and move, still grant us the friend we trust and the fair we love.

> I'll act with prudence as far as I'm able,
>   But if success I must never find,
> Then come misfortune, I bid thee welcome,
>   I'll meet thee with undaunted mind . . .

> The pie-bald jacket let me patch once more,
> On eighteen pence a week I've lived before.

[Gilbert says—this would be in the spring of 1782—'Robert had a 'pet ewe and two lambs. The ewe was tethered in a field adjoining the 'farm. He and I were going out with our teams and our two younger

'brothers to drive for us, when the boy Hughoc,¹ a curious looking
'awkward boy usually clad in plaiding, came to us with much anxiety
'in his face, saying that the ewe called Mailie had entangled herself in
'the tether and was lying in a ditch. Robert was much tickled. Poor
'Mailie was set to rights. And when we returned from the plough in
'the evening he repeated to me her Death and Dying Words pretty much
'as they now stand.']

THE DEATH AND DYING WORDS OF POOR MAILIE
THE AUTHOR'S ONLY PET EWE

As Mailie and her lambs thegither
Were ae day nibblin on the tether
Upon her cloot she cast a hitch
And owre she warst'd in the ditch.
There, groanin, dying, she did lie
When Hughoc he came doytin by.

Wi' glowrin een and lifted hands
Poor Hughoc like a statue stands
He says her days were near-hand ended
But wae's my heart, he could na mend it.
He gaped wide but naething spak
At length poor Mailie silence brak.

O thou, whose lamentable face
Appears to mourn my woeful case,
My dying words attentive hear
And bear them to my master dear.

Tell him he was a master kin'
And aye was good to me and mine
And now my dying charge I gie him,
My helpless lambs, I trust them wi' him.
O bid him save their harmless lives
Frae dogs and tods * and butchers' knives.   [*Foxes]

¹ *oc is the Gaelic diminutive; see also Davoc, p. 37.*

And now, my bairs, wi' my last breath
I leave my blessing wi' you baith
And when you think upon your mither
Mind to be kind to ane anither.

This said, poor Mailie turn'd her head
And closed her een amang the dead.

[A second poem was written about Mailie. This time ' Poor Robin '
has ' lost a friend '.]

Thro' a' the town she trotted by him.
A lang half-mile she could descry him.
Wi' kindly bleat when she did spy him
    She ran wi' speed.
A friend mair faithful ne'er cam nigh him
    Than Mailie dead.

[' Robert also had a dog, a collie, a great favourite, called Luath '[1]
says Gilbert.]

His breast was white, his tousie * back   [*Tousled]
Weel clad wi' coat o' glossy black,
His gawsie † tail wi' upward curl   [†Handsome]
Hung owre his hurdies wi' a swirl.

Lochlea. Sept. 7th.   *To Thomas Orr.*
Dear Thomas—I am to blame for not returning an answer to your
kind letter. But such has been the backwardness of our harvest and so
seldom are we at Ayr that I have scarcely had one opportunity of sending
a line to you. Believe me, Tom, I have nothing to tell you of news.
For myself I am going on in my old way—taking as light a burden as
I can of the cares of the world. I hope you will write me soon. Your
friend   Robert Burness.

Jan. 15th. Lochlea.
What has been the result of all the pains of an indulgent father and
a masterly teacher ? I hope my conduct will not disgrace the education
I have gotten.

[1] *Luath is the Gaelic for Swift.*

[At the dinner hour country neighbours ' would usually find the ' family, father, brothers and sisters, sitting each with a book in one hand ' and a spoon in the other'.]

One would have thought that, bred as I have been, I might have been a pushing fellow; but, to tell the truth, there is hardly anything more my reverse.

Robert Burness is a man of honesty and good will, who has little art in making money and still less in keeping it. Even the last, worst shift of the unfortunate does not much terrify me. To beg . . . to lie in barns . . . I would learn to be happy even *then*. I am not lazy.

[Gilbert recalls ' delightful days when we had to go, with one or two ' companions, to get peats for the winter fuel. Robert was always sure ' to enliven the work with a fire of witty remarks'.

' It would hardly be possible', writes James Gray, Schoolmaster, ' to ' conceive any being more interesting and delightful.']

Here you have a few lines of my first attempt (A Winter's Night) in that irregular kind of measure in which many of our finest odes were wrote. How far I have succeeded I don't know.

> Ae night the storm the steeples rocked
> Poor Labour sweet in sleep was locked,
> While burns wi' snawy wreaths up-chocked
>   Wild-eddying swirl
> Or thro' the mining outlet bocked
>   Down headlong hurl.
>
> Listening the doors an' winnocks rattle
> I thought me on the ourie cattle . . .
> Dim-dark'ning thro' the flaky show'r
>   Or whirling drift . . .

In many things I am a strict economist; not indeed for the sake of the money, but from a kind of pride. I scorn to fear the face of any man living.   I abhor as hell the idea of sneaking in a corner to avoid a dun. 'Tis this that endears economy to me.

In the matter of books I was and am very profuse. My favorite authors at this period were of the sentimental kind, such as Shenstone, Thomson, MacKenzie, Sterne, MacPherson's Ossian &c. These were the glorious models after which I endeavoured to form my conduct.   While reading I could forget that I was a poor insignificant devil, unnoticed and unknown.   In markets, the men of business jostled me on every side as an idle encumbrance in their way.

The clouds of misfortune were now gathering thick round my father's head.   He was visibly far gone in a consumption.

June 21st. Lochlee.   *To James Burness, Montrose.*
Dear Cousin—My father has been for some months very poorly in health.   In his own opinion and indeed in almost everybody's else, he is in a dying condition.   He sends you, probably for the last time, his warmest wishes.

My Mother sends you a small present of a cheese.   'Tis but a very little one, as our last year's stock is sold off; but we will send you a proper one in the season.   Mother and the rest of the family desire to inclose their kind compliments to you.

Your affectionate cousin   Robert Burness.

Eight months later my father was snatched away to where the weary be at rest by Phthisical Consumption. This just saved him. But for Death—the poor man's last and often best friend—he might have ended his days in a Debtors' Jail.

[Isbal remembered afterwards how, as their father was dying, he murmured ' There's only ONE of my family for whose future conduct I fear.' He repeated this. Robert came up to the bed and asked ' O father, is ' it me you mean ? ' The old man said it was. Robert turned to the ' window with the tears streaming down his cheeks '.]

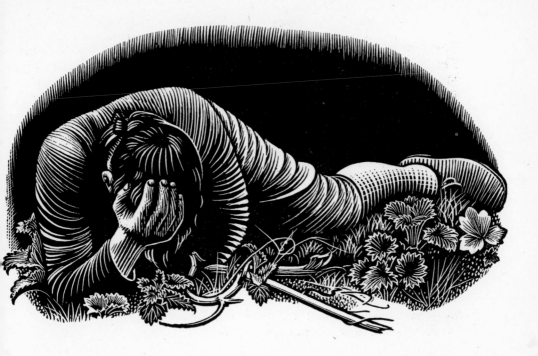

Feb. 17th. Lochlee.   *To James Burness.*

Dear Cousin—On the 13th current I lost the best of fathers, the best of friends, the ablest of instructors—a man whose memory I will ever honor and revere.   We have long had warning of the impending stroke. He is now at rest from the many buffetings of an evil world against which he so long and bravely struggled.   R. B.

My father used to say that in his whole life, whatever he was fondly set on almost always failed him.   I am afraid it is all the heritage he has left me.

April.   Lochlee.   The following song is miserably deficient in versification, but as the sentiments are the feelings of my heart, I have particular pleasure in conning it over—

My father was a farmer upon the Carrick border
And carefully he bred me in decency and order.
He bade me act a manly part though I had ne'er a farthing,
For without an honest, manly heart no man was worth regarding.

Then out into the world my course I did determine,
Tho' to be rich was not my wish, yet to be *great* was charming.
My talents they were not the worst nor yet my education—
Resolved was I at last to try to mend my situation.

In many a way and vain essay I courted Fortune's favour:
Some cause unseen still stept between to frustrate each endeavour . . .
Then sore harrass'd and tir'd at last with Fortune's vain delusion,
I dropt my schemes like idle dreams and came to this conclusion—

When sometimes by my labour I earn a little money
Some unforeseen misfortune comes gen'rally upon me
Thus, all obscure, unknown and poor, thro' life I'm doom'd to wander
Till down my weary bones I lay in everlasting slumber.

No help nor hope nor view have I nor person to befriend me
So I must toil and sweat and broil and labour to sustain me,
To plough and sow, to reap and mow . . .

April. Lochlee. There is scarcely any earthly object gives me more—
I don't know if I should call it pleasure—than to walk in the sheltered side
of a wood in a cloudy winter day and hear a stormy wind howling among
the trees and raving o'er the plain. It exalts me, enraptures me. In one
of these seasons I composed the following.

> The wintry west extends his blast
>   And hail and rain does blaw,
> Or stormy north sends driving forth
>   The blinding sleet and snaw.
> Wild-tumbling brown the burn comes down
>   And roars frae bank to brae,
> While bird and beast in covert rest
>   And pass the heartless day.
>
> The sweeping blast, the sky o'ercast,
>   The joyless winter day
> Let others fear, to me more dear
>   Than all the pride of May.

The tempest's howl; it soothes my soul,
   My griefs it seems to join,
The leafless trees my fancy please.
   Their fate resembles mine.

When my father died, his all went among the rapacious hell-hounds
that growl in the Kennel of Justice. But we made a shift in the family
to scrape a little money amongst us to keep us together. With this Gilbert
and I took a neighbouring farm [called Mossgiel].

Octr. 18th. Mossgiel.   *To Mr. Gavin Hamilton.*
Sir—As you are pleased to give us the offer of a private bargain of
your cows that you intend for sale, my brother and I this day took a look
of them. If you are still intending to let us have them, please appoint
a day that we may wait on you.
          I am, Sir, your humble servant Robert Burns.

P.S. Whatever of your dairy utensils you intend to dispose of we
will probably purchase. R. B.

[Gilbert makes this note about the flitting to Mossgiel: ' During the
' whole of the time we lived in the farm of Lochlea, my father allowed
' my brother and me such wages for our Labour as he gave to other
' labourers. When my father's affairs drew near a crisis, Robert and I
' took the farm of Mossgiel as an asylum for the family in case of the
' worst. It was stocked by the property and individual savings of the
' whole family and was a joint concern among us. Every member of the
' family was allowed ordinary wages. Robert's allowance and mine was
' £7 per annum each. I was intrusted with the keeping of the family
' accounts.
  ' During the whole time this family concern lasted, as well as at Lochlea,
' Robert's expenses never exceeded his slender income. His temperance
' and frugality were everything that could be wished.
  ' When addressed about a business matter, he always turned it off
' with " Oh talk to my brother Gilbert about that."]

April. With anything like business I am totally unacquainted.

The aim and end of human life is to cultivate an intercourse with the Being to whom we owe life, that unknown Almighty Cause—and to maintain an integritive conduct towards our fellow creatures. . . .

I write in my miscellaneous way and know not why I have got into this preaching vein.

Mossgiel. Gilbert wants my hare-brained imagination as well as my social and amorous madness, but in good sense and every sober qualification, he is far my superiour.

Poverty and Obscurity

I entered on this farm with a full resolution. I read farming books; I calculated crops; I attended markets. But, from unfortunately buying in bad seed last year and from a bad harvest this year, we have lost half of both our crops.

[Some notes written at the time.] Our markets are exceeding high—oatmeal 17*d.* and 18*d.* pr peck and not to be got even at that price. We have been pretty well supplied with pease from England and elsewhere, but that resource is likely to fail us and if it does, what will become of us —particularly the very poorest sort—heaven only knows.

> Then farewell hopes of laurel boughs
> To garland my poetic brows !

Farming (in Scotland) is at a very low ebb. Our lands, generally speaking, are mountainous and barren. Our landholders, full of ideas of farming gathered from English and other rich soils, make no allowance for the *quality* of the land and consequently stretch us much beyond what we will be found able to pay. We are also much at a loss for want of proper *methods* in our improvements of farming.

Scotland till of late was flourishing incredibly in silk, lawn and carpet weaving. We are still carrying on, but much reduced. We also had a fine trade in the shoe way, now entirely ruined. Hundreds, driven to a starving condition on account of it, go a begging with the burnt out cottager. [This is a reference to the clearances. The big landlords, finding sheep more profitable than human beings were already turning out the crofters and burning their houses down lest they should return.]

Even in higher life, imitating English and French and other foreign luxuries and fopperies has ruined many. In short this country has been and still is decaying fast.

> One night as I did wander
>   When corn begins to shoot
> I sat me down to ponder
>   Upon an auld tree root.

Auld Ayr ran by before me
And bickered to the sea
A cushat * crooded o'er me   [*Wood-pigeon]
That echoed through the trees . . .

May. Mossgiel. I don't well know what is the reason of it, but somehow or other, though I am pretty generally beloved—when I have a mind —yet I never could get the art of commanding *respect.* I imagine that it is owing to my being deficient in discretion. I am so apt to a *lapsus linguae.* N.B. to try if I can discover the causes of this wretched infirmity and if possible to mend it.

August 3rd. Mossgiel.   *To James Burness. Montrose.*
Dear Cousin—I ought to have acknowledged the receipt of your last kind letter before this time. Our family are all in health at pres^t. We were very happy with John [another cousin]. We have been enjoying his company for near two weeks and I must say he is one of the most agreeable, facetious, warm-hearted lads I was ever acquainted with. I expect to hear from you soon.
Your affectionate cousin   Robert Burness.

August. Mossgiel. I want to be thought a *wise* man. I wish to be rich. I would be generous. But I am obscure and obscure I must *be* it seems. I am afraid I am but a ne'er-do-weel, though no young poet nor young soldier's heart ever beat more fondly for fame than mine.

Sept. 13th. Mossgiel.   *To John Tennant Junr.*
My unlucky illness of Friday last did not do me a greater disservice than in disappointing me of the pleasure I had promised myself in spending an hour with you. I got so much better on Saturday as to be able to ride home. But I am still in a kind of slow fever.   R. B.

[Heart affected. Fainting fits, particularly at night. Cold baths prescribed as a remedy. A tub of cold water to be placed by the bedside;

and the patient, whenever threatened with faintness, immediately to plunge in.

Doctor's orders strictly obeyed.]

I rarely hit where I aim and if I want anything I am almost sure never to find it where I seek it. For instance, if my pen-knife is needed, I pull out twenty things, a plough-wedge, a horse-nail, an old letter or a tattered rhyme, in short everything but my pen-knife. And at last after a painful, fruitless search it will be found in an unsuspected pocket as if on purpose thrust out of the way.

It is a good while now since I began to be known in this neighbourhood as a maker of rhymes. The first of my poetic offspring that ever saw the light [but of course only in manuscript] was a burlesque Lamentation on a quarrel between two Revd. Calvinists. I had some idea myself that the piece (The Twa Herds) had some merit. It met with a roar of applause. 'Holy Willie's Prayer' next made its appearance and it has alarmed the Kirk-Session so much that they have held several meetings to look over their holy artillery if any of it is pointed against profane rhymers. I have spoken with such heat and indiscretion that I have raised a hue and cry of Heresy against me. Perhaps I am doing what I ought not to do—a predicament I have more than once been in before. But I detest illiberality, and I detest this wrangling between the two great parties that divide our Scots ecclesiastics. Polemical divinity is putting the country half mad. Heresy . . . I do not care three farthings for Authorities. You mim-mou'd priesties lifted up with Hebrew lore, you who believe in John Knox, you who are so accustomed to the wild goose heights of Calvinistic theology—

> Let me sound an alarm to your conscience,
>   A heretic blast
>   Has been blown in the west,
> That what is not sense must be nonsense!

We talk of *air* and *manner*, of *beauty* and *wit* and lord knows what; but to have a woman [This time a milk-maid, Lizzie Paton, employed on the farm at Mossgiel and answering as often as not to the name of Betty] to lye with when one pleases without risk of the cursed expence of bastards . . .

Betty

She is not the fairest altho' she is fair.
O' nice education but small is her share.
Her parentage humble as humble can be,
But I love the dear lassie because she loves me.

That riotous passions may still make me zig-zag in my future path is far from being improbable, but come what may . . .

Now blooms the lily by the bank,
The primrose down the brae,
The hawthorn's budding in the glen
And milk-white is the slae.
The meanest hind is fair Scotland
May rove their sweets among . . .

Mossgiel. Nov. 11th.   *To Thomas Orr.*

Dear Thomas—I am at present so cursedly taken in with an affair of gallantry [Betty Paton], that I am very glad Peggy [Peggy Thomson] is off my hand. I am embarrassed enough without her. I don't chuse to enter into particulars in writing, but I should be glad to see you to tell you about it.

         R. B.

[The 'riotous passions' had produced a daughter. The child was brought by her father to Mossgiel.]

Thou's welcome wean—my sweet wee lady . . .

Welcome my bonie sweet wee dochter,
Tho' ye come here a wee unsought for
Yet by my faith ye're no unwrought for—
That I shall swear !

Poverty and Obscurity

Wee image o' my bonie Betty
As dear and near my heart I set thee
As all the priests had seen me get thee
    That's out o' Hell—

Gude grant that thou may ay inherit
Thy mither's looks and gracefu' merit
And thy poor worthless daddie's spirit
    Without his failins.

What tho' they call me fornicator . . .

No man can say in what degree any person besides himself can be called wicked.   Let the strictest of conduct examine impartially how many of their virtues are owing to constitution and education, how many of the weaknesses of mankind they have escaped because they were out of the line of such temptation—and how much they are indebted to the world's good opinion because the world does not know all.   Any man who can thus think, will scan the failings of mankind around him with a brother's eye.

But the cold-blooded bigot cannot forgive *anything*.

After having been summoned three times before the Kirk-Session, finally I put a Sunday's face on and went.   I owned that the tale [about Betty Paton] was true.   I scorned to lie.   There is something so mean and unmanly in falsehood.   Telling the truth is not only the safest but actually the *easiest* way.   I said ' I fear that unless ye geld me I'll ne'er be better ! ' and came away.

O ye douce folk that live by rule
Grave, tideless-blooded, calm an' cool,
Your hearts are like a standing pool,
    Ye *never* stray . . .

But I—I have been made a Sunday's laughing-stock [by sitting, as ordered by the Kirk-Session, for hours on the Stool of Repentence—the Cutty Stool or Creepie Chair—to be preached at in front of the whole congregation] and abused like a pick-pocket.

5

If there be any truth in the Orthodox Faith of these Churches, I am damned past redemption, but ·

> . . . de'il ma' care about their jaw . . .
> I'll cock my nose aboon them a' !
> On my ain legs thro' dirt and dub
> I independent stand.

No churchman am I.

But I have long had a wishing eye to that inestimable blessing a wife [not Betty, who would have been unsuitable].

Often at weddings my mouth has watered deliciously to see a young fellow, after a few idle commonplace stories from a gentleman in black [the Minister], strip and go to bed with a young girl—whilst *I*, for just the same thing—only wanting the ceremony—am abused like a pickpocket. *I* am a fornicator. *I* am wild and wicked and have scarcely any vestige of the image of God left me !

> In vain he struggles, the Fates behind him press
> And clamorous Hell yawns for her prey below . . .

[' My mother believes that never woman loved a man ', says Isbal, ' with ' more devotion than that poor creature (Betty Paton) did him. She was an ' exceedingly handsome figure, but rude and uncultivated to a great degree. ' She married, some time after, a farm servant-lad named Andrew.']

Mossgiel. Now comes the six and twentieth summer I've seen, I, Rob, wild and wicked, with scarcely any vestige of the image of God left me. . . .

(*This same autumn.*) But it is *natural,* as I have said, for a young fellow to like the acquaintance of the females and customary for him to keep them company when occasion serves.

One of the Mauchline belles [Jean Armour, aged 20, the daughter of Mr. Armour the builder] is more agreeable to me than the rest. . . .

The weather has brightened up a little. I may learn to be, if not happy, at least easy.

When I came roun' by Mauchline toun
   Not dreadin anybody
My heart was caught before I thought,
   And by a Mauchline lady . . .

Wi' bonnet aff quoth I ' Sweet lass,
   I think ye seem to ken me . . .'

My poor country Muse, all rustic, awkward and unpolished as she is, has
more charms for me than any other of the pleasures of life. I hope she will
not desert me. The words come almost before I know . . .

In Mauchline there dwells six proper young belles,
   The pride of the place and its neighbourhood a';
Their carriage and dress, a stranger would guess
   In London or Paris they'd gotten it a'.
Miss Miller is fine, Miss Markland's divine,
   Miss Smith she has wit and Miss Betty is braw,
There's beauty and fortune to get with Miss Morton,
   But Armour's the jewel for me o' them a'.

There is something, I know not what, pleases me, I know not why, in her company. It warms me, it charms me, it heats me but to mention her name—Jean,

> I saw thee dancing o'er the green
> Thy waist sae jimp, thy limbs sae clean,
> Thy tempting lips thy roguish een—
> By Heaven and Earth I love thee !

But I am deep in the guilt of being unfortunate [i.e. poor], for which good and lawful reason the lady's parents have broken all our measures.

> Ah woe is me, my mother dear
> A man of strife ye've born me . . .

Wae on the siller, I was never canny for hoarding it. They scorn my low estate.

> But at twel at night
> When the moon shines bright
> My dear, I'll come and see thee . . .

My darling Jean ! Her willing mou' was sweet as sugarcandie ! And did na her heart leap light and joy blink in her ee as Robie told a tale of love ! A woman to lye with when one pleases . . .

> When first I saw fair Jeanie's face
> I couldna tell what ail'd me.
> My heart went fluttering pit-a-pat
> My een they almost fail'd me.
>
> She's aye sae neat, sae trim, sae tight
> All grace does round her hover,
> Ae look depriv'd me o' my heart
> And I became her lover.

A woman to lye with. . . .

Like that great poet and great gallant (and by consequence great fool) Solomon, I have, with all the ardour of a warm imagination, shaken hands with folly. Men of grave geometrical minds may cry up reason as much as they please. For myself I would always take it as a *compliment* to have it said that my heart ran before my head.

> But what could ye other expect
> Of one that's avowedly daft ?

I have a sore warfare with the Devil, the world and the Flesh. The first I generally fly from ; the second, alas, generally flies from me ; the third is my plague, worse than the plagues of Egypt.

> Robin was a rovin boy
> Rantin, rovin, rantin, rovin,
> Robin was a rovin boy
> Rantin, rovin Robin.

Autumn. Mossgiel.   *To Miss Peggy Kennedy of Daljarroch.*
Madam—Permit me to present you with the inclosed song. Your most obedient and very humble serv[t].   R. B.

> Young Peggy blooms our boniest lass,
> Her blush is like the morning
> The rosy dawn the springing grass
> With early gems adorning.
>
> Her smile is as the evening mild
> When feathered pairs are courting
> And little lambkins wanton wild
> In playful bands disporting . . .

[' Robert ', says Gilbert, composed without any regular plan. If ' he hit on two or three stanzas to please him, he would then think of ' introductory and concluding stanzas. Hence the middle of the poem ' was often first produced. In the course of one Sunday walk, he repeated ' to me the " Cotter's Saturday Night ". I was electrified.']

Autumn. Mossgiel. I am meditating to publish my Poems.
[' He informed me ', writes a later acquaintance, one Josiah Walker, ' that having the advantage of a most exact and retentive memory, he never

' committed his verses to writing till he had touched and re-touched them in
' his mind and had brought them to that state in which he would admit no
'further alteration.   His hours of composition, he said, were desultory and
'uncertain.']

November.   Mossgiel.

TO A MOUSE
ON TURNING UP HER NEST WITH THE PLOUGH

Wee sleekit cowrin tim'rous beastie
Oh what a panic's in thy breastie !
Thou need na start awa sae hasty
    Wi' bickering brattle,
I wad be laith to rin and chase thee
    Wi' murdering pattle * . . .   [*Plough staff]

Thou saw the fields laid bare an' waste
An' weary winter coming fast,
An' cozie here beneath the blast
    Thou thought to dwell
Till crash ! the cruel coulter passed
    Out thro' thy cell.

That wee bit heap o' leaves and stibble
Has cost thee monie a weary nibble.
Now thou's turned out for a' thy trouble
    But † house or hold,   [†Without]
To thole the winter's sleety dribble
    An' crancreuch ‡ cold.   [‡Hoar frost]

But, mousie, thou art no thy lane §   [§Alone]
In proving foresight may be vain.
The best laid schemes o' mice and men
    Gang aft agley
And leave us nought but grief and pain
    For promised joy.

Still thou art blest compared wi' me.
The present only toucheth thee
But och ! I backward cast my e'e
    On prospects drear.
And forward, tho' I canna see,
    I guess and fear.

Poverty and Obscurity

Nov. 11th. Bleak-faced Halloween returns again.

In the West of Scotland All Hallow Eve is thought to be a night when Witches and other mischief-making beings are all abroad on their baneful midnight errands. And particularly those aërial people the Fairies are said on that night to hold a grand anniversary. A favourite haunt of the Fairies are certain little romantic rocky green hills called Cassilis Downans.

> Upon that night when Fairies light
>   On Cassilis Downans dance,
> Or owre the leas in splendid blaze
>   On sprightly coursers prance . . .
> Some merry friendly country folks
>   Together did convene
> To burn their nuts and pull their stocks
>   And hold their Halloween
>   Full blythe that night.

The first ceremony of Halloween is pulling each a stock or plant of kail. The lads, with love-knots well knotted on their garters, must go out hand in hand with the neat lasses and with eyes shut they must pull the first stock they meet with; it's being big or little, straight or crooked, is prophetic of the size and shape of the grand object of all their spells—their future husband or wife.

They then go to the barnyard and pull each a stalk of oats. If the third stalk wants the 'top-pickle'—that is the grain at the top of the stalk—the party in question will come to the marriage-bed anything but a maid. So

> . . . Rab slips out and jinks about
>   Behind the muckle thorn.
> He grippet Nelly hard and fast.
>   Loud skirl'd the lasses
> And *her* top-pickle maist * was lost   [*Almost]
>   When kiutlin † in the fause-house ‡   [†Cuddling]
>   Wi' him that night.

‡ *The fause-house. When corn is in a doubtful state by being too green or wet, the stack builder, by means of old timber, &c., makes a large apartment in his stack, with an opening in the side exposed to the wind. This is the 'false-house'.*

61

The old guidwife's weel-hoarded nuts
  Are round and round divided,
And monie lads and lasses fates
  Are there that night decided.
Some kindle, couthie, side by side
  And burn the gither trimly
Some start awa wi' saucy pride
  And jump out-owre the chimlie
    Full high that night . . .

Wi' merry sangs and friendly cracks
  I wat they didna weary—
And unco' tales and funnie jokes
  Their sports were cheap and cheary
Till butter'd sowens * wi' fragrant lunt †   [† *Steam*]
  Set a' their gabs a-steerin. ‡   [‡ *Wagging*]
Syne wi' a social glass o' strunt §   [§ *Whisky*]
  They parted off careerin
    Full blythe that night

    * *Sowens, with butter instead of milk to them, is always the Halloween supper. Sowens are made from the liquor got by steeping oats in water. When it has soured, it is boiled to the thickness of porridge.*

Feb. 17th 1786. Mossgiel. Some very important news, not the most agreeable.

A few days later. Mossgiel. Jean has jilted me—and with peculiar circumstances of mortification.

[Her parents, realising that an infant was inevitable, had sent her to Paisley, where there was just a chance that another admirer, Robert Wilson, a young weaver, with fair enough prospects, might yet, in spite of what had happened, be willing to marry her. This last item of gossip naturally reached Mossgiel.] But she pledged her *soul* to meet me in matrimony. I had taken steps to a private marriage and made up a Form of Wedlock. [In Scots law ' Marriage may be declared by writing. The proof of marriage is ' not confined to the testimonies of the clergyman and witnesses present at the 'ceremony. The subsequent acknowledgment of it by the parties is 'sufficient' (*Erskine*).] She had pledged her soul and I loved her near to distraction.

> Falsest of womankind
> Cans't thou declare
> All thy fond plighted vows
> Fleeting as air ?

> To thy new lover hie
> Laugh o'er thy perjury
> Then in thy bosom try
> What peace is there !

I loved her near to distraction, but her parents got the hint. And in detestation of my guilt of being a *poor* devil, not only forbade me her company and their house but prevailed with the lawyer to mutilate that unlucky Paper [the Form of Wedlock]. When the lawyer told me that the names were all cut out of the Paper, I was stark staring mad. My maddening passions, roused to fury, bore over their banks, carrying every check before them. Reason was a screaming elk and religion a feebly-struggling beaver down the roarings of Niagara.

But a storm naturally overblows itself. I am sunk into a lurid calm silent, sullen, staring, like Lot's wife besaltified in the plains of Gomorha.

> She's fair and she's false that causes my smart
> I loved her meikle and lang,
> She's broken her vow, she's broken my heart
> And I may e'en gae hang.

Against one thing, after Jean's damnable conduct, I am now fixed as fate—owning her conjugally. That, by hell, I will *never* do. I now have not a hope nor even a wish to make her mine. I curse that fatal night. Perdition sieze her falsehood and perfidy ! But God bless her, my poor, once-dear, misguided girl. She is ill advised.

As for the old harridan her mother, may all the Furies await her until her latest hour. May hell rouse the infernal flames to welcome her approach. I write in a moment of rage. I can write no more.

Early March. Mossgiel.

The morn that warns the approaching day
    Awakes me up to toil and woe.
I see the hours in long array
    That I must suffer, lingering slow.
My toil-beat nerves . . .

Of late I have been confined with some
lingering complaints originating as I take
it in the stomach.

    I have been all my life one of the
rueful-looking sons of disappointment as
my father was. He used to say that in
his whole life, whatever he was fondly
set on almost always failed him.

    Ye tiny elves that guiltless sport
      Like linnets in the bush
    Ye little know the ills ye court
      When manhood is your wish.

The regions of my fancy are dreadfully subject to baleful east-winds which
at times for months together wither every bud and blossom and turn the
whole into an arid waste. From which good Lord deliver us. Amen.

    I have lost—I have lost a wife and by degrees I am subsiding into the
time-settled sorrow of the widower, who wiping away a decent tear, lifts
up his eye to look—for *another wife.* . . .

TO ANDREW

*whose father Mr. Aiken the well known lawyer in Ayr is pleased to profess great
approbation of my works. Indeed he is now my chief Patron.*

    Ye'll try the world soon, my lad
      And Andrew dear, believe me,
    Ye'll find mankind an unco squad
      And muckle they may grieve ye.

March 20th. Mossgiel. I hope sometime before we hear the gowk [the
cuckoo] to send my proposals for publishing to the press.

And Andrew dear believe me again . . .

> Ay free, off-hand, your story tell
> When wi' a bosom cronie,
> But still *keep something to yoursel'*
> Ye scarcely tell to onie.

[Something not to be told to any, not even to a bosom crony; what might this refer to ? ' Most of my poems are connected with my own story,' says Robert later on quite frankly. And it seems that Andrew is now being reminded to be secretive simply because Robert has a secret of his own. This new and absorbing secret is a Highland nursery-maid called Mary Campbell.]

Mary is a charming young creature, a warm hearted, charming young creature as ever blessed a man with generous love . . .

> O were yon hills and vallies mine
> Yon palace and yon gardens fine,
> The world then the love should know
> I bear my Highland lassie O !

My sweet Highland Mary, my faithful lassie. I know *her* heart will never change.

April 2nd. Extract from the Mauchline Kirk-Session Records : ' Being ' informed that Jean Armour, an unmarried woman is said to be with child ' and that she has gone off to reside elsewhere, the Session think it their duty ' to enquire . . .'

April 9th. A further extract : ' Mrs. Armour, mother to Jean Armour, ' says that she does not suspect her daughter to be with child and that she is ' only gone to Paisley to see her friends and will soon return.'

Against *two* things I am now fixed as fate—owning Jean and staying any longer at home.

May 17th. Mossgiel. In about three or four weeks I shall probably set the press a-going. I am to commence poet *in print*.

Love is the Alpha and Omega of human enjoyment. All pleasures, all happiness flow immediately from this delicious source. I am indeed a fool, but *knave* is an infinitely worse character than anybody, I hope, will dare to give the unfortunate Robt. Burns. Many and piercing of late have been my sorrows, but I have a pretty large portion of honour still left me and an enthusiastic, incoherent benevolence. [For Mary had promised to become Mrs. Burns and it was now agreed that she should return for a short visit to her people to arrange about her marriage.] I took farewell of the dear girl on the second Sunday in May in a sequestered spot on the banks of the Ayr. [This 'sequestered spot', according to the Rev. Mr. Hamilton Paul, was 'just where the Fail disembogues into the Ayr'.]

How sweetly bloom'd the gay green birk
How rich the hawthorn's blossom,
As underneath the fragrant shade
I clasp'd her to my bosom.

The golden hours on angel wings
Flew o'er me and my dearie
For dear to me as light and life
Is my sweet Highland Mary.

Wi' monie a vow and lock'd embrace
Our parting was full tender,
And pledging aft to meet again
We tore ourselves asunder.

Meanwhile unluckily for me that black affair [with Jean] which I cannot yet bear to recollect, has led me point-blank within reach of the Kirk-Session's heaviest metal. Already the holy beagles begin to snuff the scent and I expect every moment to see them cast off and hear them after me in full cry. But as I am an old fox, I shall give them dodging and doubling for it and bye and bye I intend to earth among the mountains of Jamaica.

[A marvellous way of escape from all entanglements—and a way too of making some money—had recently been revealed through the agency of an influential doctor in Ayr. This was the chance of a post as book-keeper on an estate in Jamaica, an easy job at no less than £30 a year, very tempting indeed in comparison with £7 a year for all the hard labours of farming at Mossgiel.]

As soon as I am master of nine guineas, the price of wafting me there, I shall bespeak a passage in the very first ship that is to sail.

> Alas ! misfortune stares my face
> And points to ruin and disgrace.
> I must go . . .

I am giving up my part of the farm to Gilbert and I am making what little preparation is in my power for Jamaica.

Before leaving my native country for ever I am resolved to publish my Poems. I think they have merit and t'would be a delicious idea that I might be called a clever fellow, even though it should never reach my ears in that inhospitable clime. At the worst the roar of the Atlantic and the *novelty* of West Indian scenes will make me forget neglect.

July 9th. Mossgiel. I am just going to put on sackcloth and ashes this day. No Churchman am I, but Mr. Auld the Minister—

> Daddie Auld, Daddie Auld,
> There's a tod * in the fauld . . .   [*A fox]
> Ye'll be in at the death Daddie Auld !

—will, if I comply with the rules of the Church (by sitting once again on the Creepie-Chair to be preached at before all the congregation), give me a certificate as a single man. The Lord stand wi' the righteous, Amen, but

> When I mount the creepie-chair
> Who will sit beside me there ?

July 10th. Mossgiel. I have appeared publickly in Church. I did this to get the certificate as a bachelor, which Mr. Auld the Minister had promised me. [Mr. Auld is later referred to as ' that Boanerges of Gospel Power '.]

A letter to the Kirk-Session : ' I am heartily sorry that I have given your ' Session trouble on my account. I acknowledge that I am with child. ' Robert Burns in Mossgiel is the father. I am with great respect your ' humble servant   (*Signed*) Jean Armour.'

Extract from the Kirk-Session Records : ' Robert Burns appeared before
' the congregation, professing his repentance for the sin of fornication.'

The Rev. Mr. Auld said : ' Robert Burns—You appear there making
' profession of repentance for ye sin of fornication.   The frequency of this sin
' is just matter of lamentation among Christians and of deep humiliation to
' the guilty persons themselves.   We call you to reflect in contrition of heart
' on all the instances of your sin and guilt, in their numbers and unhappy
' consequences—and to say that what you have done you will do no more.
' Beware of returning to your sin, like the dog to his vomit or the sow to her
' wallowing in the mire.'

July 17th. Mossgiel. I am now fixed to go for the West Indies in
October.

My book will be ready in a fortnight—anyhow before I leave the country.
I have been so throng with the printing . . .

July 22nd. Mossgiel. Gilbert binds himself to aliment, clothe and
educate my natural child Elizabeth (begot upon Elizabeth Paton) in a
suitable manner as if she was his own.   To enable him to make good this
engagement I have assigned to him sundry goods, gear, cattle, furniture and
all other effects that I shall leave behind me after allowing for my part of the
debts due by him and me as joint tacksmen of the farm—and particularly
the profits that may arise from the publication of my poems.

July 30th. Jean's father has got a warrant to throw me in Jail till I find
security for an enormous sum.   So I am sculking from covert to covert—
from one friend's house to another.

Aug. 10th. Kilm^{ck}. I have at last made my public appearance [in
print]—six hundred copies, of which I have got subscriptions for about
three hundred and fifty.

' These poems ' [*extract from the Preface*] ' are not the productions of a
' poet who, with all the advantages and amid all the elegancies and idleness
' of upper life looks *down* for a rural theme, but of one who, bred to the
' plough, and amid the toil and fatigues of a laborious life, has found poetry
' its own reward. He begs his readers—particularly the Learned and Polite—
' that they will make every allowance. . . .'

Burns—by Himself

I am in such a bustle preparing for my West-India voyage. I expect a letter every day from the Master of the vessel to repair directly to Greenock. My chest is already on the road.

> The gloomy night is gath'ring fast,
> Loud roars the wild inconstant blast.
> Yon murky cloud is filled with rain,
> I see it driving o'er the plain.
> The hunter now has left the moor
> The scatt'red coveys meet secure,
> While here I wander prest with care
> Along the lovely banks of Ayr.

> The Autumn mourns her rip'ning corn
> By early Winter's ravage torn
> Across her placid, azure sky
> She sees the scowling tempest fly.
> Chill runs my blood to hear it rave.
> I think upon the stormy wave,
> Where many a danger I must dare
> Far from the bonie banks of Ayr.

> Farewell my friends, farewell my foes
> My peace with these, my love with those . . .

I composed this song, a farewell to my native land, as I conveyed my chest so far on the road to Greenock.

Another farewell—written on the blank leaf of a copy of my Poems, which I have presented to an old sweetheart Peggy Thomson [of Kirkoswald]. Poor Peggy ! She was married two years ago to an old acquaintance of mine and a most worthy fellow John Neilson, farmer. When I took farewell of her, neither she nor I could speak a syllable. John escorted me three miles on my road and we *both* parted in tears.

> Once fondly lov'd and still remember'd dear,
> Sweet early object of my youthful vows,
> Accept this mark of friendship, warm, sincere—
> Friendship—'tis all cold duty now allows.

And when you read the simple artless rhymes
    One friendly sigh for him—he asks no more—
Who distant burns in flaming torrid climes
    Or haply lies beneath th' Atlantic roar.

Aug. 14th. My plans all derang'd. The Nancy, in which I was to have gone, did not give me warning enough.

I have been very throng (mainly with the publication of the Poems) and two days' notice was too little for me to wind up my affairs. I am now to be a passenger aboard the Bell, Captn· Cathcart, who sails the end of next month.

Aug. 30th. Mossgiel.   *To William Niven.*

My Dear Friend—I have been very throng ever since I saw you and have not got the whole of my promise performed to you. But have patience and I will pay you all.

Make my friendly compl^{nts} to the lads and particularly to spunkie youthful Tammie. I will perform the rest of my promise soon. I am ever, my dear Willm your obliged   Robt Burns.

Sept. 1st. Mossgiel. I am under little apprehension now about Mr. Armour. The Kirk folks darena touch me; for although the warrant is still in existence, some of the First Gentlemen in the County have offered to befriend me. Jean will not take any step [and I am sure she will see that her parents do not take any step] against me without letting me know, as nothing but the most violent menaces could have forced her to sign the petition. I have seen her once again. She is at this moment threatened with the pangs of approaching travail. I cannot help being anxious, very anxious for her. To tell the truth I feel a miserable blank in my heart with want of her and I don't think I shall ever meet with so delicious an armful again. She has her faults and so have I and so has everybody.

Jean

Sept. 1st. Mossgiel.   *To John Richmond.*

I saw your Jenny of late and she complains bitterly against you. You are acting very wrong, my friend. Her happiness or misery is bound up in your affection or unkindness. Poor girl, she told me with tears in her eyes that she had been at great pains learning to write better, just on purpose to be able to correspond with you. I know you to be a man of honour, but this conduct of yours to a poor girl who distractly loves you and whom you have ruined . . . Forgive me for saying this. I beg your pardon. 'Tis taking an improper liberty.

I present you with my book. Never lend it, but keep it for my sake. Your ever faithful friend   R. B.

Sunday, Sept. 3rd. Mossgiel.   *To John Richmond.*

Wish me luck, dear Richmond. Jean has just brought me a fine boy and girl at one throw. God bless the little dears!   R. B.

Green grow the rashes O
Green grow the rashes O
The sweetest hours that e'er I spend
Are spent among the lasses O!

For you sae douce, ye sneer at this;
Ye're nought but senseless asses O
The sweetest hours that e'er I spend
Are spent among the lasses O!

Friday morn. Sept. 8th. Mossgiel.   *To Robert Muir.*

My Friend, my Brother—You will have heard that poor Jean has repaid my amorous mortgages *double*. A very fine boy and girl have awakened a thousand feelings that thrill, some with tender pleasure, some with foreboding anguish thro' my soul.

I believe all my hopes of staying at home will be abortive, but more of this when, in the latter end of next week, you shall be troubled with a visit from your most devoted   R. B.

On the eve of my going to Jamaica.   *To Mrs. Stewart of Stair.*

Madam—I shall ever with grateful pleasure remember the reception I got when I had the honor of waiting on you.

I am little acquainted with Politeness, but surely, did those in exalted stations know how happy they could make some classes of their Inferiours, they would never stand so high, but condescend as sweetly as did Mrs. Stewart of Stair. . . .

[Gilbert says that ' Sir William Cunninghame was also paying Robert ' some attention at this time.']

My vanity is highly gratified by the reception I have met with from the [Ayrshire] publick.

[' Even plough boys ', Robert Heron aged 22 writes, ' and maid-servants ' would gladly bestow the wages which they earn the most hardly and which ' they need for necessary cloathing if they might procure the Poems. I got ' hold of the book on Saturday night and closed it not till a late hour on the ' rising Sunday morn, after I had read over every syllable.']

Sept. 27th.   *To John Richmond.*
I am going perhaps to try for a second edition of my book. If I do, it will detain me a little longer in the country. If not I shall be gone as soon as harvest is over. God bless you.   R. B.

Bettsy M—— [Eliza Miller, another of the Belles of Mauchline] waits me.
That eternal propensity I always had to fall in love ! But the ship is on her way home that is to take me out to Jamaica; and then farewell, farewell Eliza dear and farewell dear old Scotland.
[The Poems might be a small local success, but they could not possibly be expected to bring in enough to live on or anything like it.]

Sept.   *To John Ballantine E^{re}.*
Sir—I am at a loss for expression suited to the state of my heart. God knows I know very little of great folks and as little care, but such a cordial welcome, an apparent joy at having it in your power to befriend

a man whose abilities you were pleased to honor with some degree of applause . . .

I have taken the liberty to inscribe the inclosed poem to you as all that a poet who owes you much can give.   R. B.

Poor hairum-scairum poet !

Wednesday morning. Oct.   *To Dr. MacKenzie.*

Dear Sir—I never spent an afternoon among great folks with half the pleasure as when, in company with you, I had the honor of paying my devoirs to Professor Dugald Stewart.   I would be delighted to see him perform acts of kindness and friendship even if *I* were *not* the object ; he does it with such a grace.

Your very humble serv^t Robt Burns.

Oct. 23rd.   A ne'er to be forgotten day.   I, Rab Burns, I, stumpin on ploughman shanks, I dinnered with a Lord [Lord Daer] but with a *Lord*, a Peer, an Earl's son !   Up higher my bonnet !

I watched, but I marked nought uncommon except good sense and (what surprised me) modesty.

> One rank's as well's another
> Nae honest worthy man need care
> To meet with noble youthful Daer
> For he but meets a brother.

To tell the truth I have little reason for complaint.   The [Ayrshire] world in general has been kind to me fully up to my deserts.   I was for some time past getting into the pining, mistrustful snarl of the misanthrope. However I might possess a warm heart and inoffensive manners (which last, by the way, is rather more than I could well boast), I saw myself alone.

Late October.   I was with Wilson my printer t'other day.   I made him the offer of a second edition.   He declines.   By his account the paper of a thousand copies would cost about £27 and the printing about £15 or £16.   He offers to agree for the printing if I will advance for the paper ; but this is out my power, so farewell hopes of a second edition till I grow richer, an epocha which I think will arrive at the payment of the National Debt.

[' One day after the work of the season was over '—this is how Isbal makes a first mention of the death of Highland Mary—' and I had as usual ' taken to the spinning wheel at which my mother or one of my sisters was ' assisting me—Robert and Gilbert being also present—a letter for the former ' was handed in. He went to the window to open and read it. I was ' struck by the look of agony which was the consequence. He went out of ' the room without uttering a word.']

My spirit is broke.

> O pale pale now those rosy lips
> I aft hae kiss'd sae fondly,
> And clos'd for ay the sparking glance
> That dwalt on me sae kindly,
> And mouldering now in silent dust
> That heart that loved me dearly . . .

At the close of this autumn my Highland lassie died of a malignant fever. The fever hurried my dear girl, my fairest and dearest, to the grave in a few days, before I could even hear of her illness.

> The day comes to me, but delight brings me none.
> The night comes to me, but my rest it is gone.

[Mary Campbell was buried in the West Kirkyard, Greenock. ' Robert wrote a moving letter to her father ', says John Kerr of Glasgow, ' but the stern old man neither answered it nor allowed anyone to speak ' about it in his presence. He disliked all allusions to her or to her lover.']

> Dark is the dwelling of the Dead
> And sad their house of rest . . .
> The chill blast passes swiftly by
> And flits around thy bier . . .
> Thy earthly house is circumscribed
> And solitary now . . .

If there is another life, a world to come (and would to God I as firmly believed it as I ardently wish it), there should I, with speechless agony

of rapture, again recognise my lost, my ever dear Mary, whose bosom was fraught with truth, honor, constancy and love.

> Eternity cannot efface
> Those records dear of transports past,
> Thy image at our last embrace—
> Ah ! little thought we 'twas the last . . .

> The flowers sprang wanton to be prest
> The birds sang love on every spray
> Till too too soon the glowing west
> Proclaimed the speed of winged day.

> Still o'er these scenes my mem'ry wakes
> And fondly broods with miser-care.
> Time but the impression stronger makes
> As streams their channels deeper wear.

Though sceptical in some points of our current belief, yet, when the necessities of my heart give cold philosophisings the lie, I *think* I have every evidence for the reality of a life beyond the present. At any rate I have a strong *persuasion* in a future state of existence.

I have been feeling all the secret wretchedness, the pang of disappointment, the sting of pride, with some wandering stabs of remorse, which never fail to settle on my vitals like vultures.

> Tho' all my daily care thou art
> And all my nightly dream,
> I'll hide the struggle in my heart . . .

Even when called away by Society and in the hour of Social Mirth, my gaiety is the madness of an intoxicated criminal under the hands of the executioner. All this urges me to go abroad. I have seen something of the storm of mischief thickening over my head. The consequence of my follies make it impracticable for me to stay at home. What I have written here is the settled tenor of my present resolution.

[But now a diversion—an invitation to spend the night at Loudon with some people called Lowrie. Gilbert says : ' The first time ever Robert

'heard the spinnet was at the house of Dr. Lowrie.   One of the Miss Lowries
'played.   Her sisters and her brother Archie, aged eighteen, with Robert
'and the other guests all danced.   Dr. and Mrs. Lowrie led down the dance.
'It was a delightful family scene for Robert.   He left a poem in the room
'where he slept' and afterwards wrote a letter ending—]

Nov. 13th.   Mossgiel.   *To Archie Lowrie.*
. . . My respectful compliments to Mr. and Mrs. Lowrie and warmest wishes
to the young ladies, particularly the fair musician whom I think much better
qualified than ever David was to charm an evil spirit out of Saul.   R. B.

A letter from Edinburgh from Dr. Blacklock has overthrown all my
schemes.   The Doctor belongs to a set of Critics for whose applause I had
not even dared to hope.   His idea that I would meet with every encouragement in Edinburgh for a second edition of my Poems has fired me so much
that. . . .

[Extract from a letter from Dr. Blacklock to a friend : ' It were therefore
'greatly to be wished, for the sake of the young man, that a second edition,
'more numerous than the former, could immediately be printed.   It appears
'certain that its intrinsic merit and the exertion of his friends might give it a
'more universal circulation than any thing of the kind which has been
'published within my memory.']

1786

Nov. 15th.   Mossgiel.   *To Mrs. Dunlop.*
Madam—I was truly sorry I was not at home yesterday.

['This', says Gilbert, 'was the beginning of a correspondence which
'ended only with Robert's life.   He was on the point of setting out for
'Edinburgh when Mrs. Dunlop (then aged 56), having just read The
'Cotter's Saturday Night, sent off a person express to Mossgiel, distant
'fifteen or sixteen miles, with a very obliging letter, begging that Robert
'would do her the pleasure of calling at Dunlop House as soon as
'convenient.']

I was much honored by the handsome compliments you are pleased to pay
my poetic abilities.   Had you been thoroughly acquainted with me, Madam,

you could not have touched my darling heart-chord more sweetly than by noticing my attempts.

I am thinking to go to Edin[r] in a week or two at farthest, to throw off a second impression of my book. On my return, I shall certainly do myself the honor to wait on you and thank you in person for the obliging notice you have been pleased to take of, Madam, your much indebted and very humble serv[t]. Robert Burns.

Mossgiel. 18th Nov[r]. I am thinking for my Edinburgh expedition on Monday or Tuesday come se'ennight, for pos.

Mrs. Dunlop

Copy of a letter to Miss Alexander of Ballochmyle inclosing a song I had just composed on her.

Mossgiel. 18th Nov[r].

Madam—A stranger begs leave to present you with the inclosed poem.

I had roved out on the banks of Ayr to view nature in all the gayety of the vernal year. The sun was flaming o'er the distant western hills; not a breath stirred the crimson opening blossom or the spreading leaf. 'Twas a golden moment. I listened to the warblers pouring their harmony on every hand & frequently turned out of my path lest I should disturb their little songs or frighten them. Such was the scene & such the hour when I spied *one of the fairest* pieces of nature's workmanship that has ever crowned a poetic landscape. I dare say, Madam, you do not recollect it. I believe you scarcely noticed me.

The inclosed song was the work of my return home. I am going to print a second edition of my poems, but cannot insert these verses without your permission.

I have the honor to be, Madam, your most obedient & very humble serv[t] Rob[t] Burns.

79

Well Mr. Burns & *did* the Lady give you permission ? No ! She was too fine a Lady to *notice* so plain a compliment. As to her brothers, whom I have since met on more equal terms, why should I quarrel with their want of attention to me ? When Fate swore that their purse should be full, Nature was equally positive that their heads should be empty.

[According to Miss Alexander herself ' the grounds being forbidden ' to unauthorised strangers, the evening being far advanced and the encounter ' very sudden, I was startled but instantly recovered myself and passed on '.]

Mossgiel. 20th Novr. I am thinking to set out the beginning of next week for the City. [Gilbert and the rest of the family most enthusiastic.] I have pocketed, all expenses deducted, near twenty pounds. This has come very seasonable.

Mossgiel. c. Novr 22nd. Away I am posting to-morrow to Edinburgh [' on a borrowed pony', Gilbert notes], without a single acquaintance in town or a single letter of introduction in my pocket.

II

GREAT FOLKS

Edin^r c. Nov. 29th. I arrived here in town on Tuesday was se'ennight [at the lodging of young John Richmond in Baxter's Close, Lawnmarket; the joint rent 3/- a week. They shared the one bed. Richmond was now 19.] Ever since my arrival I have suffered with a miserable head-ach & stomach complaint but am now a good deal better.

I am entering the lists flushed with hope to struggle for notice, for distinction, in common with hundreds of others. But who are they? Men like myself. And seven tenths of them come short of my natural advantages! Besides I have two good pairs of breeks. My coat is Scotch of the best. And I have a Holland cravat, stockings and pumps.

That no scheme to frustrate my hopes may prosper is the prayer of Robt Burns.

> There's a youth in this city, it were a great pity
> That he from our lassies should wander awa',
> For he's bonie and braw, weel-favor'd with a',
> And his hair has a natural buckle and a'.
>
> His coat is the hue o' his bonnet sae blue
> His fecket is white as the new driven snaw,
> His hose they are blue and his shoon like the sloe
> And, his clean siller buckles, they dazzle us a' . . .

My Highland bonnet, once my proudest dress, is at present exchanged for a ten shilling *hat*. So hey brave Robin lad, cock up your beaver!

Edinburgh. 1 Dec^r.   *To Sir John Whitefoord.*
Sir—You are the first gentleman here who has interested himself for me. I am not master enough of the etiquette of these matters to know,

nor did I stay to inquire, whether propriety disallows my thanking you in this manner. But you will do me the justice to believe that this letter is not the manoeuvre of foot-licking servility. Poor as I am, I have an independent fortune at the plough-tail.

I have no return, Sir, to make to you for your goodness but one—the honest, warm wishes of a grateful heart for your happiness.

Robt Burns.

Professor Dugald Stewart and others of my learned acquaintances have put me in a periodical paper called The Lounger. [The following is an extract from a long article in the December number by Mr. Henry MacKenzie.]

' I introduce a poet of our own country, with whose writings I have
' lately become acquainted, Robert Burns, an Ayr-shire ploughman,
' whom I think I may safely pronounce a genius.

' In mentioning the circumstances of his humble station I mean not
' to urge the merits of his poetry solely in relation to the lowness of his
' birth and the little opportunity which his education could afford. His
' poetry seems to me *fully* entitled to obtain our applause.

' Against some passages in his poems it has been objected that they
' breathe a spirit of libertinism and irreligion. But when we consider
' the ignorance of the lower classes of the people, when we reflect on his
' rank in life, the habits to which he must have been subject and the society
' in which he must have mixed, we regret—perhaps more than wonder—
' that delicacy should be so often offended in perusing a volume in which
' there is much to interest and please us.']

[And here is the *Edinburgh Review* :
' There are peculiarities in his work which remind us of the lowness
' of his origin, and faults for which the defects of his education afford an
' obvious cause. There is a want of polish or at least of respectfulness
' in the general tone of his gallantry. He writes with more passion perhaps
' on the subject of love than any other poet whatever—but with a fervour
' that is sometimes indelicate and seldom accomodated to the timidity and
' sweet austere composure of women of refinement. In Burn's work there
' is much to censure as well as much to praise. But it is impossible to
' read his productions without forming a higher idea of the intelligence,

83

'taste and accomplishments of our peasantry than most of those in the
'higher ranks are disposed to entertain.']

[And the *Monthly Review*:
  'Great efforts have been made by the inhabitants of Scotland of the
'superior ranks to approximate in their speech to the pure English standard;
'and this has made it difficult to write in the Scottish dialect without
'exciting in them (the superior ranks) some feelings of disgust. Mr.
'Burns . . .']

  Edin^r Dec. 7th. My poor unfortunate songs! Well, I care not, not
I. I am in a fair way of becoming as eminent as Thomas à Kempis or
John Bunyan. So let the critics go whistle! ('The lowness of his origin'
. . . 'the ignorance of the lower classes' . . . 'the want of polish' . . .
'feelings of disgust' . . .)

> Now deil ma care about their jaw . . .
> I'll cock my nose aboon them a'!

I was until just lately *too* obscure. But now I tremble lest I should be
ruined by being dragged too suddenly into the glare of polite and learned
observation.

  Dec. 13th Edin^r. Here at Edinburgh I mingle among many classes
of men, all of them new to me. I am in a new world. I am all attention.
I have been introduced to a good many of the Noblesse. My avowed
patrons are amongst others the Duchess of Gordon, Lord and Lady
Glencairn with my Lord & Lady Betty, The Earl of Buchan, the Earl
of Eglinton, the Honble Henry Erskine, Sir John Whitefoord, Professor
Dugald Stewart of Catrine (who fills the Moral Philosophy Chair at the
University, a gentleman who has treated me with peculiar kindness,
entering into my interests with so much zeal that I shall ever regard his
patronage & kindly good offices as a most valued consequence of my
success here)—and Mr. Henry MacKenzie, author of 'The Man of Feeling'. Dr John Moore also is doing me the honor to interest himself very
warmly on my behalf. As for Dr Blacklock, whom I see very often,
I have found in him what I would have expected, a clear head and a
warm heart. We all know *his* merit—though his Poems are rather silly.

Through my Lord Glencairn's influence the Caledonian Hunt one & all subscribe for the 2ⁿᵈ Edition—to be published by Creech.

An unknown hand left ten guineas 'for the Ayrshire Bard' this morning. I have since discovered my generous unknown friend to be Patrick Miller Esq. brother of Lord Glenlee, the Lord Justice Clerk. I drank a glass of claret with him by invitation at his own house yesternight.

Also I have met in Mr. Dalrymple of Orangefield a friend closer than a brother. The warmth with which he interests himself in my affairs is of the same enthusiastic kind which Mr. Aiken and the few patrons of my earlier days showed.

I saw Andrew Aiken today. He is very well.

[Fashionable Mrs. Alison Cockburn of Fairnilee—'an old lady', Robert calls her ' a Mrs. Cockburn of I forget what place'—authoress of a new version of Flowers of the Forest, writes: ' The town is at present 'agog with the ploughman poet, who receives adulation with native 'dignity and is the very figure of his profession, strong and coarse, but 'he has a most enthusiastic heart of love. He has seen the Duchess of 'Gordon and all the gay world. The man will be spoiled, if he can 'spoil, but he keeps his simple manners and is quite sober. No doubt 'he will be at the Hunt Ball tomorrow. His favourite for looks and 'manners is Eliza Burnet—no bad judge indeed !']

Dec. 27th. Edinʳ. Heavenly Miss Eliza Burnet ! There has not been anything nearly like her, in beauty, grace and goodness since Eve on the first day of her existance. She is daughter to Lord Monboddo at whose house I have been more than once.

[Professor Dalzel writes, ' We have got a poet in town just now, whom 'everybody is taking notice of—a ploughman from Ayrshire—a man of 'unquestionable genius. He is a fellow of strong common sense. But 'he runs the risk of being spoiled by the excessive attention paid him 'just now by persons of all ranks. I saw him at an assembly t'other 'night. The Duchess of Gordon and other ladies of rank took notice 'of him. He behaves wonderfully well, very independant, though not 'forward.']

1787

Jan 7th. Edinr. I have met a very pretty girl, a Lothian farmer's daughter, whom I have almost persuaded to accompany me to the west country, should I ever return to settle there. I had a most delicious ride from Leith to her house yesternight in a hackney-coach with her brother and two sisters and brother's wife. We dined all together at a common friend's house in Leith and danced, drank and sang till late enough. The claret was good and I thirsty.

[Josiah Walker, tutor to the Marquis Tullibardine, who first met Robert at breakfast at Dr. Blacklock's, is among those obviously impressed—
' His person, though strong and well knit and much superior to what
' might be expected in a ploughman, is still rather course in outline. His
' emotions are firm and decided, though without any pretentions to grace.
' In conversation he is powerful. His conceptions and expression are of
' corresponding vigour and on all subjects are as remote as possible from
' commonplaces.
   ' After breakfast I requested him to communicate some of his unpub-
' lished pieces. I paid particular attention to his recitation, which was
' plain, slow, articulate and forcible but without any eloquence or art.
' He was standing during the time with his face towards the window to
' which—and not to his auditors—he directed his eyes.
   ' The day after this I supped in company with him at Professor Blair's.
' The other guests had each been invited to have an opportunity of meeting
' with the poet-ploughman. Though he therefore furnished the greatest
' proportion of the conversation he did no more than what he saw evidently
' was expected. Men of genius are often prone to comit blunders in
' company from ignorance or negligence of the laws of conversation.
' From singularities of this sort Burns is unusually free.']

Sat.   *To Lord Monboddo.*

I shall do myself the honor, Sir, to dine with you tomorrow as you obligingly request.
   My conscience twitting me with having neglected to send Miss Eliza a song which she wished to have, I inclose it for her—with one or two more. I have the honour to be, my Lord, your very humble servt

Robt Burns.

Great Folks

[Professor Dugald Stewart thinks that 'the attentions he has received
'during his stay in town from all ranks are such as would have turned
'any head but his own. He has retained the same simplicity of manners
'and appearance which struck me so forcibly when I first saw him in the
'country. The variety of his engagements while in Edinburgh have
'prevented me from seeing him as often as I could have wished. He has
'called on me once or twice at my request early in the morning and walked
'with me to the Braid Hills, when he charmed me still more by his private
'conversation than he had ever done in company, even though his praise
'of those he loved was sometimes indiscriminate and extravagant.
' In his political principles he is a Jacobite, perhaps owing partly to
'the fact that his father was originally from one of the Earl Marischall's
'estates (Inverugie).']

I suspect that my political tenets, such as they are, may be rather heretical
in the opinion of some of my best friends here. But I would not have
a dissocial word about it with any one of God's creatures, although I
have a few first principles in politics which I believe I would not
easily part with. I cannot rise to the exalted ideas of a Citizen-of-the-
World-at-large. I have all those national prejudices which I believe glow
peculiarly strong in the breast of a Scotsman.

[Mrs. Walter Riddell later describes Robert thus : 'His figure cer-
'tainly bears the authentic impress of his birth and original station in life.
'His features are stamped with the firmness of conscious though not arrogant
'pre-eminence. The animated expressions of his countenance are peculiar
'to himself, the rapid lightnings of his eye, the fiery glances, harbingers
'of some flash of genius. His voice alone can improve upon the magic
'of his eyes. Sonorous, with the finest modulation, it captivates the ear.']

['I should pronounce him', Professor Dugald Stewart goes on, 'fitted
'to excel in whatever walk of ambition he had chosen to exert his
abilities.']

Dr. Dugald Stewart is the most perfect character I ever saw for generosity,
strength of mind, manly dignity and wit. In telling a story he excels. He
is one of the very first public speakers.

[John Syme, with Alexander Cunningham ('my dear and much valued friend') and others agree that 'He is of a form that indicates agility 'as well as strength. His dark and haughty countenance easily relaxes 'into the most extravagant mirth.']

I am still undetermined as to the future and usually never think of it.

My honoured friend and first patron Mr. Aiken [the lawyer in Ayr, Andrew's father] thinks a hint about the mischevous nature of intoxicated vanity not unseasonable. Alas, he is wide of the mark. And Mrs. Dunlop—she is afraid that I shall grow *intoxicated* with my prosperity. Dr. Lowrie [Archie's father], he too sends friendly hints. I thank all my friends but I do not need these hints as much as they imagine. They are dazed by newspaper reports.

Indeed it is not easy to imagine a more helpless state than his whose poetic fancy gives him some pretentions to the politesse of life, yet is as poor as I am.

> Yon, bustling and justling,
>   Forget each grief and pain.
> I, listless yet restless,
>   Find every prospect vain.

Till lately I looked on every side for a *ray* of light; and the consequences of my follies may perhaps still make it impracticable for me to stay at home. I look down on the future as I would into the bottomless pit.

[But in *The Lounger* Mr. Henry MacKenzie again comes forward: 'I have learned that he has been obliged to form the resolution of 'leaving his native land. I trust that means may be found to prevent 'this.']

Lord Glencairn has sent a parcel of subscription bills (for the new edition of the Poems) to the Marquiss of Graham with downright orders to get them filled up with all the first Scottish names about Court. He has likewise wrote to the Duke of Montague and is about to write to the Duke of Portland on my behalf.

Few of the sore evils under the sun give me more uneasiness than how I am received when I have the honour to be called to the tables of the Great. Conscious that men are born equal I meet with the self-sufficient stately stupidity of a Squire Something or a Sir Somebody. How it mortifies me to hear the fellow's shallow idiot attempts at wit applauded —a fellow whose abilities would scarcely have made an eightpenny tailor and whose heart is not worth three farthings—while my remark is neglected.

The noble Lord Glencairn showed so much attention—engrossing attention—one day to a dunderpate that I was within half a point of throwing down my gage of contemptuous defiance. But Glencairn took my hand and looked so benevolently good at parting that I shall love him until my dying day.

['A sort of dignified plainness and simplicity' is what young Walter Scott notices particularly. 'I was a lad of fifteen when he first came to 'Edinburgh. His person was strong and robust, his manners rustic but 'not clownish. His features are represented in Mr. Nasmyth's picture; 'but to me it conveys the idea that they are *diminished* as if seen in perspective.

'There was a strong impression of shrewdness in all his lineaments; 'the eyes alone, I think, indicated the poetical temperament. They were 'large and dark. They glowed (I say literally glowed) when he spoke 'with feeling and interest. I never saw such eyes in a human head, though 'I have seen the most distinguished men. His conversation expressed 'perfect self-confidence without the slightest presumption. He was much 'caressed in Edinburgh, but the efforts made for his relief were extremely 'trifling.

'In general society he often permitted his determination of vindicating 'his personal dignity to hurry into unjustifiable resentment of slight or 'imagined neglect. This ill-judged jealousy of precedence led him often 'to place his own pretensions to notice in competition with those of the 'company who, he conceived, might found theirs on birth or fortune.

' On such occasions it was no easy task to deal with him. The dignity,
' the spirit, the indignation of Burns was that of a plebian, of a high-souled
' plebian indeed, but still a plebian.

' Although so poor as to be ever on the very brink of absolute ruin,
' looking forward now to the situation of a *foot-soldier*, now to that of a
' *common beggar*, he was as proud and independent as if he possessed a
' prince's revenue.

' In the society of men of taste who could relish his conversation he
' was eloquent, impressive and instructing. But it was in female circles
' that his powers of expression displayed their utmost fascination.']

[Josiah Walker goes so far as to say: ' In no man is sexuality more
' powerful or apparent. The presence of women produce an instant
' revolution in his manner. The tone of his conversation and demeanour
' changes and he endeavours to recommend himself by other powers of
' pleasing. Nor are these powers employed without success, even with
' those who could not for a moment admit a thought of him as a lover.'

The Duchess of Gordon for example said that ' *she had been completely
' carried off her feet*'.

Josiah writes further of Robert's ' dark and luxuriant sensibility '—' his
' luminous expression ' and declares that ' he indeed is favoured in personal
' appearance.'

Alexander Peterkin adds : ' He is applauded, carressed and befriended
' by the most eminent and he adorns the circles of literature and fashion
' with the native charms of his unaffected and masculine powers.']

Never did Saul's armour sit so heavy on David as does the encumbering
robe of public notice with which friendship and patronage have invested
me. I do not say this in affected modesty. I have long studied myself
such as I lately was and such as I believe I had better still have been, and
I think I know pretty exactly what ground I occupy both as a man and
a poet; and however the world or a friend may sometimes differ from
me in that particular, I stand for it in silent resolve.

With better health and more spirits I shall write an account of my
every step.

Great Folks

[Young John Richmond, with whom Robert is still sharing the one bed in their lodgings, says ' I help him transcribe his poems for the ' press. When he comes in of a night, jaded, I read aloud to him till he ' falls asleep. He keeps good hours and he lives soberly.

' After a brief residence in town his plain dress has been exchanged for ' a suit of blue and buff, with buckskin breeches and top boots. He con-'tinues to wear his hair tied behind and spread upon his forehead, but ' without powder, though powder is now nearly universal. On the ' whole his appearance is modest and becoming.

' It is remarked that he shows no sign of embarrassment in refined ' society.']

Edinr Jan. A man of consequence and fashion shall richly repay a deed of kindness with a nod and a smile or a hearty shake of the hand; while a *poor* fellow's gratitude, like a copper coin, is of small account in the currency of the world.

Edinr. Jann 11th. A Gentleman waited on me yesterday and gave me, by Lord Eglingtoun's order, ten guineas by way of subscription for my 2nd Edition.

I met with Lord Maitland and a brother of his today at breakfast. They are exceedingly easy, accesible, agreable fellows and seemingly pretty clever.

Sir John Whiteford's son John, who calls very frequently on me is in a fuss today like a coronation. This is the Great day—the Assembly and Ball of the Caledonian Hunt; and John has had the good luck to engage the hand of the beauty-famed and wealth-celebrated Miss MacAdam. John is desparately in for it there—and, I am afraid, will be desperate indeed.

[Alexander Smellie the printer's son, notes how in the printing office Burns ' will walk up and down cracking a whip that he carries. There ' is a particular stool which he uniformly occupies while correcting his

Miss Chalmers

' proof-sheets. He will not sit on any
' other. It is known as Burns's stool.
' One day it happened that Sir John
' Dalrymple, who was printing an Essay,
' occupied the stool. Burns came in.
' Before he could say anything he was
' requested to walk into the composing
' room. The opportunity was taken to
' request Sir John for the stool (but
' without mentioning Burns's name). Sir
' John said " I will not give up my seat
' " to yon impudent staring fellow."
' Upon which he was informed that the
' impudent staring fellow was Robert
' Burns the poet. " Good gracious ! "
' exclaimed Sir John, instantly leaving
' the stool, " Give him all the seats in
' your " house ! " ']

Jan. Edinr.   *To Miss Peggy Chalmers.*[1]

I know you will laugh when I tell you that your pianoforte and you
together have play'd the deuce somehow about my heart. I am not sure
what is the matter with me. When you whisper or look kindly to another
it gives me a draught of damnation. I have a kind of wayward wish to be
with you ten minutes by yourself; though what I would say Heaven above
knows. You may perhaps give yourself airs of distance on this. That
will *completely* cure me.   R. B.

Jan. 14th. Edr. I am still dark as was Chaos in respect to Futurity.
My generous friend Mr. Patrick Miller (Lord Glenlee's brother) has been
talking with me about the lease of some farm or other near Dumfries—the
third town of importance and elegance in Scotland. But Mr. Miller is no
judge of land ; and though I dare say he means to favour me, yet he may give

---

[1] [*Daughter of a gentleman whose farm had been within easy walking distance of Lochlea. Visits to
Miss Peggy, now living with her cousins the Hamiltons in Edinburgh, are becoming frequent.*]

me a bargain that may ruin me. I have promised to meet him on his lands some time in May.

Charlotte Hamilton also (Peggy Chalmers's cousin) is lovely. Her features have the smile of sweetness. Her complexion is equal to that of Miss Eliza Burnet (Lord Monboddo's daughter). Her lips are fascinating. The two girls are luxuriantly happy with one another without apparently that commonly necessary appendage to female bliss, a *lover*. They are angelic creatures.

I went to a Mason-Lodge yesternight. The meeting was most numerous and elegant. The Grand Master, who presided with great solemnity, among other general toasts gave ' Caledonia's Bard, Brother B——', which rung through the whole assembly with multiplied honors and repeated acclamations. As I had no idea such a thing would happen, I was downright thunderstruck and, trembling in every nerve, made the best return in my power. As I finished some of the Grand Officers said just so loud as I could hear (and with a comforting accent) ' *Very well indeed !* ' which set me something to rights again.

I have just now had a visit from my landlady, a staid sober piously-disposed widow who firmly believes that her husband is in heaven ; and having been very happy with him on earth, she vigorously and perseveringly practices some of the most distinguishing Christian virtues such as attending Church, railing against vice etc. so that she may be qualified to meet her dear quondam bedfellow in that happy place where the unclean and the ungodly shall never enter.

She is at present in sore tribulation respecting some ' daughters of Belial ' who are on the floor immediately above. As the floors are low and ill-plaistered, we can easily distinguish our laughter-loving, night-rejoicing neighbours—when they are eating, when they are drinking, when they are . . . &c. My landlady told me that we should not be envious. ' These 'base jades' she said 'shall one day be in hell, gnashing their teeth over a 'cup of God's wrath !'

Jan. 15th. Edinr.   *To Mrs. Dunlop.*

Madam—The word you object to does not strike me as an improper epithet.   On your finding fault with it, I distrusted my own judgment and applied for the opinion of some of the *literati* here who honour me with their critical strictures.   They *all* allow it to be proper.   R. B.

By far the most agreable hours I spend in Edinr. must be placed to the account of Miss Lowrie [Archie's sister] and her pianoforte.   The other night at the concert I saw her in a seat not very distant and went up to pay my respects to her.   On my return Mr. Henry MacKenzie asked me who she was.

I am determined to go to the Play.   I shall call on Archie [now a student at Edinburgh University], and if Miss Lowrie can come too I shall be *very* happy.   If not I suppose Archie will have no objection to take a seat with me in the pit.

While Wisdom has been chalking out the straight way, I have zigzagged over the path.   I have compromised matters of late by uncoupling my heart and fancy for a sight-chance after *a certain Edinr. belle.*   My devotions proceed no farther than a forenoon's walk, a sentimental conversation, now and then a squeeze of the hand and, when sequestered propriety will allow, a kiss. 'Kissing is the key o' love' was an old song of my Mither's.

There is nothing in the whole frame of man which seems to me so unaccountable as conscience.   Were conscience efficient to *prevent* a mischief, it might be of use; but at the beginning of the business its feeble efforts are to the workings of passion as the infant frosts of an autumnal morning to the unclouded fervor of the rising sun.   And no sooner are the tumultuous doings of the wicked deed over than in the very vortex of our horrors, up starts conscience and harrows us with the feelings of the damned.

Feb. 24th Edinr.   I am getting my phiz done by an eminent engraver Mr. Beugo, and if it can be ready in time I will appear in my book, looking like other *fools*, to my title-page.

[*March 8th Edinburgh.* A letter received from Peter Stuart saying—' Next
' week I hope I may have the pleasure of seeing you over a morning cup of
' tea, but by all accounts it will be a matter of difficulty to see you at all unless
' your company is bespoke a week beforehand. There is a rumour here
' concerning your great intimacy with the Duchess of Gordon and other
' ladies of distinction.']

It is not yet three months since home was so hot for me that I was on the
wing for the western shore of the Atlantic, not to make a fortune but to hide
my disgrace. I knew no other employment than following the plough nor
could I boast anything higher than a distant acquaintance with a country
clergyman. Now I am distinguished, patronised, befriended. Today the
noble Earl of Glencairn took me by the hand and interested himself further
in my concerns. I still often feel myself embarrassed.

I shall soon be in print (the Second Edition) in a week or ten days at
farthest.
I guess that I shall clear between two and three hundred pounds. With
that sum I intend—so far as I may be said to have any intention—to return
to my old acquaintance the plough and to commence Farmer. I do *not*
intend to give up Poesy ! While following the plough or building up my
shocks I shall in my wonted way have leisure to woo my rustic Muse, who
gave me the notice of Caledonia.
I have seen a little of the luxuries of upper stations here in Edinburgh.
I can live without them. I shall never blush for my own poverty nor for the
poverty of my country. A country fellow at the plough, his acre well tilled
is right enough.

March 21st Edinr.   To my dear James Candlish, Mauchline.
You will think by my delaying to write to you, who are almost the earliest
friend that I have on earth, that I am so drowned in the intoxication of good
fortune as to be indifferent to old and once dear connections. The truth is,
(for I am awkward at a fib) I was determined to write a good letter full of
argument, erudition and all that. I thought of it and thought of it, but for
my soul I cannot, and lest you should mistake the cause of my silence, I just
sit down to tell you so. I shall expect to hear from you ; welcome sense,

welcome nonsense. Dont impart my brevity to a wrong cause. I am still as when we were together sporting about the lady-thorn. With the warmest sincerity, my dear old friend, your   R. B.

March Edinr.   *To Archie Lowrie.*

I cannot be with you at tea, as I have just got a summons to wait on Lord Glencairn in the afternoon. But I expect to do myself the pleasure of calling on you between seven and eight.   R. B.

March 22nd Edinr.   *To Mrs. Dunlop.*

Madam—I was honoured by yours of the 26th Feb. In giving me your friendship you have given me a solid permanent addition to my happiness. I have today corrected the last proof sheets of my Poems and have now only the Glossary and subscribers names to print. Printing this last is much against my will, but some of my friends whom I do not choose to thwart will have it so.

Should the profits afford it I *would* take your hint of a military life as the most congenial to my feelings and situation, but I have a fond aged mother to care for and some other bosom ties perhaps equally tender, so I shall return to my rural shades, in all likelihood never more to quit them.   R. B.

April 19th. Edinr. It is impossible, at least I find it impossible to be *always* entertaining and witty, though I am very willing to admit that I have poetical abilities. I generally like pretty well to hear myself speaking—at least *fully* as well as anybody else.

Few if any other writers are so intimately acquainted with my walks of life and with the classes among whom I have chiefly mingled. I have now seen a good deal of life here in Edinburgh and though I am honoured by the many civilities, the kindness, the friendship of all these illustrious Lights of Literature, I *still* claim this priviledge of thinking for myself.

I know very well that it is only the *novelty* of my character, my awkard rusticity and crude unpolished ideas that have raised this partial tide of public notice. And too surely do I see that time when the same tide will leave me and recede. I hate to presage ill luck, but I have made up my mind that neglect will not surprise me. I come abroad in print for certain on Wednesday.

April 23rd Edinr. I leave Edinr. in the course of ten days or a fortnight for a leisurely pilgrimage with Robert Ainslie, my most intimate friend here [a lawyer's apprentice]. We are to visit some of the classic ground of Caledonia.

April 30th Edinr.   *To Mrs. Dunlop.*

Your criticisms, Madam, I understand very well and could wish to have pleased you better. You are right in your guess that I am not very amenable to counsel. Poets much my superiors have so flattered those who possessed wealth and power that I am determined to flatter no created being, so help me God. I never will crouch to any man. I set as little by kings, lords, clergy, critics, &c. as all these respectable gentry do by my bardship. I know what I may expect of the world by and by—abuse and perhaps neglect.

As for my Dream poem, which has unfortunately incurred your displeasure, I hope to appear in its defence at Dunlop House in four weeks or less. I have the honour to be, Madam, your very highly indebted humble servant   Robt. Burns.

Improper stanzas. I do not really object to leaving out improper stanzas where that can be done *without spoiling the whole*.

[Josiah Walker says that ' At a literary party that spring the conversation
' turned to Gray's " Elegy ", a poem of which Robert was enthusiastically
' fond. A clergyman who was present made an ill timed attack on it.
' Robert defended it, urging the clergyman to bring forward passages which
' he thought exceptionable. The clergyman made several attempts to quote
' the poem, but always in a blundering inaccurate manner. At length
' Robert roused himself and with an eye flashing contempt called the
' clergyman a " damned blockhead ".
' His hostess beside whom he was sitting had a child on her knee.
' Robert turned to the child and said " I beg your pardon my little dear." ']

Monday morning May 1st Edinburgh.   *To Patrick Miller Esqre.*

When you kindly offered to accomodate me with a farm, I was afraid to think of it. But now when by the appearance of a second edition of my book, I may reckon on a middling farming capital, there is nothing I wish for more than to resume the plough.

Indolence and innatention to business I *have* sometimes been guilty of, but extravagence never. If therefore, Sir, you could fix me in any sequester'd romantic spot and let me have such a lease as by care and industry I might live in humble decency and have a spare hour now and then to write out an idle rhyme . . . I am still afraid Sir, to dwell on the idea lest Fortune have not such happiness in store for me,   R. B.

R. B. by Mr. Miers

May 6th. I was so hurried leaving Edinburgh [with Robert Ainslie, the lawyer's apprentice] that I absolutely forgot several things I ought to have minded.

Lammermuir Hills miserably dreary but at times very picturesque. Reach Berrywell. Old Mr. Ainslie (Factor to Lord Douglas) an uncommon character, his hobbies agriculture, philosophy and politics, very intelligent. Mrs. A. an excellent, sensible, cheerful, amiable old woman. Miss A. a little *embonpoint* but handsome; her face—particularly her eyes—full of sweetness and good humour. Douglas, the youngest, a clever, fine, promising young fellow. The family meeting with Robert (my *compagnon de voyage*) very charming. The whole family remarkably attached to their menials.

May 7th. Coldstream. Went over to England. Dined with Robert Ainslie and Mr. Foreman. Beat Mr. F. in a dispute about Voltaire.

May 8th. Breakfast at Kelso. Fine bridge over the Tweed. Enchanting views on both sides of the river, particularly on the Scotch side.

['The weather charming'—this from some jottings by young Ainslie— 'the travellers youthful and in good spirits.']

> The chanting linnet or the mellow thrush
> Hailing the setting sun, sweet in the green thorn bush,
> The soaring lark, the perching red-breast shrill
> Or deep toned plovers grey wild-whistling o'er the hill
> Some warbler's dying fall . . .

Ruins of Roxburgh Castle—a holly bush growing where James II of Scotland was accidentally killed by the bursting of a cannon. A small religious ruin and a fine old garden, planted by the religious, rooted out and *destroyed by an English hottentot, a Mr. Cole.*

Bad roads. Turnip and sheep husbandry—great improvements. Mr. MacDowal at Caverton Mill with whom we dined to-day, sold his sheep, ewe and lamb together at two guineas a piece. Wash their sheep before shearing. Magnificence of farmers and farm houses.

Up Teviot and up Jed to Jedburgh and so wish myself goodnight.

> Clamorous craiks * at close of day   [*Corn-crakes, of course]
> 'Mang fields o' flowering clover gay . . .

May 9th. Breakfast in Jedburgh. Dine with a Captain Rutherford, a polite, soldier-like gentleman who showed a particular respect to my Bardship. My name has made a small noise in the country.

Miss Rutherford too far gone woman to expose so much of a swelling bosom, but her face very fine.

May 10th. Return to Jedburgh. Walk up Jed with some ladies. Introduced to the clergyman of the place, a gentleman sadly addicted to punning. The two elder ladies are ugly and stupid and bore me most shockingly.

But there is also a Miss Isabella Lindsay, a good-humoured girl, rather short, but handsome and extremely graceful—beautiful hazel eyes. Shook myself loose (after several unsuccessful efforts) of the elder ladies and somehow or other got hold of Miss Lindsay's arm. Miss seemed very well pleased. After some little chit-chat of the tender kind, I presented her with a proof-print of my *nob*, which she accepted with something more than gratitude. Was waited on by the magistrates and presented with the freedom of the burgh.

Took farewell of Jedburgh with some melancholy. Disagreeable sensations. Sweet Isabella Lindsay! That love-kindling eye must beam on another; that graceful form must bless another's arms, not mine.

> Her smiling, sae wyling,
>   Would make a wretch forget his woe,
> What pleasure, what treasure
>   Upon those rosy lips to grow.

Like harmony her motion
  Her pretty ankle is a spy
Betraying fair proportion
  Would make a saint forget the sky.

Sae warming, sae charming
  Her faultless form and graceful air
Ilk feature—auld Nature
  Declared that she could do nae mair.

May 11th. Kelso. Farmers Club—all gentlemen. Each of them keeps a hunter and attends the fox-hunting in the country. Dine with Sir Alexander Don, a pretty clever fellow, but far from being a match for his divine lady.

May 12th. A very wet day. Dined with Lady Hariot.

[John Syme, Writer to the Signet, expatiates on ' the electric flashes of the ' poet's eloquence at table and the burning satiric shafts which he launched ' at those whom he disliked or who had betrayed any affectation or meanness ' in their behaviour.

' His expression varied perpetually and it was beautiful how his lips ' indicated the sentiment he was about to utter. His eyes and lips—the first ' remarkable for fire and the second for flexibility—formed at all times an ' index to his mind.']

May 13th. Visit Dryburgh, a fine old ruined abbey. Still bad weather. Up Tweed to Melrose. Dine there and visit that far-famed glorious ruin.

Selkirk. In a solitary inn. I am jaded to death. A miserable wet day's riding . . . [The Post just in, letters to answer and some newspapers to read] . . . Mrs. Fame is very idle to tell so many lies. I have *not* been at Glasgow, *nor* do I intend for London.

May 14th. Come to Inverleithing, a famous Spa in the vicinity of the palace of Traquair. Here, having dined and drank some Galloway-whey, I remain till tomorrow. Saw Ellibanks and Ellibraes, on either side of the Tweed.

May 15th. Drank tea yesternight at Pirn. Breakfasted today with Mr. Ballantyne of Hollowlee. Dine at a country inn at Earlston, the birthplace and residence of Thomas the Rhymer. Saw the ruins of the castle.

May 16th. Dine at Dunse with the Farmers' Club. Impossible to do them justice.

May 17th. Breakfast at Berrywell and walk in to Dunse to see a famous knife made by a cutler there. Presented to an Italian prince.

May 18th. Ride to Berwick—an idle town, rudely picturesque. Meet Lord Errol in walking round the walls. His Lordship's flattering notice of me. Dine with Mr. Clunzie, merchant.

After dinner we came up a bold shore and over a wild country to Eyemouth. Sup and sleep at Mr. Grieve's. Spent the day at Mr. Grieve's. The Miss Grieves very good girls. Take a sail after dinner. My heart got a brush from Miss Betsey.

May 20th. Set out to Dunbar. Call at Mr. Sheriffs, where Robert Ainslie and I dine. Mr. S. talkative and conceited. I talked of love to Nancy the whole evening.

May 21st. Sir James Hall of Dunglass, having heard of my being in the neighbourhood, came to breakfast. Took me to see his fine scenery on the stream of Dunglass—the most romantic place I ever saw. Sir James and his Lady a happy couple.

Pass through the most glorious corn-country till I reach Dunbar, a neat little town. Dine with Provost Fall. Mrs. F. a genius in painting, fully more clever in the fine arts and sciences than my friend Lady Waucope, without her consumate assurance of her abilities.

May 22nd. Breakfast at Skateraw.

May 23rd. Leave for Duns. Found the sweet Miss Ainslie all alone at Berrywell. How well-bred, how frank, how good she is. Charming Rachel. Heavenly Powers who know the weakness of human hearts, support mine! What happiness must I see, only to remind me that I cannot enjoy it . . .

> False flatterer, Hope, away
> Nor think to lure us as in days of yore.

Lammermuir Hills, from East Lothian to Duns very wild. Dine with the Farmers' Club at Kelso. Sir John Hume there.

May 24th. I am taken extremely ill, with strong feverish symptoms. *A servant to watch me all night.* Gloomy forebodings of death.

May 25th. Went to see a roup [a bankrupt sale] of an unfortunate farmer's stock. May rigid economy and decent industry preserve me from ever being the principal dramatis persona in such a scene of horror.

May 26th. This day I feel warm with gratitude to the Great Preserver of men, who has kindly restored me to health and strength once more.

A pleasant walk with my friend Douglas Ainslie, aged sixteen, a sweet, modest, clever young fellow.

May 27th. Cross Tweed and traverse the moors through a wild country to Alnwick. Alnwick Castle, a seat of the Duke of Northumberland, furnished in a most princely manner. A Mr. Wilkin, agent of His Grace's, showed us the house and policies. Mr. Wilkin a discreet, sensible man.

May 28th. Through by-ways to Warkworth, where we dine. Hermitage and old castle. Warkworth situated very picturesque.

On to Newcastle. Old Mr. Hood has been persuaded to join our partie. Mr. Kerr and he do very well.

I dare not talk nonsense lest I should lose dignity.

May 29th. Next morning. Sir James Hall of Dunglass came to breakfast with us and carried me away with him. His charming Lady and he did me the honor to accompany me the whole forenoon through the glorious Deane of Dunglass. I would not stay dinner.

When I returned to my horse, I found Miss ready equipped to escort me to Dunbar, with the view of making a parade of me as a Sweetheart among her relations by the way and at Dunbar. She was *bien poudre, bien frise* in her fine cream-coloured riding clothes, mounted on an old horse that had once been fat. Nothing could prevail with her, no distant insinuation, no broad hint would make her give over her purpose. At last, vexed, disgusted, enraged to a high degree, I pretended a fire-haste and rode so hard that she was almost shaken to pieces on old Jolly and, to my great joy, found it convenient to stop at an uncle's house by the way. I refused to call with her. And so we quarrelled and parted.

May 30th. Left early in the morning and rode over a fine country to Hexham to breakfast. From Hexham to Wardrue, the celebrated Spa where we slept.

Thursday May 31st. Reach Longtown to dine. A hiring-day in Longtown—I was uncommonly happy to see so many young folks enjoying life.

Friday June 1st. Carlisle. Met a strange, romantic adventure by the way, falling in with a girl who after some overtures of gallantry on my side, offered to take me in for a Gretna-green affair. I, not being such a gull as she imagined, made an appointment with her. I gave her a brush of caressing and a bottle of cyder. Her fingers I lovingly squeezed. I kissed her and promised her . . . nothing.

So finding herself *un peu trompé* in her man, she sheered off.

> Wantonness for evermair,
>   Wantonness has been my ruin,
> Yet for a' my dool and care
> It's wantonness for evermair.
>   I hae loved the Black, the Brown,
> I hae loved the Fair, the Gowden,
>   A' the colours in the town . . .
> Wantonness has been my ruin.

Saturday June 2nd. Met my good friend Mr. Mitchell and walked with him through his printing works—four or five hundred people employed, many of them women and children.

June 3rd. By coast to Annan. Overtaken on the way by a curious old fish, a shoemaker-miner from Cumberland.

> We labour soon, we labour late
>   To feed the titled knave, man,
> And a' the comfort we're to get
>   Is that ayont the grave, man.

June 11th. Mauchline. I arrived on Friday last in my native country again after a very agreeable jaunt. It rejoices my heart that I have met such a fellow as Robert Ainslie. I have set him down as the staff of my old age when the whole list of my friends will have forgot me. All well at home.

The stateliness of the patricians of Edin[r]. and the servility of my plebeian brethren here (who perhaps formerly eyed me askance) have nearly put me out of conceit altogether with my species. Since my return to Mauchline, I am *now* made very welcome to visit Jean. The servility . . . If anything had been wanting to disgust me completely at Armour's family, their mean servile compliance would have done it. 'Tis true I have just now a little cash . . .

I have bought a pocket Milton, which I carry perpetually about with me in order to study that great personage Satan, a favorite hero of mine.

I cannot settle. Farming, the only thing of which I know anything, I dare not risk—on farms as they are. If I do not fix, I will go for Jamaica.

I have been with Mr. Patrick Miller. My hopes in that business [a farm known as Ellisland] are but slender.

The poetic mind finds itself miserably deranged in and unfit for the walks of business. I detest business.

June 25th. Arrochar. Argyll-shire. I write this on another tour (partly an account of some business I have to settle in various places)—this time through a country where savage streams tumble over savage mountains, thinly overspread with savage flocks which starvingly support as savage inhabitants.

My last stage was Inveraray. [Entirely neglected there by the inn-keeper whose whole attention seemed to be occupied by some company on a visit to the Duke of Argyll. No invitation from the Duke to Mr. R. B.]

> Whoe'er he be that sojourns here
> I pity much his case
> Unless he come to wait upon
> The Lord their God ' His Grace '.

I am out of temper. My social disposition, when not checked by some modification of spited pride makes me generally a *welcome* guest. Well, one virtue I shall ever claim as mine. To no man, whatever his station in life or his powers to serve me have I ever crouched.

How wretched to shrink at the approach of a lordly piece of self con-sequence, who amid all his stately glitter is formed as you are (and perhaps not so well formed !) who came into this world as you did and must go out of it a stinking corpse.

June 30th. Linlithgow. On our way here, at a Highland gentleman's hospital mansion, [on the western shore of Loch Lomond] we were a merry party and danced till the ladies left us at three in the morning. Our dancing was none of the French or English insipid formal movements.

The ladies sung Scotch songs like angels, at intervals. Then we flew at ' Bab at the Bowster' ' Tullochgorum' etc., like midges sporting in the mottie sun.

When the dear lassies left us, we ranged round the bowl till the good-fellow hour of six; except a few minutes when we went out to pay our devotions to the glorious Lamp of Day peering over the towering top of Ben Lomond. We all kneeled, each man a full glass in his hand; and I, as priest, repeated some rhyming nonsense.

We spent the day on Loch Lomond and reached Dumbarton in the evening. We dined at another good fellow's house. When we went out to mount our horses, we found ourselves ' no vera fou but gaylie yet '.

My two friends and I rode soberly down the Loch side, till by came a Highlandman at a gallop on a tolerably good horse which had never known iron or leather.

We scorned to be out-galloped by a Highlandman, so off we started after him whip and spur. My companions, though well mounted, fell astern. But my old mare Jenny Geddes, one of the Rosinante family, strained past the Highlandman in spite of all his efforts. Just as I was passing him, Donald wheeled his horse as if to cross before me to mar my progress, when down came his horse and threw his rider's breekless arse in the clipt hedge and down came Jenny Geddes over all. I came off with a few cuts and bruises and a thorough resolution to be a pattern of sobriety for the future.

I have yet fixed on nothing with respect to the serious business of life. I am an aimless fellow with a vicious bent to idleness. However, I shall somewhere have a farm soon—I was going to say a wife too, but that will never be my blessed lot. I may intrigue if I choose to run risks, but I must not marry.

All my earlier love songs were the breathings of ardent passion, but now my Muse has jilted me. My heart no more glows with feverish rapture. I have at present no paradisaical evening interviews stolen from the restless cares and prying inhabitants of this vile, bleak, barren, weary world. I have only Miss —— [Chalmers ?], a *distant* acquaintance of Jamie Smith [the 'Trusty Trojan' of boyish days, now established in a small calico business at Linlithgow].

I do like her a good deal. She has a fine figure and elegant manners and has seen the politest quarters of Europe in the train of some Great Folks. At the commencement of our acquaintance I frequently visited her. And after passing regularly between the distant formal bow and the familiar grasp round the waist, I ventured in my careless way, to talk of friendship in rather ambiguous terms. I wrote to her in the same style. Miss, construing my words farther I suppose than even I intended, flew off in a tangent of female dignity and reserve, like a mounting lark in an April morning; and wrote me an answer which measured out very completely what an immense way I had to travel before I could reach the climate of her favour.

But I am an old hawk at the sport and wrote her such a cool, deliberate, prudent reply as brought my bird from her aerial towerings pop down at my foot like Corporal Trim's hat.

July 7th. Mossgiel. Of late I have been confined with that lingering indisposition, originating, as I take it, in the stomach. It has hung about me for some time and has almost beaten me out of the use of pen & ink.

July 29th. Mossgiel. A letter from Creech just now received oblidges me to be in Edin^r against this day or tomorrow se'ennight, though my stay will be but a few days.

July 31st. Mossgiel. I am going for Edin^r by way of Paisley and Glasgow tomorrow morning.

[A Paisley boy called Taylor describes the traveller as ' a big athletic ' man of a brown ruddy complexion, broad chested and standing firmly ' on his legs which were rather clumsy though hid in top boots. He ' was dressed in a blue coat and buckskin breeches '. He made a highly favourable impression on Dr. Taylor, the boy's father. But Mrs. Taylor was struck with ' a certain gloominess in his countenance and bearing '.]

Aug. 14th. Edin^r. Here I am again. I sit in the attic story, alias the garret. The clock is just striking twelve forenoon. What I am thinking I myself cannot tell. What I am usually saying is not worth telling.

> Out over the Forth I look to the north,
>   But what is the north and its Highlands to me ?
> The south nor the east gie ease to my heart,
>   The far foreign land nor the wide rolling sea,
> But I look to the west when I gae to rest,
>   That happy my dreams and my slumbers may be.

I ate some Newhaven broth—in other words boiled mussels—with Mr. Farquharson's family t'other day.

Great Folks

Aug. 23rd. Edin^r. Tomorrow I leave Edin^r for a tour of the High-lands with Mr. William Nicol, one of the masters of the High School here. For our tour Mr. Nicol thinks it more comfortable in a chaise than on horseback, to which I say Amen. So Jenny Geddes goes back to Ayr-shire ' wi' her finger in her mouth ', to use a phrase of my mother's.

August 25th, Linlithgow. I am delighted with the fertile carses of Stirling and Falkirk, rich waving crops of wheat, barley &c.; but the more the elegance and the luxury among farmers, I always observe in equal propor-tion the rudeness [penury, illiteracy] and simplicity of the peasantry.

Soil about Linlithgow light and thin. The town carries the appear-ance of decayed grandeur—charmingly rural retired situation. The old palace a tolerably fine but melancholy ruin sweetly situated on a small elevation by the brink of a loch. Shown the room where Mary Queen of Scots was born.

The infamous Stool of Repentance standing in the old Romish way on a lofty situation.

A pretty good old Gothic church. See a horserace.

Through Falkirk. Nothing remarkable there except the tomb of Sir John the Graham. Camelon, the ancient metropolis of the Picts now a small village.

Past Larbert and admire a monument of cast-iron erected by Mr. Bruce, the African explorer, to his wife. He used her very ill and I supposed he meant the monument as much in gratitude to Heaven as anything else.

Dine at Achinbowie.

Aug. 26th. Stirling. Here the Stewarts once reigned in glory.

Bannockburn. Shewn the old house where James III finished so trajically his unfortunate life.

The Field of Bannockburn. The hole where glorious Bruce set his standard. I said a fervent prayer for Old Caledonia over the hole. No Scot can pass here uninterested. I saw my countrymen coming down upon the murderers of their fathers, noble revenge and just hate glowing in their veins. I saw them meet on the victorious field, exulting

III

in their royal leader and rescued liberty and independance. But now, alas !

> Fareweel to a' our ancient fame,
> Fareweel our ancient glory,
> Fareweel ev'n to the Scottish name
> Sae famed in martial story . . .

August 27th. *Stirling.* Rode up the meandering Devan's banks to pay my respects to some Ayr-shire folks. After breakfast we made a party to go and see the Rumbling Brig and the Deil's Mill and the famous Caudron Linn, a remarkable cascade; and after spending one of the most pleasant days I ever had in my life (though Lady MacKenzie being rather a little alarmingly ill of a sore throat somewhat marr'd our enjoyment), we returned to Stirling in the evening. I shall not be back in Ayr-shire for four weeks.

August 28th. Breakfast with Captain Forrester. On to Crieff. Dine and go to Arbruchil—cold reception. A most romantically pleasant ride up Earn by Auchtertyre and Comrie.

> The winds were laid, the air was still
> The stars they shot along the sky
> The tod was howling on the hill
> And the distant-echoing glens reply . . .

Sup at Crieff.

> The paly moon rose in the livid east . . .

August 29th. Glen Almond. Ossian's grave. Loch Fruoch. Glen-quaich. Meet the Hon. Charles Townshend.

August 30th. Down Tay to Dunkeld. Glenlyon House, a seat of the Duke of Athole.

Druids' Temple—three circles of stones, the outer-most sunk. The second circle has thirteen stones, the innermost eight. Two large detached ones, like a gate, to the south-east. Said prayers in it.

Castle Menzies. Sup.

I composed these lines standing under the Falls of Moness—

Now summer blinks on flow'ry braes
And o'er the crystal streamlets plays
Come, let us spend the lightsome days
In the birks * of Aberfeldie.   [*Birch woods]

The braes ascend like lofty wa's,
The foaming stream deep-roaring fa's,
O'er hung with fragrant-spreading shaws,†   [†Woods]
The birks of Aberfeldie.

The hoary cliffs are crowned wi' flowers.
White o'er the linn the burnie pours
And, rising, wets wi' misty showers
The birks of Aberfeldie.

August 31st. Walk to Burnam top. Fine prospect down Tay. Wrote with a pencil over the chimneypiece in the parlour of the Inn at the outlet of Loch Tay—

O'er many a winding dale and painful steep
Th'abodes of covey'd grouse and timid sheep
My savage journey curious I pursue . . .

The meeting cliffs each deep-sunk glen divides
The woods wild scattered clothe their ample sides
The incessant roar of headlong tumbling floods . . .

Craigieburn Hills. Hermitage on the Bran Water. A picture of Ossian.

Breakfast with Dr. Stewart. Neil Gow plays—a short, stout built, honest Highland figure, with his grayish hair shed on his brow—an interesting face marking strong sense & kind openheartedness mixed with unmistrusting simplicity. Visit his house.

Ride up Tummel River to Blair, another of the Duke of Athole's seats. Wild grandeur of the pass of Gillecrankie. Visit the gallant Lord Dundee's stone.

Blair Castle. Sup with the Duchess of Athole. Easy and happy from the manners of the family. My Lord Duke's kind hospitality, markedly kind indeed. Flattered by the recollection of all that polite agreable company.

Sept. 1st. Visit the scenes round Blair—fine but spoiled with bad taste—in company with Josiah Walker [the Ducal children's tutor] and Sir William Murray of Auchtertyre, an honest, worthy man, but tormented with hypochondria. [An invitation from Sir William to stay at Auchtertyre—accepted for early October.]

Dine at Blair Castle with the Duke & Duchess again. Company— The Duke & Duchess, General Murray, Captain Murray, Sir William Murray, Mrs. Graham, *belle et aimable* and the lovely Miss Cathcart (the Duchess's sisters), Mrs. Murray who is a painter, Mrs. King, the Duchess's fine family, the Marquis of Tullibardine, Lords James, Edward and Robert, Ladies Charlotte, Emilia and children. I wish I had the power of Guido. Dance. Sup. Miss Cathcart one of those ministering spirits who delight in doing kind offices. Charms of Grahame of Fintrie's conversation.

Have spent nearly two days here.

[Josiah Walker, the tutor, relates how the Duke and Duchess were as much pleased with Robert as he was with them and that ' the ladies ' in their anxiety to have a little more of his company sent a servant to ' bribe the driver to loosen or pull off one of the horse's shoes '. But the attempt failed.]

Sept. 2nd. Up the Garrie. Falls of Bruar. Dalnacardoch. Hospitably entertained.

> When Death dark stream I ferry o'er . . .
> In Heaven itself I'll ask no more
> Than just a Highland welcome.

No corn from Loch Garrie to Dalwhinnie.

> Lone on the bleaky hills the straying flocks
> Shun the fierce storms among the sheltering rocks.
> Down foam the rivulets, red with dashing rains,
> The gathering floods burst o'er the distant plains . . .

Many miles through a wild country amid gloomy, savage glens and grey
cliffs. Snow on the hills 17 feet deep.

> Th' increasing blast roared round the beetling rocks,
> The clouds, swift-winged, flew o'er the starry sky.
> The groaning trees untimely shed their locks
> And shooting meteors caught the startled eye.

Sept. 3rd. Cross Spey. Ruthven Barracks magnificent.
Breakfast at Aviemore, a wild spot. Wild mossy mountains where
the grouse lead their coveys through the heather to feed. Moors red brown
with heather bells.

> The thundering guns are heard on every side;
> The wounded coveys, reeling, scatter wide . . .
> Sires, mothers in one carnage lie . . .

Down Strathspey, so famous in Scotch music, to Grant Castle where
I spent half a day with Sir James Grant and family. Lady Grant a sweet
pleasant body.
Come through mist and darkness to Dulsie to lie.

Sept. 4th. Call at Castle Cawdor, where Macbeth murdered King
Duncan. Saw the identical bed in which King Duncan was stabbed.
Dine at Kilravock. Mrs. Rose a true chieftain's wife. Thence to
Inverness. Wont leave Inverness till Thursday morning. Jaded to
death with the fatigue of today's journey.

Sept. 5th. Heard an admirable Gaelic air from an Inverness lady. The tune is called ' Phannerach dhon na chri' ['A bhannarach dhonn a' chruidh' (O brown milkmaid of the cows)]. I am so charmed with it that I have begged her to write me a set of it from her singing. I am not musical scholar enough to prick down the tune properly myself. I am writing words for it. I wont say the poetry is first rate, though I am convinced it is very well.

Loch Ness. Falls of Fyers. Urquhart Castle. Sup with the Provost, Mr. Inglis, Mrs. Inglis and three young ladies.

LINES ON THE FALLS OF FYERS, NEAR LOCH NESS,
written with a pencil on the spot.

Among the heathy hills and ragged woods
The roaring Fyers pours his mossy floods.
As high in air the bursting torrents flow;
As deep recoiling surges foam below.
Dim-seen through rising mists and ceaseless show'rs
Still thro' the gap the struggling river toils
And still, below, the horrid cauldron boils . . .

Also have just had time to write out a poem on Bruar Water, having brushed it up as well as the jogging of the chaise and Willie Nicol's chat would allow.

Sept. 6th. Culloden Muir. Reflections on the field of battle and on Princes [the Duke of Cumberland] whose cumbrous pride was all their worth. Here is part of a Birthday Ode for Prince Charles.

Afar the illustrious Exile roams
   Whom kingdoms on this day should hail,
An inmate in the casual shed
On transient pity's bounty fed,
   Haunted by busy Memory's bitter tale . . .

Breakfast at Kilravock. The beautiful wild scenery of Kilravock delights me, the venerable castle, the woods, the winding river, the Fairy Walk at the bottom of the garden.

Mrs. Rose and Mrs. Grant accompany us to Kildrummie. Miss Rose, who sung two Gaelic songs, beautiful. Miss Sophia Brodie, daughter of the famous Brodie of Brodie, most agreable. Brodie House to lie.

Sept. 7th. Forres. Famous stone. Mr. Brodie tells me that the muir of Macbeth's witch-meeting is still haunted. The country folks wont pass it at night.

Venerable ruins of Elgin Abbey. Cross Spey to Fochabers. Gordon Castle a fine palace, worthy of the generous proprietor. Dine. Company —Duke and Duchess, Ladies Charlotte and Magdeline, Colonel Abercrombie and Lady, and a clergyman. The Duke affable, gay and kind. The Duchess witty and sensible. God bless them.

[Dr. Couper of Fochabers says that ' Burns left Mr. Nicol at the inn
' while he himself went to the castle. The family was about to sit down
' to dinner. He was invited to take his place at table as a matter of course.
' But after a few glasses of wine he proposed to withdraw. On being
' pressed to stay he mentioned his engagement with his fellow traveller.
' The Duke offered to send a servant to conduct Mr. Nicol to the castle,
' but Burns insisted on undertaking that himself. A gentleman, a par-
' ticular friend of the Duke went with him and the invitation was delivered
' in all the forms of politeness. It was too late. The pride of Mr. Nicol
' was inflamed into a high degree of passion by the neglect to which he
' thought he had been subjected. He had ordered the horses to be put
' in, determined to proceed on his journey alone. They found him parading
' the street before the door of the inn, venting his anger on the postillion
' for the slowness with which he obeyed his commands. As no explana-
' tion nor entreaty could change Mr. Nicol's purpose, Burns had either to
' separate from his fellow-traveller entirely or to proceed with him instantly
' on their journey. Burns chose the latter of these alternatives, and, seating
' himself beside Mr. Nicol in the post-chaise, with regret turned his back
' on Gordon Castle, where he had promised himself some happy days.']

My curse on the unlucky predicament which hurried me away from Castle Gordon. May that obstinate Nicol be damned.

Come to Cullen to lie. The country here is sadly poor and unimproven.

Sept. 8th. Breakfasted at Banff. [' During breakfast ', says a schoolboy who was present, ' Burns played off some sportive jests at his touchy com-
' panion about some misunderstanding between them at Fochabers.']
Through Buchan to Old Deer (which formerly belonged to the Earls Marischall). Lie.

Sometime on Monday the 10th inst. I shall be in Stonehive when I shall see my father's relations.

Sept. 9th. Set out for Peterhead. Along the shore by the famous Bullars of Buchan and Slains Castle. The soil rich—crops of wheat, turnips &c. Aberdeen to lie.

Sept. 10th. Meet among others the author of 'Jamie and Bess', a little decripid body—also Bishop Skinner, and Professor Gordon, good natured, jolly-looking. Aberdeen a lazy town.

On to Stonehive. Near here the coast a good deal romantic. Meet my relations. My cousin Robert Burness one of those who love fun. His wife a sweet hospitable body without any affectation of town breeding. Also my cousin James Burness and my aunts Jean and Isbal, hale old women.

Sept. 11th. Howe of the Mearns a rich cultivated but still uninclosed country. I have now spent two days with my relations.

Sept. 12th. Montrose. Finely situated handsome town. Meet more Cousins. Willie Nicol took some freak in his head to wake me before six o clock this morning to continue our journey in the rattling chaise by some other road and breakfast by the way. I had to come. Very sorry to leave Montrose. Breakfast at Muthie. Sail along that wild rocky coast and see the famous caverns. Arbroath. Stately ruins of Abbey.

Sept. 13th. Dundee. A low-lying but pleasant town. Old Steeple. Tayfrith. Broughty Castle a finely situated ruin jutting into the Tay.

Sept. 14th. Breakfast with the Miss Scotts. Miss Bess Scott—almost in love with her.

Come through rich harvests and fine hedge-rows to Perth. Fruitful, hilly, wooded country round Perth. Castle Huntley. Sir Stewart Thriepland.

Sept. 15th. Leave Perth. Scoon. Picture of the Chevalier and his Sister. Queen Mary's bed, the hangings wrought with her own hands. Castle Gowrie.

Up Strathearn to dine with the Belches of Endermay.

Yon silent towers . . .
Where at moonshine's midnight hours
O'er the dewy bending flowers
Fairies dance sae cheery . . .

Mrs. B. gawcie, frank, affable, fond of rural sports, hunting &c.   Come
to Kinross to lie.   Reflections on a fit of colic.

Sept. 16th.   Pass through a cold, barren country to Queensferry.   Dine.
Cross the ferry and on to Edinburgh.

Sept. 28th.   Edin^r.   My journey through the Highlands has been
perfectly inspiring.

The wind blew hollow from the hills . . .

I hope I have laid in a good stock of new poetical ideas.
I am determined not to leave Edin^r till I have wound up my matters
with Mr. Creech, my Publisher.   It will, I am afraid, be a tedious business.

Sept. 29th Edin^r.   I have been trying for a birth for William.

[*At the beginning of October* three short visits—the first to the Hamiltons
of Harvieston, the second to Sir William Murray of Auchtertyre (Strathearn), the third to Mr. John Ramsay of Auchtertyre (near Stirling), accompanied by Mrs. Dunlop's young relative James MacKittrick Adair, who
says ' Burns and I left Edinburgh and rode by Linlithgow and Carron,
' with which he was forcibly struck.']

Great Folks

CARRON IRONWORKS

We cam na here to view your works
In hopes to be mair wise,
But only lest we gang to Hell
It may be nae surprise.

['At Stirling', Adair relates, 'we met with a company of travellers.
'Many songs were sung. When Burns was called on in his turn, he
'recited one of his own poems instead of singing, but with a tone and
'emphasis which, though not correct, were impressive and pathetic.
    'From Stirling to Harvieston. During our residence there Mrs. Bruce
'of Clackmannan Tower a lady of above ninety, who believes herself
'to be a descendant of the Bruce, being in possession of the hero's two-
'handed sword, conferred the order of knighthood on Burns, remarking
'that she had a better right to do so than *some people*. At Dunfermline
'we visited the ruined abbey and the abbey church, now consecrated to
'Presbyterian worship. Here I mounted the Cutty Stool or Stool of
'Repentance, assuming the character of a penitent for fornication, while
'Burns from the pulpit addressed to me a ludicrous reproof and exhorta-
'tion parodied from that which had been delivered, so he assured me,
'to himself in Ayr-shire.']

Oct. 8th. Auchtertyre. Very comfortable here with Sir William Murray,
neither oppressed by ceremony nor mortified by neglect. Lady Augusta
most engaging. The family just notice me enough to make me easy but
not embarrass me. What a blessed fireside ! How happy should I be
to pass a *winter* evening under this roof and smoke a pipe of tobacco or
drink water-gruel with them.
    During a solitary forenoon's walk from Auchtertyre among the hills
I scared some water fowl in Loch Turit.

Why, ye tenants of the lake
For me your wat'ry haunt forsake ?
Peaceful keep your dimpling wave,
Busy feed or wanton lave
Or beneath the sheltering rock
Bide the surging billow's shock.

The eagle from the cliffy brow
Marking you his prey below,
In his breast no pity dwells.
Strong necessity compells . . .
But if Man's superior might
Dare invade your native right,
Swiftly seek on clanging wings
Other lakes . . .

I leave on wednesday or thursday. I shall spend a day or two with Mr. John Ramsay near Stirling, as I return to Edinburgh.

[A few days later Mr. Ramsay writes, ' I was never more delighted ' than with his company for two days tête-à-tête.']

*Oct. 20th. Edin*ʳ*.* I have been unlucky in catching a miserable cold for which the medical gentlemen have ordered me into close confinement under pain of death. In two or three days, if I get better, I will take a ride to Dumfries to explain my ideas about a farm to Mr. Patrick Miller. I want to be in a small farm, about a plough-gang, in a pleasant country under a good landlord. I have no foolish notion of being a tenant on easier terms than another. To find a farm where one can live at all is not easy, but I would wish to call Mr. Patrick Miller landlord sooner than any landed gentleman I know.

*Oct. 25th. Attic Storey No. 2. St. James Sq*ʳ*. Edin*ʳ*.*
I am busy at present assisting with a Collection of Scotch Songs set to music. It is to contain all the native songs that can be found. Sometimes I am to make a stanza to a fine air when it has no words. I am absolutely crazed about it, collecting old stanzas and every information remaining respecting their origin, authors &c. &c. I am vexed to think that those men of genius, for such they certainly were, who composed our fine Scottish lyrics should be unknown. There is something in the old Scotch songs which peculiarly marks them from English songs.

The collection is to be called ' The Scots Musical Museum ', pathetic & lively songs adorned here & there with vignettes.

[Josiah Walker, the Blair Castle tutor, about the end of October writes —' I called for him at the house of Mr. Cruickshank, one of the Masters

' at the High School, whose twelve year old daughter was a promising
' pianist. I found him seated by the harpsichord while Jenny (' Sweet
' Rose-bud ' he called her) sang and accompanied his verses. He kept
' adjusting them to the music by repeated trials of the effect. He was so
' totally absorbed that it was difficult to draw his attention from it for a
' moment.']

This is from a song ' A rosebud in my early walk ' that I composed
on Miss Jenny Cruickshank to an air by Davie Sillar.

> Within the bush her covert nest
> A little linnet fondly pressèd.
> The dew sat chilly on her breast
>   Sae early in the morning.
>
> She soon shall see her tender brood
> The pride, the pleasure of the wood
> Amang the fresh green leaves bedew'd
>   Awake the early morning.
>
> So thou, sweet rose-bud, young and gay . . . ~

Nov. 6th. Edin. This day will decide my affairs with my Publisher
Creech. Things are—like myself—not what they ought to be.

That eternal propensity I always had to fall in love . . . Peggy
Chalmers, how divine she is ! Her face, her charm . . . [This is that
same Peggy Chalmers, the Ayrshire farmer's daughter, now in Edinburgh

with her cousins the Hamiltons, who agree that ' Peggy has charm. Her
' hazel eyes are large and bright. Her teeth are white and regular. She
' is little, but her figure is perfect '] . . . her form, her native grace, her
worth, her mind . . . [' She greatly likes reading ', the amiable description goes on, ' but she rarely talks of books. She prefers listening. Her
' conversation has a favourable influence on Mr. Burns.'] . . . her gentle
look, her angel air . . .

> Where, braving angry winter's storms
> The lofty Ochills rise,
> Far in their shade my Peggy's charms
> First blest my wondering eyes . . .

I have just seen a letter from Peggy to a young gentleman, heir to a
fortune, a mere schoolboy, who professes a passion for her. Her letter
was severe, but he did not seem to take it amiss. On the contrary, he
talked of being with her in the Christmas days—a mere volatile schoolboy,
but in mind and manners a Gentleman—*tant pis*. I fear I am something
like undone, but I hope for the best.

Nov. Edin^r*.*   *To Miss Peggy Chalmers.*
My Dear Madam—I have just now read yours. The poetic compli-
ments I pay *cannot be misunderstood*. Shall I be plain with you ? I will,
so look to it . . .   R. B.

[And soon after this, ' still hoping for the best ', Robert apparently
made a definite proposal of marriage, which, in the kindest possible way,
Miss Peggy had to refuse. She was already engaged—not to the volatile
schoolboy but to someone else, a very decent man, a bank clerk.]

Nov. 23rd 1787. Edin^r*.*   *To Robert Ainslie.*
You will think it romantic when I tell you that I find the idea of your
friendship almost necessary to my existence. You assume a proper length
of face in my bitter hours of blue-devilism and you laugh fully up to my
highest wishes at my good things. I dont know if you *are* one of the
first fellows in God's world, but *you are so to me*. I tell you this just now

in the conviction that some inequalities in my temper and manner may perhaps sometimes make you suspect that I am not so warmly as I ought to be your friend   R. B.

Wherever you are God bless you & lead you not into temptation but deliver you from evil.

I would give my best song to my worst enemy to have Peggy by me now.   That ardent love for which I have so often sought a return from my fellow creatures . . .

[Young Ainslie recollects how ' he called for me one day and said ' " We'll take a ramble over Arthur's Seat to admire the beauties of nature ' " and come in to a late tea." We did so and I have never known his ' conversation so amusing, and altogether delightful as during that cheerful ' stroll we had over the hill and during the sober tea-drinking which followed.']

[But Miss Peggy did not see why her engagement need make any difference.   The agreable friendship is to be resumed.] Well, this is not amiss ! Two or three strides across my room. By heavens, that there is an incomprehensible Great Being intimately acquainted with my internal machinery and consequent deportment is evident.

Dec. Edin^r.   *To Miss Peggy Chalmers.*
My Dear Madam—I must tell you that I have to the best of my power now compleated the poem to Charlotte. I am fixed that it shall go into the ' Scot's Musical Museum ', and neither of you need spend your precious time in contradicting me about this. On the contrary I look for high compliments from you both.   R. B.

Dec. St. James Sq. Edin^r. I have been at Dumfries and at one visit more shall be decided about a farm in that country. I am rather hopeless in it. If this Dumfries business fail me I am determined to return into partnership with Gilbert. And at our leisure we will take another farm in the Mauchline neighbourhood. A certain sour-faced old acquaintance called Glauber's Salts hinders me tonight from supping abroad.

Dec. Edin'. I am an odd being. I lie so miserably open to the incursions of passion (and prudence and forethought move so very very slow) that I am almost in a state of perpetual warfare and, alas, frequent defeat.

I have lately composed some verses for Miss Isabella MacLeod of Raasay—

> Raving winds around her blowing
> Yellow leaves the woodlands strowing
> By a river hoarsely roaring . . .

—on the death of her sister and the still more melancholy death of her sister's husband the Earl, who shot himself out of sheer heart-break at some mortifications owing to the deranged state of his finances.

Dec. Edin'.   *To Gavin Hamilton Esq'.*
My Dear Sir—It is indeed with the highest pleasure that I congratulate you on the return of days of ease after the horrid hours of misery I saw you suffering when I was last in Ayrshire. It is needless for me to advise you to have a reverend care for your health. I know you will make it a point never at any one time to drink more than a pint (I mean an English pint) of wine.

As you are now in habits of intimacy with that Boanerges of Gospel power, Mr. Auld [the Minister], be earnest with him that he will wrestle in prayer for you that you may see the vanity of charity, generosity and forgiveness.

Most fervently do I beseech the Holy Trinity or Holy Somebody that directs the world that you may live long and be happy but live no longer than you are happy. Yours in the Lord   Rob* Burns.

I have again gone wrong in my unguarded way. I am just the same Will-o'-wisp I used to be. About the first and fourth quarters of the moon I generally set in for the trade winds of wisdom; but about the full and change I am the luckless victim of mad tornadoes which blow me into chaos. With passions wild and strong I am too much the prey of giddy inconsistencies. I am at this moment ready for hang myself for a young Edin^r widow, Mrs. MacLehose [a cousin of Lord Craig and also related, though more remotely, to Lord Dreghorn], who has wit and beauty more murderously fatal than the assissinating stiletto of the Sicilian banditti or the poisoned arrow of the African savage. My Highland dirk I have removed into a closet, the keys of which I cannot command—in case of spring-tide paroxysms. I am shocked at life.

She is amiable, young, and deserted by a husband who was bound by every tie of Duty to protect and cherish her. I never met with a person whom I more anxiously wished to meet again.

> Her air sae sweet, her shape complete
> Wi' nae proportion wanting—
> The Queen of Love could never move
> Wi' motion mair enchanting.

Dec. 7th. Met with an accident owing to the drunken stupidity of a coachman. I fell and dislocated the cap of my knee, which has laid me up a cripple. A serious, agonising, damned hard knock. I cannot stir my leg off a cushion.

Dec. 8th No. 2 St. James' Sq.   *To Mrs. MacLehose.*
I can say with truth Madam, that I never met with a person in my life whom I more anxiously wished to meet again than yourself. Tonight I was to have had that very great pleasure. I had set no small store by my tea-drinking with you and have not often been so disappointed—but an unlucky fall from a coach has so bruised one of my knees that I cant stir. I am under the care of a surgeon.

If I dont see you again I shall not rest in my grave for chagrin. I know not how to account for it but I am strangely taken with some people; nor am I often *mis*taken.

> Sae sweetly move her genty limbs
> Like music notes o' lovers' hymns.
> The diamond dew in her een sae blue
> Where laughing love sae wanton swims . . .

Dec. 12th. No. 2 St. James' Sq.   *To Mrs. MacLehose.*

My Dearest Madam—Had I been so blest to have met you *in time*, your friendship might have led me—God knows where. Tomorrow and every day till I see you again you shall hear from me. Time is too short for ceremonies. May you enjoy a better night's repose than I am likely to have.   R. B.

Dec. 20th. No. 2 St. James' Sqr.   *To Mrs. MacLehose.*

Pay my addresses to a married woman! My dear Madam! 'Tis true, I never saw you but once; but how much acquaintance did I form with you in that once! I cannot positively say whether my heart might not have gone astray a *little*.

I have written you this scrawl because I have nothing else to do and you may sit down and find fault with it, if you have no better way of consuming your time. I daresay you will throw it into the fire and call me a stupid idle fellow, but whatever you think of my brains, believe me, to be, with the most sacred respect, your humble servant.   R. B.

> I rede you beware at the hunting, young men!
> I rede you beware at the hunting, young men!
> Take some on the wing and some as they spring,
> But cannily steal on a bonie moor-hen.
>
> The heather was blooming, the meadows were mawn,
> Our lads gaed a-hunting one day at the dawn,
> O'er moors and o'er mosses and monie a glen.
> At length they discovered a bonie moor-hen.
>
> Sweet-brushing the dew from the brown heather bells
> Her colours betrayed her on yon mossy fells,
> Yet in spite of her plumage she sat in their sight
> Then whirr! she was over a mile at a flight.
>
> I rede you beware at the hunting young men!
> I rede you beware at the hunting young men!
> Take some on the wing and some as they spring . . .

[A letter received from Mrs. MacLehose, saying ' Do not publish the ' Moor-Hen. Do not for your sake *and mine*.' The poem was published.]

Dec. 21st. My limb now allows me to sit in some peace; to walk I have as yet no prospect of, as I cant mark it to the ground.

A letter from Gilbert. He has written me to assist him a little in money matters. Dare I ask Mr. Ballantine to accomodate him? I could not raise as much as he wants without my personal presence and I cannot stir out, not even in a chair. Dare I ask Mr. Cowan?

Crossed room on crutches.

1787–8

Dec. 28th No. 2 St. James' Sqr.   *To Mrs. MacLehose.*

I beg your pardon my dear Clarinda. [She has asked to be called Clarinda—her real name being Nancy.] I really dont know what I wrote.

I do love you if possible still better for having so fine a taste for Poesy. Erase the word love and put esteem or any other tame expression you please in its place, but I believe there is no holding converse or carrying on correspondence with an amiable woman, much less a *gloriously amiable fine woman*, without some mixture of that delicious passion. Adding a little love to friendship is like adding cream to strawberries.   R. B.

> In vain would Prudence with decorous sneer
> Point out a censuring world and bid me fear
> Above the world on wings of love I rise
> I know its worst and can that worst despise.

My limb is vastly better, but I still have not any use of it without crutches. As soon as I can walk—and I think I shall walk in ten days or a fortnight —I must return to Ayrshire.

Jan 3rd. St. James Sqr.   *To Mrs. MacLehose.*

Did you but know what I feel when you talk of your sorrows! Good God, that one who is so amiable to her fellow creatures should be so unhappy . . .

As soon as I can go so far, even in a *coach*, my first visit shall be to you.

Jan 14th St. James Sqr.   *To Mrs. MacLehose.*
Why have I not heard from you, Clarinda ? I well expected a letter.
I am determined to see you, if at all possible on Saturday evening.

My limb has been so well today I have gone up and down stairs without
my staff.

1788

Jan. 16th No. 2 St. James' Sqr.   *To Mrs. MacLehose.*
Friday evening about eight expect me. If I cant walk all the way
I'll take a chair. Oh my angel ! I fear, I fear my acquaintance with
you is too short to make the lasting impression on your heart I could
wish.   R. B.

Jan. 19th Edinr. Sparkling was the rosy wine and private was the
chamber . . . What luxury of bliss I was enjoying this time yesternight !

Not the bee upon the blossom
  In the pride o' sunny noon
Not the little sporting fairy
  All beneath the summer moon
Kens the pleasure, feels the rapture
  That thy presence . . .

Clarinda you have stolen away my soul.

Next morning—Edinr. A little alarm today that I am mortal has joined with a return of my old indisposition to make me good for nothing.

Jan. Edinr.   *To Mrs. MacLehose.*
  Your letter finds me writing to you, Clarinda. That you have faults I never doubted. But Oh why will you wound me by hinting that last night must have lessened my opinion of you ? I am vexed that you are complaining.   R. B.

Jan. 21st Edinr. Much better this morning on the whole, but I still have a horrid languor on my spirits.

Jan 21st. Edinr. St. James' Sqr.   *To Mrs. MacLehose.*

We have no ideas almost at all of another world. But I have often amused myself with visionary schemes. For instance : suppose you and I just as we are at present, with the same reasoning powers and even desires, the same curiosity for knowledge. And imagine our bodies free from pain. Imagine further that we were set free from the laws of gravitation and could at pleasure fly without inconvenience through all the yet unconjectur'd bounds of Creation—what a life would we lead in our mutual friendship and love !

I see you laughing at my fairy fancies and calling me a voluptuous Mahometan ; but don't you see us hand in hand—or rather my arm about your lovely waist, making our remarks on Sirius or surveying a comet flaming inoxius by ?   R. B.

Oh what a fool I am in love ! What an extravagant prodigal of affection ! The tender sex—I never have met *one* who can repay me in passion. They are either not so rich in love as I am, or they are niggards when I am lavish.

> Oh wha can prudence think upon
> And sic a lassie by him ?
> Oh wha can prudence think upon
> And sae in love as I am ?

After six weeks I am beginning to walk. They have been six horrible weeks. Low spirits have made me unfit to read, write or think.

I have a hundred times wished that one could resign life as an officer resigns a commission.

I am ashamed of all this ; for though I do not want bravery, I could wish to have the cunning to conceal my cowardice.

About the middle of next week I leave Edinburgh.

Jan. 22nd. Edinr. I have broke measures with Creech (the Publisher) and last week I wrote him a frosty, keen letter. He replied upon his honour that I should have the account on Monday. But this is Tuesday. God have mercy on me, a poor damned, incautious, duped, unfortunate fool.

Jan 24th. Edinr. Pretty hearty after a bowl. I have no distinct ideas of anything.

Jan 25th. St. James' Sqr.   *To Mrs. MacLehose.*
Clarinda, my Life, I propose bringing my bosom friend Robert Ainslie tomorrow evening at his strong request to see you. Put off tea till about seven.   R. B.

Jan 29th. St. James's Sqr.   *To Mrs. MacLehose*
My Dearest Love, could you think I *intended* to hurt you by anything I said yesternight? I thought the devotion of love might make you happy. Will I be mistaken? I send you a poem to read.   R. B.
This night about nine. Do not wound our meeting with any averted looks or restrained caresses.

Feb. 1st Edinr. I am miserably stupid this morning. Yesterday I dined with a baronet and sat pretty late at the wine.

Feb. 7th Edinr. Nothing worth mentioning. Everything going on as usual, houses building, bucks strutting, blackguards sculking, ladies flaring, whores leering &c in the old way.
I have been a cripple now near three months, though I am getting vastly better and have laid aside my crutches. A lame poet is unlucky; lame verses . . .
Saw Jamie Smith lately, hale and hearty as formerly. Melancholly accounts of Jean. God knows, I am no saint.

Feb. 12th. Edinr. I have been to Lady Wallace's. I shall certainly call *there* again.

Feb. 13th. Edinr.   *To Mrs. MacLehose.*
I make a numerous dinner-party wait me while I read yours and write this. Do not require that I should cease to love you. 'Tis impossible. I loved you at first sight.
I'll be with you tomorrow evening.   R. B.

The charms of the mind, the langer they shine,
The mair admiration they draw,
While peaches and cherries and roses and lilies
They fade and they wither awa.

After a wretched day I am preparing for a sleepless night. I am a discontented ghost, a perturbed spirit. I have been torturing my philosophy to no purpose.

Gloomy conjectures in the dark vista of futurity only make me more conscious of my inability for the struggle of the world.

Mrs. MacLehose, by Mr. Miers

Feb. 14th Edinr.   *To Mrs. MacLehose.*
Tell me, are you under the least shadow of an obligation to Mr. MacLehose ? If not, in the name of common sense, can it be improper to bestow your affections on another ?

I thank you for going to Miers [the Profile-painter]. Urge him to have it done by the middle of next week. I want it for a breast-pin to wear next my heart. When I sat to him I'm sure he did not exceed two minutes.   R. B.

[Miers did silhouette portraits for from 6s. to 10s. each—frame included.]

Feb 14th. Edinr.   *To Mrs. MacLehose.*
Clarinda—matters are grown very serious with us. I leave Edinburgh tomorrow to take the decisive look of the farm near Dumfries. I am yours for life. Never be discouraged. Look forward.   R. B.

Feb. Edinr. Last night at Lady Wallace's. The happiest by much, of all that I have spent in Edin[r].

Feb. 17th Mossgiel.
I have altered all my plans.
On my return here I found my mother, my brothers Gilbert and William and my sisters on the brink of ruin with their farm. The lease

is a wretched one, but as I am certain that it will be worth holding and that Gilbert will probably weather out the remaining seven years of it, I advanced £180, nearly one half of my capital, to keep the family together. I give myself no airs on this, for it was mere selfishness on my part. I was conscious that the wrong scale of the balance was pretty heavily charged.

After the necessary support my brothers and the rest of the family require, I guess my remaining all will be about £200.

I have weighed seriously my own situation, my hopes and turn of mind and am fully fixed. I wish (with a word from Lord Glencairn) to get into the Excise.

There is a certain stigma affixed to the character of an Excise Officer, but I do not intend to borrow honour from any profession. I have chosen after mature deliberation. It is immediate bread—£35 a year.

The future is still before me. I have many difficulties to encounter, but they are not all absolutely insuperable.

III

I BEGIN AS A FARMER

Tomorrow I leave Edinburgh for Glasgow.

Feb. 18th. Glasgow.   *To Mrs. MacLehose.*
I have just met my old friend Richard Brown now a Ship's Captain.
Guess my pleasure. My brother William too, the young Saddler, has
come to Glasgow to meet me and here are we three spending the evening.
I am just going to propose your health.   R. B.

> So much laughter, so much life enjoyed . . .
> While . . .
> The tide-swol'n Firth * with sullen-sounding roar   [* *of Clyde*]
> Thro' the still night dashed hoarse along the shore.

[Isbal says 'he sent from Glasgow a gown for my mother and one
'for me as well as a quantity of Mode Silk sufficient to make cloaks and
'bonnets for me and my two sisters'.
When he arrived back at Mossgiel 'he came in and was in the midst
'of us before we knew.
'He wore a breast-pin with a miniature of Mrs. MacLehose in it.']

Feb. 23rd. Mossgiel.   *To Mrs. MacLehose.*
I have just now delivered your kind present to my sweet little Bobbie,
a very fine fellow. Your letter was waiting me.
Now for a little news that will please you. I this morning called on
a certain woman [Jean]. I am disgusted with her. I cannot endure
her! I tried to compare her with my Clarinda. *Here* was tasteless insi-
pidity, vulgarity of soul and mercenary fawning: *there* polished genius

and the most delicate, the most tender passion. I have done with her and she with me.

What signifies a young man's love an't dinna last for ay ?

Feb. 24th. Mossgiel. Hither and yon, happy-go-lucky has been my progress through the mosses and moors. I am a wanderer, a Will-o-wisp. Life is a fairy scene. Almost all that deserves the name of enjoyment is only a charming delusion.

> Ambition is a meteor-gleam
> Fame a restless airy dream
> Pleasures insects on the wing . . .

March 2nd. Cumnock.   *To Mrs. MacLehose.*
I hope and am certain that my generous Clarinda will not think my silence has been in any degree owing to forgetfulness. I have been about through the country ever since Feb. 22nd.; and am here, returning from Dumfriesshire, at an inn, the post-office of the place, with just so long time as my horse eats his corn to write you.

I am thinking my farming scheme will yet hold. A worthy, intelligent farmer, my father's friend and my own, has been with me on the spot. He thinks the bargain practicable. I am myself, on a more serious view of the lands, much better pleased with them.   R. B.

March 3rd. Mossgiel. Just returned from visiting Mr. Patrick Miller's farm (Ellisland), I have fought my way through the savage hospitality of this country—the object of all hosts being to send every guest drunk to bed if they can. The hospitality which knocks a man down with strong liquors is the devil.

March 5th. Mossgiel. Life has been one continued hurry. Headach & low spirits. My knee rather worse.

Jean I found forlorn, destitute, friendless—all for the old cause.

I have reconciled her to her fate. I have reconciled her to her mother. I have taken her a room [in Mauchline]. I have taken her to my arms. I have given her a mahogany bed. I have given her a guinea. I swore her solemnly never to attempt any claim on me as husband. She did this like a good girl.

I have been prudent and cautious to an astounding degree.

March 6th. Mossgiel. Eight o'clock at night. Just walked the ten minutes into Mauchline to wait the Post in hope of hearing from Clarinda. The driver of the Post-chaise comes—with his red jacket Whip-jee-woa ! A letter. Hers of this night's post is the third I have got from her.

I call over the idea of her as a miser counts over his treasure. How rich am I ! I will dare affirm that such an attachment as mine to Clarinda and such evenings as she and I have spent are what the most deeply experienced judges of love never dreamed of. She knows how to make one happy. A hundred times a day do I figure her, her book laid aside as I get within the room.

Just had my little Bobbie inoculated in the smallpox, as they are in the neighbourhood. He is as yet doing very well. I intend breeding him up for the Church ; and from an innate dexterity in secret mischief which he possesses & a certain hypocritical gravity as he looks on the consequences, I have no small hopes of him in the sacerdotal line. That no scheme to overthrow the credit of Orthodoxy may prosper is the prayer of Robert Burns !

March 7th. Mossgiel. If my offer to Mr. Patrick Miller is accepted, I commence farmer at Whitsunday. The Excise salary would pay half my rent. I shall build a house, drive lime &c and heaven be my help ! It will take a strong effort to bring my thoughts into the routine of farming, but perhaps after all I may settle, though my late scenes of idleness and dissipation have enervated my mind to an alarming degree. I am earnestly busy to bring about a revolution in myself and have dropt all conversation and all reading but what tends in some way or other to my serious aim.

With the world of wits and *gens comme il faut* I never again will intimately mix. I never again will appear in the circle of the fashionable herd who come either to show their consequence or to borrow consequence . . .

Firmness both in suffering and exertion I would wish to be thought to possess, for I have always despised the whining yelp of complaint. Away

then with these disquietudes ! I shall sit down a plain farmer, the happiest of lives when a man can live by it.

Poetry must be laid aside for some time.

[A letter received from Mr. Crawford of Cartsburn—

' *March 16th*—I hazard inviting you to an agreeable rural retirement at
' a convenient distance from a town where there are many of your admirers,
' a library I hope not ill chosen, a cellar not ill stored and most cordially
' at your service. Welcome; and I will add that if you should be dis-
' appointed, I shall be much more so. Shall I then be blest with your
' society ? Answer me, dear boy. Will you allow me to send a servant
' and a horse for you ? Your hearty friend

T. Crawford.']

I shall certainly write to Mr. Crawford in answer to his friendly epistle, but not now, as so many perplexing farming arrangements await me.

I stay in the West about three weeks and then return to Edin^r for six weeks' instructions [in the Excise job].

March 17th. My Excise affair is just concluded and I have received my instructions.

The Excise Commission, which I got without any hanging-on or mortifying solicitation, I regard as my sheet anchor in life, a certain maintenance, a certainty of employment. The salary should pay half my rent. £35 a year is no bad *dernier ressort*—and luxury to anything the first five & twenty years of my life taught me to expect. So far good. My poverty is changed to comfortable independance. Besides the Commissioners are some of them my firm friends.

Also I have at last fairly signed my tack with Mr. Patrick Miller. Yesternight I compleated the bargain. I commence farmer at Whitsunday.

I now have the two plans before me and I wish to adopt the one most likely to procure me independance.

I Begin as a Farmer

March 18th. An indifferent night. Care & anxiety sat on my spirits. But I am better today.

The chearfulness of this morning is the fruit of some serious ideas that lie in their realities beyond the ' dark and narrow house ' as Ossian, prince of poets, calls it.

March 19th.   *To Mrs. MacLehose.*

Clarinda, do not be uneasy. Do not accuse me. You know I am a cool lover. Your hopes, your fears are mine. don't mind them. Excuse this hurried scrawl.   R. B.

> Let not women e'er complain
>   Of inconstancy in love.
> Nature's almighty law is Change.
> Mark the winds and mark the skies,
>   Ocean's ebb and ocean's flow.
> Sun and moon but set to rise.
>   Round and round the seasons go.
> Why then ask of silly Man
> To oppose great Nature's plan ?

I have just now written that arch-rascal Creech my Publisher such a letter that my own goose-feather in my hand shrunk back. I was convulsed with rage a good part of the day.

March 31st. Mossgiel. I am so harassed with anxiety about this farming project of mine. Fatigue and a load of care almost too heavy for my shoulders have in some degree actually fever'd me.

March 31st. Mossgiel.   *To Mrs. Dunlop.*

I am truly sorry to tell you, Madam, that I fear it will not be in my power to come to Dunlop House on Sunday. But I am never better pleased than when I see a letter from you, wrote out till there is hardly blank paper enough to close it !   R. B.

April 7th. Mossgiel. I have been roving over the country hiring farm hands. Yesterday I was riding thro' a parcel of damn'd melancholy, joyless muirs between Galloway and Ayr-shire, it being Sunday.

Thursday night. Mossgiel. A bruised finger has hindered me from writing.

I am cursed with a melancholy prescience which makes me the veriest coward. There is a foggy atmosphere native to my soul in which dreary objects seem larger than life. Extreme sensibility, irritated and prejudiced on the gloomy side by a series of misfortunes and disappointments just at that period when the soul is laying in her cargoe of ideas for the voyage through life is I believe the principle cause of this unhappy frame of mind.

I am so harassed, I have been positively crazed, mis-spending my strength like a bull goring a bramble bush.

April 28th. Mauchline. By the blessing of the God of my Fathers I am now a married man! I have married my Jean.

> I hae a wife o' my ain!
> I hae a penny to spend.
> I'll borrow frae naebody.
> I'll be merry and free.
> I'll be sad for naebody
> Naebody cares for me.
> I care for naebody.
> I hae a wife o' my ain!

I was fined for the previous irregular marriage by a Justice of the Peace. I have just now waited on Mr. Auld the Minister. He says if I bring an attestation of this by the two witnesses, there shall be no more about it.

I was not under the least verbal obligation to her, but her happiness or misery were in my hands; and who can trifle with such a deposite? Jean now has a *legal* matrimonial title to the best blood in my body. And so farewell rakery. Let the kirk-folk ring their bells!

[The miniature of Mrs. MacLehose is now removed from the breast-pin, Isbal notices, and one of Jean (done during a brief visit to Glasgow with William) is put in its stead.]

> The lily it is pure and the lily it is fair
> And in her lovely bosom I'll place the lily there.

This song I composed out of compliment to Jean during the honeymoon.

> . . . I see her in the dewy flowers
> I see her sweet and fair
> I hear her in the tuneful birds
> I hear her charm the air.
>
> There's not a bonie flower that springs
> By fountain shaw or green,
> There's not a bonie bird that sings
> But minds me o' my Jean.

There was a certain period of my life that my spirit was broke by repeated losses and disasters, which threatened the utter ruin of my future. But a truce now with this peevish poor complaining. Love grasps his scorpions : stifled they expire.

May 4th. Mauchline. I am impatient to know if the Ailsa Craig fowling be commenced this season yet, as I want 3 or 4 stone of feathers.

> I see thee dancing o'er the green
> Thy waist sae jimp, thy limbs sae clean,
> Thy tempting lips, thy roguish een—
> By Heaven and Earth I love thee !

May 25th. Mauchline. I am really uneasy about that money which my publisher Mr. Creech owes me. I want it much at present both for myself and for Gilbert. A hundred guineas can be but a trifling affair to Mr. Creech. 'Tis a matter of most serious importance to me.

May 27th. Last afternoon I had the honor to spend an hour or two at a good woman's fireside, where the homely planks that composed the floor were decorated with a splendid carpet and the gay table sparkled with silver and china. 'Tis now about Term-day, Rent day. We talked about the insignificant creatures who (tho' in all appearance partakers and equally noble partakers of the same nature as Madame) have *vulgar souls.* Thus does pampered Luxury eye the simple rustic whose toil upholds the glittering show.

Alas, against stupidity and self-conceit, against the fashioned marble of the polished mind, humor is the peck of a sparrow and satire the pop-gun of a schoolboy. We must pocket our pearls.

The snowdrops and primrose our woodlands adorn
And violets bathe in the wet o' the morn.

I have some favorite flowers in Spring, among which are the mountain-daisy, the hare-bell, the fox-glove, the wild brier-rose, the budding birk & the hoary hawthorn. These I hang over with particular delight.

May 31st. Mauchline. Once much loved (I lov'd her to distraction) and still loved, my girl has been *doubly* kinder to me than even the best of women. Of the four children she bore me in seventeen months, two sets of twins, my eldest boy only is living. But I reckon on twelve brace of children against I celebrate my twelfth wedding day—twentyfour christenings, twentyfour useful members of society! I am so enamoured of her prolific twin-bearing merit that I have given her the legal title which I now avow to the world.

I intend to present *Mrs. Burns* with a printed shawl.

Circumstanced as I am, I could never have got a female partner for life who could have entered into my favorite studies, relished my favorite authors &c without entailing on me at the same time expensive living, caprice, affectation, with all the other blessed boarding-school requirements of Misses of the Would-be-Gentry.

Friendship must be my social channel.

I am pleased with my conduct and really more and more pleased with my choice. If I have *not* got polite tattle, modish manners and fashionable dress, I *have* got a clean-limbed, bewitching young hussey with the soundest constitution, the most placid good nature, the sweetest temper, vigorous health and sprightly chearfulness set off to the best advantage by a more than common handsome figure and a warm heart.

A wife's head is immaterial compared with her heart. My Jean has the kindest heart in the county, gratefully devoted with all its powers to love me. Indeed the poor girl has the most sacred enthusiasm for me and has not a wish but to gratify my every idea of her deportment. She believes as firmly as her creed that I am *le plus bel esprit et le plus honnête homme* in the universe.

She scarcely ever in her life spent five minutes together on either prose or verse. But though she should never read—nor have danced in a brighter Assembly than a Penny Wedding—she has the finest ' wood-note wild' I ever heard.

> The primrose I will pull, the firstling o' the year,
> And I will pull the pink, the emblem o' my dear,
> For she's the pink o' womankind and blooms without a peer.

The air for this song was taken down from her voice. It is well known in the west country; but the old words are trash.

Her sweetness and in housewife matters her aptness to learn and activity to execute, should, with my long and deep-rooted affection, make her a tolerable good wife.

During my absences in Nithsdale she is to be regularly & constantly apprentice to my Mother & sisters in their dairy & other rural business. In short I can easily *fancy* a more agreable companion for my journey of life but I have never *seen* the individual instance.

> My love she's but a lassie yet
> My love she's but a lassie yet

I am just going for Nithsdale to the Ellisland farm again.

June 1st. Ellisland. I am six miles from Dumfries here and as yet have little acquaintance in the neighbourhood. Very busy with farm enclosures & improvements to tend. And with the dwelling house a-building there is scarce any opportunity of calling at the Post Office in Dumfries.

I have just put the last hand to a song & I think I may say of it ' Here is a work of mine finished in my very finest style.'

TO JEAN

O my love is like a red red rose
　That's newly sprung in June,
O my love is like a melodie
　That's sweetly play'd in tune.

As fair art thou, my bonie lass,
　So deep in love am I,
And I will love thee still, my dear,
　Till a' the seas gang dry.

Till a' the seas gang dry, my dear,
　And the rocks melt wi' the sun,
And I will love thee still, my dear,
　While the sands o' life shall run.

And fare thee weel, my only love,
　And fare thee weel, a while,
And I will come again, my love,
　Tho' it were ten thousand mile.

The same day. Ellisland, near Dumfries.　　　　*To Robert Ainslie.*
My Dear Friend—Almost my first welcome to this place was the inclosed letter [from one Mary Cameron, an Edinburgh servant girl saying that she is destitute, out of a job and about to have an infant].

Please call and send for the wench and give her ten or twelve shillings, but dont for Heaven's sake meddle with her. I insist on this on your honour. Advise her out to some country friends.

You may not perhaps like the business, but I just tax your friendship so far.

Call immediately or at least as soon as it is dark, for God's sake, lest the poor soul be starving. Ask for a letter I wrote her—by way of token. It is unsigned.

I am very sorry for this—but what is done is done. Except Jamie Smith there is not any person in the world I would trust so far.

Write me after the meeting. R. B.

I am vexed about this affair, and were it not for the terrors of my ticklish situation respecting provision for a family of children . . .

God knows that I, with such appetites and with such a famine of provision for them, am not the thing I should be, nor am I even the thing I *could* be ; yet Man is naturally a kind animal. We of the rougher, the barbarian sex come (by some miscarriage or other) into this vexatious world with a disposition to do good for it. But the scrapes into which our indiscretions so often bring us . . .

> Such is the fate of artless maid
> By Love's simplicity betrayed.

Love's simplicity . . . A damned star has almost all my life squinted out the rays of its malign influence, and behold whatever I do shall not prosper. And so it is with me always. With such voracious appetites. . . .

> . . . Hawks will rob the tender joys
> That bless the little lintwhites nest,
> And frost will blight the first flowers
> And love will break the soundest rest.

I want books. Of the novelists I have perused Fielding beyond any other. Richardson—unhappily his characters are beings of some other world, however much they may captivate the inexperienced romantic fancy of a boy or girl. I want Smollet's works for the sake of his incomparable humour. The veriest ordinary copies will serve. I am only nice about the appearance of the Poets. I forget the price of Cowper's Poems, but I believe I must have them.

Dryden's Virgil has delighted me. The Georgics are to me by far the best of Virgil. It is indeed a species of writing entirely new to me and has filled my head with a thousand fancies. But when I read the Georgics and then survey my own powers 't is like the idea of a Shetland Pony by the side of a thoroughbred hunter. I own I am disappointed in the Aeneid. I think Virgil is in many instances a servile copier of Homer. Nor can I think there is anything of this owing to the translators.

I like to mark the passages that strike me most in every book I read. I have not perused Tasso enough to form an opinion.

I have been extremely fortunate in all my bargainings hitherto, Jean not excepted. I am truly pleased with this last affair. It has indeed added to my anxieties for futurity, but it has given a stability to my mind and resolutions unknown before.

We generally grow so attentive to ourselves and so regardless of others that I have often looked on this world as one vast ocean occupied by unnumerable vortices each whirling round its own centre.

June 11th. Ellisland. Tomorrow I begin my operations as a farmer, and God speed the Plough !

June 13th. Ellisland. This is the second day that I have been on my farm. I am the solitary inmate of the hovel that I shelter in while here, [Jean being still at Mauchline]. It is pervious to every blast that blows and every shower that falls, the force of the wind only mitigated by being sifted through numberless apertures in the walls and I am only preserved from being chilled to death by being suffocated with smoke.

An indifferent night.

(TO A GAELIC AIR)

How lang and dreary is the night
   When I am frae my dearie.
I restless lie frae e'en to morn
   Tho' I were ne'er sae weary.

I Begin as a Farmer

How slow ye move, ye heavy hours,
The joyless day how dreary,
It was na sae ye glinted by
When I was wi' my dearie.

June 14th. Ellisland. This is now the third day I have been in these
parts, far from every object I love nor any acquaintance older than yesterday
except Jenny Geddes, the old mare.

Lord, what a capricious kind of existence Man has here! I am such a
coward, so tired that I would almost at any time lay me down and be at peace.
But a wife and children—these bind me to struggle with the stream till some
chopping squall overset the silly vessel or its own craziness drive it to a wreck.

Wedlock, the circumstance that buckles me hardest to care, was what
in a few seasons I *must* have resolved on anyhow. In the present case it
was unavoidably necessary. Humanity, generosity, justice to my own
happiness in after life, so far as that could depend (which it surely will a
great deal) on internal peace—all these joined with a rooted attachment
to urge the step I have taken.

Jean is still at Mauchline. She does not come from Ayrshire till the
new house which I am building here be ready. So I am eight or ten
days at Mauchline and this place alternately. The new house is not a
palace but a plain sensible domicile.

June 23rd. Ellisland.   *To Robert Ainslie.*

This is only a business scrap. Mr. Miers, Profile-Painter; call there
and sit to him for me. You must not refuse to sit. When I sat for him
I am sure he did not exceed two minutes.

I propose hanging the profiles of Lord Glencairn, Dr. Blacklock and
yourself in trio over my new chimney-piece. Adieu.   R. B.

PS. Miers leaves town soon.

I have just now been interrupted by one of my new neighbours, who
has made himself absolutely contemptible in my eyes by his silly garulous
pruriency.

Let me pry more narrowly into this. Have I *nothing* of a Presbyterian
sourness, a hypercritical severity when I survey my neighbours? There

is a great deal of folly in talking unnecessarily of one's private affairs, but this has been a fault of my own too. From this moment I abjure it.

> Let me fair nature's face descrive
> And I wi' pleasure
> Shall let the busy grumbling hive
> Bum owre their treasure.

I seldom see a newspaper.

My existence or non-existence is now of as little importance to that Great World I lately left as a parcel of ditchers. I foresaw this from the beginning and yet . . . What thin-skinned animals, what sensitive plants poor poets are ! How we do add another cubit to our stature on being applauded—and shrink when neglected !

Self conceit is the overweening opinion of a fool who fancies himself to *be* what he would wish himself to be *thought*.

Give me to act up to the dignity of my nature.

June 30th. Mauchline.   *To Robert Ainslie.*

Another business scrap. You have been imposed upon in paying Miers for a profile of young Mr. Hamilton. I never gave Miers any such order. I went there once indeed with young Hamilton, but he sat to Miers of his own accord. He said he wished to send the profile to a sweetheart. I would as soon think of ordering a profile of Tibby Nairn or Julie Rutherford as such a contemptible puppy. I beg you will return the profile to Mr. Miers. I have no objection to lose the money, but I wont have any such profile in my possession.   R. B.

> Hope not sunshine every hour
> Fear not clouds will always lour . . .
> For the future be prepared
> Guard whatever thou canst guard,
> But, thy utmost duty done,
> Welcome what thou canst not shun . . .
> Keep the name of Man in mind
> And dishonour not thy kind.

July 17th. Mauchline. My WIFE waiting to welcome me back to Ayrshire. I met her with the sincerest pleasure.

A bachelor state would have ensured me more friends, but peace in the enjoyment of my own mind . . . and confidence . . .

The scale of good-wifeship I divide into ten parts—good nature 4, good-sense 2, wit 1, personal charms 1, education, fortune, connections, family-blood &c, &c,—these must be expressed in *fractions*.

I write in my miscellaneous, reverie manner. When I am in a scribbling humor, I know not when to give over.

[It was not till now that the Church at last decided to ratify the marriage. The Kirk-Session held a Purgation Ceremony at which ' Robert ' Burns with Jean Armour his alledged spouse both acknowledged their ' irregular marriage and their sorrow for that irregularity, desiring that the ' Session would take such steps as might seem to them proper with a view ' to the Solemn Confirmation of the said marriage. The Session, taking ' this affair under their consideration, agreed that they both be rebuked for ' this acknowledged irregularity. And the Session, having a title in law ' to exact a fine (on behalf of the Poor) agreed to leave the amount of this ' fine to Mr. Burns's generosity. Mr. Burns gave a guinea-note.']

Aug. 5th. Mauchline.   *To Mr. MacIndoe, Silk Merchant, Glasgow.*
My Dear Sir—If you will send me fifteen yds of black lutestring silk, such as they used to make gowns and petticoats of, the same kind as that of which I bought a gown and petticoat from you formerly, I shall send you the money, when John Ronald the carrier goes again to your good town.   R. B.

Aug. 16th. Ellisland. I was yesterday at Mr. Patrick Miller's to dinner, the first time since I have been his Tenant. We had a song on the harpsichord beginning

' Raving winds around her blowing '

The air was much admired. The lady of the house asked me whose were the words. ' Mine Madam ' I said. She took not the smallest notice !

Aug. 20th. Mauchline. Arrived here from Ellisland. I was on horseback by three o'clock this morning. As I jogged along in the dark by the Banks of the Firth towards Ayrshire, I began a rough sketch of a poem with the lines—

> . . . in gowany glens
> Where bonie lassies bleach their claes . . .

And I am determined from this time forth whatever I write to do it *leisurely*—

> Where stately oaks their twisted arms
> Throw broad and dark across the pool . . .

August 23rd. Mauchline. I am enquiring for a place for my young brother William among the Saddler's shops in Edinburgh. If I get him into a first rate shop, I will bind him a year or two—I almost do not care on what terms. He is about eighteen now, really very clever. I will have him a first rate hand if possible.

I am on the way to my farm again, where I will be busy for about a month with the harvest.

I have wrote to Mrs. Mac Lehose.

Here I am in the middle of my harvest, without good weather when I have reapers and without reapers when I have good weather. A tremendous thunderstorm yesternight and fog this morning.

> Alas, curst wi' eternal fogs
> And damn'd in everlasting bogs . . .

Most of my neighbours may be said to lead a vegetable life. They only know Prose in graces, prayers, &c. and the value of these they estimate as they do their plaiding webs—by the ell. They have as much idea of a poet as of a rhinocerus.

I at intervals throw my horny fist across my bi-cobwebbed lyre, much in the same manner as an old wife throws her hand across the spokes of her spinning wheel.

Sept. 9th. Ellisland.   *To Mr. Beugo, Engraver,*
                            Princes St., Edinburgh.

You are going to be married ? Depend upon it, if you have not made some damned foolish choice, it will be a very great improvement. I can speak from experience (tho' God knows my choice was as random as Blind-man's-buff).

I am here at the very elbow of existence. If you see Mr. Alexander Naesmith, to whom I sat half a dozen times for my likeness, remember me to him most respectfully.   R. B.

Sept. 10th. Ellisland. I am thinking of something in the rural way of the Drama-kind.

> Is there nae Scottish poet burning keen for fame
> Would boldly try to gie us plays at hame ?
> There's themes enow in Caledonian story
> Would show the Tragic Muse in all her glory.
> Is there no darling Bard . . .
>   . . . o' the Scottish nation
> Will gar Fame blaw until her trumpet crack
> And warsle Time and lay him on his back ?
>
>   . . . If a' the land
> Would take the Muses' servants by the hand,
> Not only hear but patronize, befriend them . . .

I Begin as a Farmer

Sept. 12th. Ellisland.   *To Jean.*

My Dear Love—I dreamed of you the whole of last night. But alas, I fear it will be three weeks ere I can hope for the happiness of seeing you. My harvest is going on. I have some to cut down still, but I put in two stacks today, so I am as tired as a dog. You might get one of Gilbert's sweet milk cheeses and send it.

I expect your new gowns will be very forward against I be home.

I believe you had best get the other half of Gilbert's web of table-linen and make it up, though I think the weaver's price is damnable dear.

Your faithful husband R. B.

PS. I have just now consulted a lady here about table-linen. She thinks I may have the *best* for two shillings per yard. So on second thoughts let it alone untill I return. Some day I will be in Dumfries and will ask the prices there.

Sept. 16. Ellisland. Busy behind my harvest folks this forenoon, but driven in later by bad weather. I bind every day after my reapers.

Sept. 16th. Ellisland.   *To Captain Robert Riddell.*

I return you my most grateful thanks for your lad today. Dare I ask for him tomorrow ? I would not ask did not necessity compel me. I have but three for my harvest. Your servant makes a fourth, which is all my forces.

R. B.

In Captain Robert Riddell's hospital mansion there is nothing gives me more pleasure than to see the minute cordial attentions and sparkling lover-like glances between him and his wife.

I have lately since harvest wrote a poem.

> While at the stook the shearers cow'r
> To shun the bitter blaudin show'r . . .

I have likewise been laying the foundation of some pretty large poetic works. I have these eight or ten months done very little that way.

> Tho' stars in skies may disappear
> And angry tempests gather
> The happy hour may soon be near
> That brings the pleasant weather.

155

Sept. 23rd. Ellisland. I am scarce able to hold up my head with this fashionable influenza which is just now the rage hereabouts.

Sunday morn. Sept.   *To Dr. Mundell.*

Dr Sir—As my symptons are continuing milder, I have not waited on you, but my liquid drug has failed. I am still using the Unction, tho' thank heaven not Extreme Unction.

                                        Your humble serv^t R. B.

Sept. 27th. Mauchline. Just arrived from Nithsdale & will be here for a fortnight. I was on horseback this morning by three o'clock. As I jogged on in the dark I was taken with a poetic-fit beginning

> Fate gave the word, the arrow sped
> And pierced my Darling's heart . . .

It is for Mrs. Fergusson of Craigdarroch—a lamentation on the death of her son, an uncommonly promising youth of 18 or 19.

I am so jaded with my dirty long journey.

I am not entirely sure of my farm's doing well. I hope for the best. But I have my Excise Commission in my pocket and so dont care three skips of a cur-dog for the gambols of Fortune.

I have been thinking that as I am only a little more than five miles from Dumfries, I might perhaps work at the Excise Office there, if the Commissioners could with propriety remove any of the other officers elsewhere (that wealthy Smith for example). But I would not injure a *poor* fellow by ousting him to make way for myself.

Oct. 14th. Ellisland.   *To Jean.*

My Dearest Love—You must get ready for Nithsdale as fast as possible, for I have an offer of a house in the very neighbourhood (with some furniture in it) which I shall have the use of for nothing till my own house be got ready. It is a large house, but we will only occupy a room or two of it. I am determined to remove you from Ayrshire immediately.

I am extremely happy at the idea of your coming, as it will save us from these cruel separations.

We will want a Maid servant. If you can hear of any to hire, ask after them.

The apples are all sold & gone.   R. B.

> The lazy mist hangs from the brow of the hill
> Concealing the course of the dark winding rill.
> How languid the scenes, late so sprightly, appear
> As autumn to winter resigns the pale year.

Nov. 5th. [Extract from a letter just received from Mrs. Dunlop.] ' A ' gentleman told me the other day that you were a sad wretch, that your ' works were *immoral* and *infamous*; you *lampooned the clergy* and were a ' *scandalous liver* in every sense of the word. I said I was *certain* he must ' be misinformed and asked if he knew you.'

. . . lampoon the clergy . . . scandalous in every sense of the word . . . immoral . . . infamous . . . Well, I have raised a hue and cry of Heresy against me which has not ceased till this hour.

I must be at the Dunlop and Kilmaurs Cow Fairs, which will happen on Halloween & Hallowday. I'll call at Dunlop House on Wednesday or Thursday, perhaps at Wednesday's breakfast hour.

Nov. 13th. Mauchline.   *To Bruce Campbell Esqre.*

Sir—I enclose you, for Mr. Boswell [*the* Mr. Boswell, recently arrived on a visit in the neighbourhood] the Ballad you mentioned, with one or two others of my fugitive Pieces. Should they procure me the honor of being introduced to Mr. Boswell, I shall think they have great merit.

There are few pleasures equal to that of having seen many of the Heroes of wit & literature of my country. And as I had the honor of drawing my first breath almost in the same parish with Mr. Boswell, my pride plumes itself on the connection. To have been acquainted with such a man as Mr. Boswell. . . .   R. B.

[This letter was passed on to Mr. Boswell, who put it aside and forgot about it after endorsing it thus:—' *13 Novr 1788.* from Mr. Robert Burns 'the Poet, expressing very high sentiments of me.']

Nov. 13th.   Mauchline.   At Dunlop House, Miss Rachel, Miss Mac-Kay and Miss Keith with their flattering attentions & artful compliments absolutely turned my head.   Their sly insinuations, their delicate innuendoes. . . .

Miss Keith much offended by four lines in my Commodore poem. Had I known that he (the Commodore) was the Godfather of my lovely young friend I would have spared him for her sake.   The four lines shall be omitted.

Miss Keith said she had never seen Gray's Poems.   I am sending her a copy of them.   I received from her by the way, a heavy complaint that Mrs. Dunlop never shows them my letters nor the poems enclosed.   I must blame Mrs. Dunlop for this.   She is at perfect liberty to show *any* of my things.

The Major made me a present of a cow.   And I am determined annually as Hallowday returns to decorate her horns with an Ode of Gratitude to the family.

Auld Lang Syne

January 25.

Sir,— In answer to Mr Russell's plea for the proper version of Auld Lang Syne (January 15), and Mr Watson's reply (January 24), let me quote from Burns's Complete Works, Kilmarnock edition.

Burns's name is not affixed to this world-famous song, and yet there can be no doubt it is chiefly his own. He admitted to Johnson that the two verses beginning respectively "We twa hae ran about the braes" and "We twa hae paidl'd in the burn" are his own, although in sending the song to Mrs Dunlop in December, 1788, and also in writing about it to Thomson in September, 1793, he speaks of it as ancient.

We are indebted to George Thomson for selecting the fine old air of Can Ye Labour Lea, which by universal consent has now become identified with the present song:

Should auld acquaintance be forgot
And never brought to mind?
Should auld acquaintance be forgot,
And auld long syne?

   For auld lang syne, my jo,
   For auld lang syne,
   We'll tak' a cup o' kindness yet,
   For auld lang syne.

And surely ye'll be your pint-stoup,
And surely I'll be mine;
And we'll tak' a cup of kindness yet,
For auld lang syne.

We twa hae run about the braes,
And pou'd the gowans fine;
But we've wander'd mony a weary fit,
Sin' auld lang syne.

We twa hae paidl'd in the burn,
Frae morning sun till dine;
But seas between us braid hae roar'd,
Sin' auld lang syne.

And there's a hand, my trusty fiere!
And gie's a hand o' thine!
And we'll tak' a right gude-willie
   waught,
For auld lang syne.

fe Geddes Drummond,
skine Avenue,
e.

V cameras ven more eedom

By Our Political Correspondent

les governing the filming of the House
ns have been slightly relaxed after the fir
onths of the experiment, with a speci
ng committee of MPs agreeing yesterd
broadcasters should be given a little mo
n.

les which allow a
shot only if an
stituency or Min-
artment has been
l will be "inter-
ss strictly" Sir
Howe, the Leader
Commons, an-
. However,
hots still will not
l during Question
r ministerial
s.

Sir Geoffrey Howe;
"Less strict."

howing the reactions of a group of MP
o a wide-angle shot will be allowed any time.
charge of filming will be allowed to zoom
n on a speaking MP or out to show the M
o nearby colleagues.
r, during disorder the cameras have still to f
eaker and cannot show the disturbance.
n operate from today, and Sir Geoffrey
odifications of the orginal directions could n

horities hope the decision will answer some
ers' complaints about over-strict rules whe
t began last November.

Health
board's
cash figh

SERIOUS failings
nancial manageme

a
en

I Begin as a Farmer

Nov. 15th. Mauchline. In a fortnight I move bag & baggage to Ellisland.

My knee, I believe, never will be entirely well; and an unlucky fall this winter has made it still worse.

If miry ridges & dirty dunghills are to engross the best part of my soul immortal, I had better been a rook or a magpie & then I should not have been plagued with any ideas superior to the breaking of clods & picking up of grubs ; not to mention barn-door cocks or mallards, creatures with which I could almost exchange lives at any time.

I am not positively certain, after all, if I shall be at Ayr Fair.

Another song begun—Dr. Blacklock commends it highly, but I am *not* just satisfied with it myself yet—

> For auld lang syne, my dear,
>   For auld lang syne,
> We'll tak' a cup o' kindness yet
>   For auld lang syne !
>
> We twa hae run about the braes
>   And pulled the gowans fine,
> But we've wandered mony a weary foot
>   Sin auld lang syne.
>
> And here's a hand, my trusty fiere *   [*Friend]
>   And gie's a hand o' thine
> And we'll tak' a cup o' kindness yet
>   For auld lang syne.

Mr. Creech owes me still about fifty pounds. He kept me hanging about Edinburgh from the 7th August 1787 until the 13th April 1788 before he would condescend to give me a statement; nor had I got it even then but for an angry letter I wrote him.

I believe I shall in whole clear about £400 & some little odds. I am still much in the gentleman's mercy.

1788–9

Dec. 22nd. Ellisland. I yesterday tried my cask of whisky for the first time.

A neighbour of mine and his wife were in my house at the time I broke open the cask. They keep a country Publick-house. They were perfectly astonished at my whisky both for its taste & strength. The whisky of this district is a most rascally liquor and by consequence only drank by the most rascally part of the inhabitants.

I *am* to be at the New Year Day Fair at Ayr.

> At the starless midnight hour
> When winter rules with boundless power,
> As the storms the forests tear
> And thunders rend the howling air,
> Listening to the doubling roar
> Singing on the rocky shore . . .

New-year-day morning. Ellisland. This is a morning of wishes.

My newest song has cost me some pains, though that is but an equivocal mark of its excellence. I have two or three others by me. These fragments, if my design succeed, are but a small part of the intended whole.

All my poetry is the effect of easy composition but of laborious correction.

[A letter from Gilbert—'*Jan. 1st 1789. Mossgiel*—Dear Brother—I
' have just finished my new-year's day breakfast in the usual form, which
' naturally makes me call to mind the days of former years. When I look
' at our family vicissitudes, I cannot help remarking to you, my dear
' brother, how good the God of Seasons is to us; and that, however some
' clouds may seem to lour, we have great reason to hope that all will turn
' out well.

' Your mother and sisters join me in the compliments of the season to
' you and Mrs. Burns, and beg you will remember us in the same manner
' to William, the first time you see him. I am, dear brother, yours Gilbert
' Burns.']

[Elizabeth Smith, farm servant, says that ' she only once at Ellisland
' saw her master affected with liquor and that was at the New Year, 1789 '.]

I Begin as a Farmer

> While winds frae aff Ben Lomond blaw
> And bar the doors wi' drivin snaw
> I set me down to pass the time
> And spin a verse or twa in rhyme.

But whether my spinning will deserve to be laid up in store like the precious thread of the Silk-worm or brushed to the devil like the vile manufacture of the Spider . . .

Jan. 4th. Ellisland. We have lost poor Uncle Robert this winter. He died yesterday. He had long been weak.

22nd Jan^{ry}. Ellisland. I muse & rhyme morning noon & night & have a hundred different poetic plans, pastoral, dramatic &c floating in the regions of fancy somewhere between purpose and resolve.
Provided the straight-jacket of criticism dont cure me . . .
Snow—and a January wind blowing cold.

> The sun had clos'd the winter day
> The curlers quat their roaring play
> And hungered Maukin * taen her way   [* *The hare*]
>   To kail-yards green
> While faithless snaws 'ilk step betray
>   Where she has been.

Necessity oblidges me to go into my new house even before it be plaistered. I will inhabit the one end untill the other is finished.

I am now able to support myself & family in a humble yet independent way.

1789

Jan. Mauchline.   *To Mrs. Dunlop.*
This morning I had set apart for a visit to my honored Friend, when behold, the snows descended and the winds blew and made my journey impracticable. I had got a hundred & fifty things to say to you.

The inclosed Ode is a compliment to the memory of the late Mrs. Oswald of Auchencruive. You probably knew her personally, an honor of which I cannot boast, though I spent my early years in her neighbourhood—a matron who, much against her private inclinations, lately left this good world and ten thousand a year behind her. Among her servants and tenants I know she was detested with the most heartfelt cordiality. However in the particular part of her conduct which roused my wrath, she was much less blameable—

I had put up, you must know, at the only tolerable Inn at Sandquhar. The frost was keen. The grim evening and howling wind were ushering in a night of snow and drift. My horse & I were both much fatigued.

I had just dispatched my dinner, glad to have found out so comfortable a place of rest, when into the courtyard wheels an immense retinue, the funeral pagentry of the late great Mrs. Oswald, and poor I am forced to brave all the horrors of the tempestuous night, the howling hills and icy cataracts and goad my jaded horse, my young, favorite horse Pegasus, twelve miles farther on through the wildest moors of Ayrshire to New Cumnock, the next Inn.

> Lo there she goes, unpitied and unblest
> She goes, but not to realms of everlasting rest.
> Note that eye, 'tis rheum o'erflows.
> Pity's flood there never rose.
> See these hands, ne'er stretched to save,
> Hands that took—but never gave.
> And are they then of no avail,
> Ten thousand glitt'ring pounds a year?
> O bitter mockery of the pompous bier!

Go to your sculptured tombs ye Great, go to your magnificent mausoleums!

I have philosophy and pride enough to support me with unwounded indifference against the neglect of my superiors, the rank & file of the noblesse & gentry, nay even to keep my vanity quite sober under the lardings of their compliments.

To soften the matter a little I have altered the title to Mrs. A—— of O——. They might suspect me for the author.

Monday even. In a week I shall be ready, with two horses, to drive lime.

I Begin as a Farmer

3ʳᵈ Feb. Ellisland. Some larger poetic plans are in my imagination or partly in execution.

I can affirm both from bachelor and wedlock experience that Love is the alpha and omega of human enjoyment. It is that spark of celestial fire which lights up the wintry hut of poverty and makes the chearless mansion warm confortable and gay. It is the emanation of Divinity that preserves the sons and daughters of rustic labour from degenerating into the brutes with which they daily hold converse.

I am distressed with the want of my house in a most provoking manner. It loses me two hours' work of my farm hands every day, besides other inconveniences. But patience. I look upon patience to be the possessing one's mind calmly in ruffling circumstances.

[A young cousin John, employed now about the farm, describes cousin Robert as ' a good master, but absent-minded and restless—very ready ' to go from one thing to another in the most unexpected fashion '.]

The circle of our acquaintance, like a wide horizon, is too large for us to make anything of it. We are amused for a little with ill-defined, distant objects, but our eye soon tires.

With whatever unconcern, after my late ramble into fashionable life, I give up a transient connection with the Self-important, I cannot lose the notice of the Learned or the Good without the bitterest regret. I returned with a few real attachments, but from my uncouthness when *out* of my native sphere and my obscurity *in* that sphere, I am oblidged to give up most of them in despair.

Early Feb. Ellisland.   *To Mr. William Dunbar. W.S.*

My Dear Sir—You made me happy once in the idea that I should enjoy your correspondence in my rustic obscurity and I shall not easily part with the hope I had induldged of your friendship as one of the enjoyments of my life. In my professional line too, my poetic line, I want you much. Before an author gets his piece finished he has viewed and reviewed it so often that he is no longer a judge of its merits. A judicious candid friend is then all he has to trust to. I had set you down as that friend.

I have the pleasure of assuring you how sincerely I am dear Sir, your most obedient humble serv^t   Robert Burns.

A little later. Ellisland. To Mr. Robert Muir, Wine Merchant, Kilmarnock.

My Dear Friend—You and I have often agreed that life is no great blessing on the whole. You know my ideas. They are not far different from yours. Now that I hope to settle with some credit and comfort at home here, there is no friendship or friendly correspondence that promises me more pleasure than yours. I hope I will not be disappointed. Adieu. God send us a cheerful meeting soon.   R. B.

5th Feb. Ellisland.   *To Mrs. Dunlop.*

I am very sorry that you should be informed of my composing, in some midnight frolic, a stanza or two perhaps not quite proper for a clergyman's reading to a company of ladies. But that *I* am the author of the verses alluded to is what I much doubt. In any case I hold it a piece of contemptible baseness for *anyone* to detail the sallies of thoughtless merriment or accidental intoxication to the ear of female delicacy.   R. B.

8th Feb. Ellisland. I am oblidged to set out for Edin^r tomorrow se'ennight.

[A letter from William—' *Feb. 15. Longtown*—As I am now entering ' the world, my inexperience, which I daily feel, makes me wish for that ' advice which you are so able to give and which I can only expect from ' you or Gilbert. I have the promise of seven shillings a week here, but ' I am to pay four shillings per week of board wages. Please write me ' often while I stay here. Please give my best wishes to my sister-in-law ' and believe me to be your affectionate and obliged brother   William. ' PS. The great coat you gave me at parting did me singular service.']

20th Feb. Edin^r. I have settled matters greatly to my satisfaction with Mr. Creech—amicably and as fairly as could have been expected. He is certainly not what he should be nor has he given me what I should have, but I clear about £440 or £450. I advanced Gilbert about £200. Their well-being is indispensible and certainly to me the same as my own.

Feb. 21st. Edin^r. I am more unhappy here in Edin^r than I ever experienced before. I love the social pleasures in moderation, but here I am impressed into the service of Bacchus. And I am *from home.* Soon I return to Nithsdale.

March 1. Ellisland. I arrived here from Edin^r yesternight.

> There was a lass and she was fair.
> At kirk and market to be seen.
> When a' our fairest maids were met
> The fairest maid was bonie Jean.
>
> And ay she wrought her country work
> And ay she sang sae merrilie.
> The blythest bird upon the bush
> Had ne'er a lighter heart than she.

To a man who has a home, however humble or remote—if that home is, like mine, the scene of domestic comfort—the bustle of the Capital will soon be a business of sickening disgust.

Often in the pomp of Prince's Street, when I must sculk into a corner lest the rattling equipage of some contemptible puppy should mangle me in the mire, I wonder what merit had these wretches in some state of pre-existance that they are ushered into this scene of being with riches in their puny fists. What demerit had I that I am kicked into the world, the sport of their folly? I have read somewhere of a monarch who was so out of humour that he said—had he been of the Creator's Council, he could have saved him a great deal of labour and absurdity.

March 2^d. Ellisland.   *To William.*

My Dear William—I arrived from Edin^r only the night before last, so could not answer your epistle sooner. I congratulate you on the prospect of employ—['Robert used to remark to me,' says Gilbert, 'that he could ' not well conceive anything more mortifying than a man seeking work ']— and I am indebted to you for one of the best letters that has been written by any mechanic lad in Nithsdale or any other dale on either side of the Border this twelvemonth. Writing a handsome letter is an accomplishment worth courting; and, with attention & practice, I can promise you that it will soon be an accomplishment of yours. If my advice can serve you, my small knowledge & experience is heartily at your service.

Taciturnity—let that be your motto. Garrulousness would lower you in the eyes of your fellow creatures.

You will receive by the carrier 2 coarse & one fine shirt, a neckcloth and your velvet waistcoat. I'll probably write you next week.   R. B.

March 9th. Ellisland.   *To Mrs. MacLehose.*

You will pardon me, Madam, if I do not carry my complaisance so far as to acquiesce in the name of villain, merely out of compliment even to *your* opinion—much as I esteem your judgment. I have already told you that at the time you allude to I was not under the smallest moral tie to Mrs. B.

I would have called on you when I was in town—indeed I could not have resisted it—but Mr. Robert Ainslie told me that you were determined to avoid your windows lest even a glance of me should occur in the street.

When I have regained your good opinion, perhaps I may venture to solicit your friendship. Be that as it may, you shall always be the object of my warmest good wishes.   R. B.

March 10th. Ellisland.   *To William.*

My Dear William—In my last I recommended taciturnity.

What mischiefs arise from garrulity or foolish confidence! There is an excellent Scots saying ' A man's mind is his kingdom '. But how few can govern that kingdom with propriety.

Now is the time of life that will either make or mar you, the time for laying in habits. At after-periods, even at so little advance as my years, one may be very sharp-sighted to one's habituall failings; but to amend them is quite a different matter. R. B.

March 23ᵈ. Ellisland. Finally settled with Mr. Creech. I must retract some ill-natured surmises and own that he has been amicable and fair with me.

March 25th. Ellisland. *To William.*

I have stolen this minute from my corn-sowing to write a line to accompany your shirt & hat. Your sister Nannie arrived here yesterday & begs to be remembered to you. Write me every opportunity.

I can no more. My head is as addle as an egg this morning with dining abroad yesterday. Forgive this foolish-looking scrap of an epistle.

If you should not succeed in your tramp to find work, don't be dejected or take any rash step. Return to us in that case. Remember this I charge you. I am ever, my dear William, yours R. B.

[A letter received from Mrs. MacLehose, in which there is this—
'I have been under unspeakable obligations to your friend Mr. Ainslie.
'He has called often.']

April 2d. Ellisland. Sore tired with the labours of the day.

I want a Shakespear. I want likewise an English Dictionary. Johnson's I suppose is the best.

April 4th. Ellisland. As I am not devoutly attached to a certain Monarch, I cannot say that my heart ran any risk of bursting with gratitude on Thursday was se'ennight.

[There had been a public Thanksgiving with Joyful Solemnity for the recovery of His Majesty George the Third from mental derangement.] Joyful Solemnity! I look on the whole business as a solemn farce of flagrant mummery.

I Begin as a Farmer

> O sing a new song to the Lord
>   Make all and every one
> A joyful noise ev'n to the King
>   His restoration !
>
> Now hear our prayer, accept our song
>   And fight Thy Chosen's battle
> We seek but little Lord from thee :
>   Thou kens we *get* as little !

April 13th. Ellisland. Much surprised last night on being told that some silly verses on the Duchess of Gordon which have appeared in a London Newspaper [The Star—also copied in the Gazette] were said to be my composition. I am not a reader of *any* London Newspaper and I am not the author of the verses in question. In fact I never composed a line on the Duchess of Gordon in my life.

I have been recollecting over the sins and backslidings of myself and my forefathers to see if I can guess why I am thus punished with this vile accusation of ingratitude in publishing a disrespectful stanza on a highly respectable personage to whom I am deeply indebted. There is one sin which Satan *cannot* throw in my teeth—ingratitude.

April 15th. Ellisland   To William.

My Dear William—I am extremely sorry at the misfortune of your leg. My house shall ever be your welcome home. If you need money, you know my direction by post. The enclosed is from Gilb^t, brought by your sister Nanny. It was unluckily forgot. I heard from them yesterday. They are all well. Adieu.   R. B.

April 19th. Ellisland. I was out today at a very early hour sowing in the fields. I heard a shot & presently a poor little hare limped by me apparently very much hurt. The inhuman fellow, who could shoot a hare at this season, when they all of them have young ones !

Indeed there is something in all that business of destroying for our sport individuals in the animal creation which do not injure us materially, that I could never reconcile to my ideas of eternal right. We are all equally creatures of some great Creator. But among the many instances of *capricious partiality* in the administration of this world, one of the most flagrant, I think, is that power which one creature has to amuse himself at the expence of another's misery, torture & death.

Wrote a poem—' ON SEEING A FELLOW WOUND A HARE WITH A SHOT, APRIL 1789.' Sent a copy of this to Dr. Gregory, Edinburgh.
Here are some of Dr. G.'s criticisms—
' The Wounded Hare is a pretty good *subject,* but the *measure* is not a ' good one. It does not *flow* well. In stanza I the first two lines are too ' coarse. " Murder-aiming " is a bad compound epithet and not very ' intelligible. " Blood-stained " has the same fault. Such epithets are ' incongruous with poetic fancy. *Form*—a hare's *form* is neither a poetic ' nor a dignified word; it is a word unsuitable to serious poetry. '" Mangled " is a coarse word ', &c &c &c.
Dr. Gregory has no bowels of compassion for a poor poetic sinner !

April 21st. Ellisland. Building, planning, planting, ploughing, sowing &c. &c. Also reading a parcel of poems by a young authoress. The poems have given me & daily give me a world of trouble in revising them. They are hopeless trash. But her forefathers once saw better days, for which consideration I submit to the horrid drudgery.

April 27th. Ellisland.   *To Mr. James Hamilton, Grocer, Glasgow.*
My Dear Sir—I have written *twice* to my brother poet Mr. Turnbull, but as I have not had a word in return from him, I suspect that he has left Glasgow. I owe him for his Poems. He sent me six copies. One of them I had paid before. The price of the rest is ready for him if he will authorise any body in Dumfries to receive it. I shall be in Mauchline at Whit-Sunday or thereabouts. Shall I send the money to you by John Ronald the Carrier ? I am not yet acquainted with any of the Dumfries Carriers. I am, dear Sir, yours sincerely   Robt. Burns.
My Rib begs her compliments to you.

I Begin as a Farmer

April 27th. Ellisland. This country has nothing new. The papers are barren of home-news and foreign. No murders or rapes worth the naming.

That strange, shifting, doubling animal Man is generally a negative & often a worthless creature. Of the men called honest and the women called chaste half of them are not what they pretend to be and many are thought to have still worse faults. But then virtue, everyone knows, is an obsolete business. Some years ago when I was young and by no means the saint I am now, I discovered that even a *godly* woman may be a . . . but this is scandal.

However respectable *individuals* in all ages have been, I look on mankind in the lump as nothing better than a foolish Mob.

> The grave sage hern thus easy picks a frog
> And thinks the mallard a sad worthless dog !

May 4th. Ellisland.   *To Mrs. Dunlop.*

I beg your pardon, Madam, for troubling you with the inclosed to John. It is to request him to look me out two milk cows, one for myself & another for Captn Riddell of Glenriddell, a neighbor of mine. John véry oblidgingly offered to do this for me. Mauchline Fair happens on the 20th curr^t. I shall be there and I hope to have the honor of assuring you in person how sincerely I am Madam, your most obedient humble serv^t

R. B.

May 5th. Ellisland.   *To William.*

My Dear Willm.—I am happy to hear that you are getting some employ.

I had a visit of your old landlord. He is high in your praises and I would advise you to cultivate his friendship as he is in his way a worthy and to you may be a useful man.

Anderson I hope will have your shoes ready to send by the waggon to-morrow. I forgot to mention about making them pumps, but I suppose good calf shoes will be no great mistake. Wattie has paid for the thongs.

Your falling in love is indeed a phenomenon ! To a fellow of your turn it cannot be hurtful. I am a veteran in these campaigns, so let me advise you always to try for *intimacy* as soon as you feel the first symptoms of

171

the passion. This is not only best as making the most of the little entertainment which the sportabilities of distant addresses always gives, but is the best preservative for one's peace.

Your sisters send their compliments. God bless you.   R. B.

P.S. I need not caution you against guilty amours. They are bad everywhere, but in England they are the very devil.

The martial clangor of a trumpet has something in it vastly more heroic than the twingle-twangle of a jews-harp. The delicate wild rose, heavy with the dawn is infinitely more beautiful than the upright stub of a burdock. These I had set down as irrefragible truths—until my faith was shaken by a book of essays on ' The Principles of Taste' by Alison. Several of his propositions have startled me. I never read a book which gave me such a quantum of information or added so much to my ideas.

May 13th. Ellisland.   *To Robt Graham Esqre of Fintry.*
Sir—I remember you talked of being this way with my honored friend Sir William Murray in the course of this summer. You cannot imagine how happy it would make me should you two do me the honor to partake of a Farmer's dinner with me. I shall promise you a piece of good beef, a chicken or perhaps a Nith salmon & a glass of punch on the shortest notice. I shall expect your Honors with a kind of enthusiasm.

Robt Burns.

May 21st. Mauchline.   *To Captain Richard Brown.*
My Dear Friend—By accident hearing of your safe arrival, I could not resist wishing you joy—wishing you would write me before you sail again—wishing you would always set me down as your bosom-friend—wishing you long life & prosperity.

There is a lad, James Miller from this place to sail your passenger. He is a good honest blunt lad by no means destitute of abilities. Should it be in your power to oblidge him in any little civility, it would oblidge me likewise. Fare well, my long-loved, dearest friend. Bless you.   R. B.

June 4th. Ellisland. I am here in my old way, holding my plough, marking the growth of my corn or the health of my dairy. I've sturdy stumps the Lord be thankit and, faith, I'm gay and hearty, sauntering at times by the delightful windings of the Nith, on the margin of which I have built my humble domicile; praying for seasonable weather or holding an intrigue with the Muses, the only gipsies with whom I have now any intercourse.

> The primrose bank, the wimpling burn,
> The cuckoo on the milk-white thorn,
> The wanton lambs at early morn . . .

June 5th. Ellisland.   *To Robert Ainslie.*

My Dear Friend—I am perfectly ashamed of myself when I look at the date of your last. It is not that I forget the friend of my heart, but I have had a collection of poems by a lady put into my hands and I am condemned to the drudgery beyond sufferance of preparing them for the press, which horrid task, with masons, wrights and plaisterers to attend to, as well as sowing corn & roaming on business through Ayrshire—all this was against me. I have not had a moment to spare from incessant toil since the 8th. Forgive me. I shall send you soon one or two rhymes.   R. B.

June 21st. Ellisland. Low spirits—I know not of any particular cause for this, but for some time my soul has been beclouded with evil imaginings & gloomy presages. Yet an honest man has nothing to fear. If we lie down in the grave, the whole man a piece of broken machinery to moulder with the clods of the valley—be it so. At least there is an end of pain, care, woes and wants. If that part of us called Mind does survive . . . but idle reasonings sometimes make me a little sceptical. Every age and every nation has had a different set of stories and it becomes a man of sense to think for himself, particularly where all men are equally interested and where indeed all men are equally in the dark.

July 17th. Ellisland. Captn. Grose, the well known author of the Antiquities of England & Wales, a chearful-looking grig of an old fat fellow, has been with Captn. Riddell, my nearest neighbour, these two months. I have to the best of my recollection of the old buildings &c. in the country, given him an itinerary thro' Ayr-shire.

I Begin as a Farmer

July 31st. Ellisland. I am deliberating whether I had better not give up farming altogether. The Excise salary is now £50 per ann., surely a much superior object to a farm. The worst of it is that leaving the farm so soon may have an unsteady, giddy-headed appearance.

. . . interrupted by the arrival of my Mother and Gilbert.

Aug. 5th. Ellisland.   *To David Sillar.*

I was half in thoughts not to have written you at all by way of revenge for the two damn'd business letters you sent me. I want to know all about your views, your hopes, fears &c. &c. in commencing poet in print. In short I wanted you to write to Robin like his old friend Davie.

I have got, I think, about eleven subscribers for you. My acquaintance in this place is yet but very limited, else I might have had more. Believe me to be, dear David, ever yours.   R. B.

Aug. 14th. Ellisland.   *To William.*

My Dear William—I received your letter and am very happy to hear that you have got settled for the winter. I inclose you the two guinea-notes of the Bank of Scotland, which I hope will serve your need. It is indeed not quite so convenient for me to spare money as it once was, but I know your situation and your worth.

Your mother and sisters beg their compliments.   R. B.

> I've little to spend and naething to lend,
> But though I be poor, unnoticed, obscure,
> I can haud up my head wi' the best . . .

Natural History is a favorite study of mine.

I never hear the loud solitary whistle of a curlew in a summer noon or the wild mixing cadence of a troop of grey plover in an autumnal morning without feeling an elevation of soul.

> Thou stock dove whose echo resounds thro' the glen,
> Ye wild whistling blackbirds in yon thorny den,
> Thou green-crested lapwing . . . screaming . . .

Aug 19th. Ellisland. I have been once more lucky. Excisemen's salaries are now £50 per ann. and I believe the Board have been so oblidging as to fix me in the Division in which I live and I suppose I shall begin doing duty at the commencement of next month. I shall have a large portion of country, but—what to me & my studies is no trifling matter— it is romantic country.

More luck still ! About two hours ago Mrs. Burns presented me with a fine chopping boy, a squalling fellow with a pipe that makes the room ring. He has a fine manly countenance and a figure that might do credit to a little fellow two months older. His Mother as usual—which, with improving the farm, building a steading of farmhouses &c. has kept me very busy.

Sept. Ellisland. The hurry of a farmer in this particular season ! Tremendous fogs this morning have driven me for refuge from the hypochondria, which I fear worse than the devil, to my Muse.

Sept. 6th. Ellisland. I had some time ago an epistle from the poetess Mrs. Little, a very ingenious composition. The fact is I know not well how to write to her. I am no dab at fine-drawn letter writing. I sit down when *necessitated* to write as I would sit down to beat hemp.

Oct. 2ᵈ. Ellisland. My little squalling son goes on improving in grace and favor. Parental partiality apart, he is in fact and very deed almost the finest boy I ever saw. He seems to say by the vigorous tossings of his little limbs that he will one day stand on the legs of independance and hold up the face on an Honest Man. He has an excellent good temper.

Nov. 1st. Ellisland.   *To Robert Ainslie.*

My Dear Friend—I had written to you ere now could I have guessed where to find you, for I am sure you have more good sense than to waste the precious days of vacation-time in the dirt of Business & Edin^r. Wherever you are, God bless you. I don't know if I have informed you that I am now appointed to an Excise Division. £50 a year for life & a provision for widows & orphans, you will allow, is no bad settlement. The appointment will not cost me above £10 or £12 per ann. of expences.

R. B.

During this autumn vacation Allan Masterton [another school-master friend] and I, being at Moffat, went to pay a visit to Willie Nicol [the Nicol of the Highland Tour].   We had such a joyous meeting.

> Oh Willie brewed a peck o' maut
> And Rob and Allan cam to see.
> Three blyther hearts that lee-lang night
> Ye wad no found in Christendie.
>
> Here are we met, three merry boys
> Three merry boys I trow are we
> And monie a night we've merry been
> And monie mae we hope to be.

Nov. 4th.   Ellisland.   *To Captain Richard Brown.*

I have been so hurried, my ever dear friend, that though I got both your letters I have not been able to command an hour to answer them. Do you come and see me. We must have a social day and perhaps lengthen it out with half the night, before you go again to sea. You are the earliest friend I now have on earth; and is not that an indearing circumstance ? You and I by being both unfortunate were entwined with one another in our growth; and blasted be the sacrilegious hand that shall attempt to undo the union. You and I must have one bumper to my favorite toast—' May the companions of our youth be the friends of our old age ! '   R. B.

Nov. 7th.   Ellisland.   *To David Newal Esqre.*

Dear Sir—The bearer is the lad who executed the drain. Four or five days more will conclude it; and these few days must, I doubt, stand over untill next Spring, as the business is impractible in wintry weather.

Seventeen pence per rood was the bargain, which, taking 85 roods as the just length, makes the account £6–0–5. But at this rate the poor fellows will scarce have 1/- per day. I know tolerably exactly how many days they were altogether & between you and me they well deserve 14^d or 15^d per day, as they wrought both hard & dirty & kept no stated hours, but from sun to sun almost.

However you & I will settle that at meeting. In the mean time they want some money. I have paid them £3–0–2½ (my half). You might,

I think, give them a couple of guineas or so untill you see the work yourself.

[William Clark, employed for six months in 1789–90 at Ellisland as ploughman states that Mr. Burns ' kept nine or ten milch cows, some ' young cattle, four horses and also several pet sheep of which he was very ' fond. During seed time he might be seen at an early hour in the fields ' sowing, but as the Excise and other business often required his attention ' from home, he did not sow the whole of the grain. He was a kind and ' indulgent master and spoke familiarly to everyone, though if anything ' put him out of humour he was very passionate for a wee while. But the ' storm was soon over and never a word afterwards. As a matter of fact ' I never saw him really angry but once, owing to the carelessness of one of ' the women. She had not cut the potatoes small enough—which brought ' one of the cows into danger of being choked. His looks, gesture and

' voice on that occasion were *terrible*. When I met him again he was per-
' fectly calm. I never saw him intoxicated.

' When at home he usually wore a blue bonnet, a blue or drab-coloured
' long tailed coat, corduroy breeches, dark blue stockings and gaiters and
' in cold weather a black and white checked plaid wrapped round his
' shoulders.

' Mrs. Burns was a good and prudent housewife, kept everything in
' neat order and was well liked by all. She provided abundance of
' wholesome food.']

Nov. 8th. Ellisland. I have somehow got a most violent cold and am
in the stupid, disagreable predicament of a stuffed aching head.

Nov. 10th. Ellisland.   *To William.*
Dear William.—I would have written you sooner, but I am so harried
and fatigued with my Excise business. I know not if you heard lately
from Gilbert. I expect him here with me on the latter end of this week.
They are all well.

The only Ayr-shire news is that Mr. Ronald is bankrupt. You will
easily guess from his insolent vanity *in his days of sunshine,* how he will feel a
little retaliation from those who thought themselves eclipsed by him.
Poor fellow, I do not think he ever intentionally injured any one—except
indeed his wife, whom he certainly has used very ill. But she is still fond
of him to distraction and bears up wonderfully.

I am very glad at your resolution of living within your income. Had
poor Mr. Ronald done so, he had not this day been a prey to the dreadful
miseries of insolvency. Go and persevere. All the family have their
complnts to you. I am, dear William, your brother   Robt Burns.

Dec. 9th. Ellisland. I have found the Excise business a great deal
smoother than I apprehended, owing a good deal to the generous friendship of my Collector and the kind assistance and instruction of my
Supervisor.

I dare to be honest and I fear no labor. Nor do I find my hurried life
greatly inimical to my correspondence with the Muses. Their visits to me
indeed, and I believe to most of their acquaintance, are short and far between,
but I meet them now and then as I jog through the hills of Nithsdale.

The following verses were the production of yesterday. I am tolerably pleased with them.

> ' Where are you gaun, my bonnie lass ?
>   Where are you gaun, my hinnie ? '
> She answer'd me right saucily
>   ' An errand for my minnie.'
>
> ' O whare live ye, my bonie lass ?
>   O whare live ye, my hinnie ? '
> ' By yon burnside, gin ye maun ken
>   In a wee house wi' my minnie.'
>
> But I went up the glen at e'en
>   To see my bonie lassie
> And lang before the grey morn came
>   She was na half sae saucy.

Another hair-breadth escape from love. Thank my stars I got off heart-whole. I believe that my heart has been so often on fire that it is now absolutely *vitrified*.

Dec. 13th. Ellisland.

Health & spirits are the greatest enjoyments on earth and wanting these all other enjoyments are of poor avail. For now near three weeks I have been so ill with a nervous headache that I have been obliged to give up for a time my Excise-books, being scarce able to lift my head, much less to ride once a week over ten muir parishes.

> Cauld blaws the evenin blast
>   When bitter bites the frost
> And in the mirk and dreary drift
>   The hills and glens are lost.

To day in the luxuriance of health, exulting in the enjoyment of existence ; in a few hours I am counting the tardy pace of the lingering moments by the repercussions of anguish. Day follows night and night comes after day with life which gives no pleasure. And yet the aweful, dark termination of that life is a something—perhaps a Nothing—at which man recoils with still more horror.

Can it be possible that when I resign this feverish being, I shall still find myself in conscious existence ? When the last gasp of agony has announced that I am no more to those that knew me & the few who loved me ; when the cold stiffened ghastly corpse is resigned into the earth to be the prey of unsightly reptiles & to become in time a trodden clod, shall I be yet warm in life, seeing & seen, enjoying & enjoyed ?

What a flattering idea is the much talk'd of world beyond the grave, the world to come. Would to God I as firmly believed in it as I ardently desire it.

Jesus Christ, thou amiablest of characters, I trust thou art no Imposter & that thy revelation of blissful scenes of existance beyond death is not one of the many impositions which, time after time, have been palmed on credulous mankind.

Dec. Ellisland.   *To William Nicol.*

I have been so ill, my ever dear Friend, that I have not been able to go over the threshold of my door since I saw you.

Your unfortunate old mare—I have tried many dealers for her & I am ashamed to say that the highest offer I got for her is fifty shillings. I tried her yesterday in the plough. The poor creature is extremely willing to do what she can, so I hope to make her worth her meat to me untill I can try her at some Fair.

Dec. 20th. Ellisland. My poor distracted mind is so torn, so racked & bedevil'd with the task of making one guinea do the business of three that I swoon at the very word Business.

Dec. 23ᵈ. Ellisland. People may talk as they please of the ignominy of the Excise, but what will support my family and keep me independant is to me a very important matter. I had much rather that my profession borrowed credit from me than that I borrowed credit from my profession.

I still have some thoughts of Drama. No man knows what Nature has fitted him for untill he try ; and if after a preparatory course of some years study, I should find myself unequal to the task, there is no great harm done. I have got Shakespeare and I shall make myself master of all the dramatic authors of any repute in both English and French, the only two languages which I know.

Jan. Ellisland. We have gotten a set of very decent Players just now in Dumfries, a company of Comedians, I have seen them an evening or two. Their manager, a Mr. Sutherland was introduced to me.

1790

Jan. 11th. Ellisland. My nerves are in a damnable state. I feel that horrid hypochondria pounding every atom of both body and soul. Yesterday my mind was in a bog, my very senses doited.

This accursed farm has undone my enjoyment of myself. Let it go to hell! If once I were clear of it, I should respire more at ease.

Besides my farm business I ride on Excise matters at least 200 miles every week.

Though I may die a very poor man, yet I hope my children shall ever boast the character of their father. These fine healthy little fellows, I have a thousand schemes about them and their future. But it will bear hard on me to give them that education I wish—at the High School fees.

['Robert,' said Jean a long while after, ' was not an early riser, except 'when he had anything very particular to do. If he lay long in bed awake, 'he was always reading. But he never lay after nine o'clock. The family 'breakfasted at nine. At all his meals he had a book beside him on the 'table. He dined at two o'clock, was fond of plain things and *hated tarts,* '*pies and puddings.* He did his work in the forenoon and was seldom 'engaged professionally in the evening when he employed his time writing 'and reading, with the children playing about him. Their prattle never 'disturbed him in the least.']

[The daughter of the Minister of Lochmaben, Jean Jaffray, to whom a poem ' THE BLUE EYED LASSIE ' was written, tells of ' How many times I 'have seen him enter the Manse in a cold rainy night after a long ride

'over the dreary moors. One of our family would help to disencumber
'him of his boots, while others brought him a pair of slippers and made
'him a warm dish of tea. He felt himself perfectly happy and enchanted
'all who had the good fortune to be present with his manly, luminous
'observations and artless manners. I never could fancy that he ever
'followed the plough because everything he said or did had a gracefulness
'and charm that was in an extraordinary degree engaging.']

Jan. 22ᵈ. Ellisland.   *To David Sillar.*
My Dear Friend—Enclosed I sent you £2-4ˢ, the price of eleven
copies of your Poems. I have been much pleased with them. I would
write you a long letter, but the bearer is in a devil of a hurry & I am in
another. I am, my dear Davie, yours sincerely   R. B.

[Professor Gillespie writes of an occasion when ' as a schoolboy I saw
'Burns' horse tied by the bridle to the sneck of a cottage door. I lingered
'some time. He was seated in an arm-chair by the fireside, listening to the
'songs of an old woman Betty Flint. She had a voice of the most over-
'powering pitch. She was neither pretty nor witty.']

[Another letter from William—'*Jan. 24th. Newcastle.* Dear Brother
'—You promised to write me some instructions about behaviour in com-
'panies rather above my station. To these instructions pray add some of
'a *moral* kind, for although (perhaps through the frigidity of my constitu-
'tion) I have hitherto withstood the temptation to those vices to which
'young fellows of my time of life are so much addicted, yet I do not
'know if my virtue will be able to withstand the more powerful tempta-
'tions of the metropolis. I sail for London in a fortnight or three weeks
'at farthest. Give the compliments of the season and my love to my
'sisters and all the rest of the family. I am &c.   W. B.']

Feb. 2ᵈ. Ellisland. Having to ride at least 200 miles every week to
inspect dirty ponds and yeasty barrels, where can I find time to write anything of importance enough to interest anybody ? I have been ill the
whole winter. An incessant head-ach, depression and all the truly miser-

able consequences of a deranged nervous system have made dreadful havoc of my health and peace.

> Oh that my father had ne'er on me smil'd,
> Oh that my mother had ne'er to me sung,
> Oh that my cradle had ne'er been rock'd,
> But that I had died when I was young.

This is from an old simple ballad. I do not remember in all my reading to have met with anything more truly the language of misery.

I am quite charmed with some of the Dumfries folk, Mrs. Burnside in particular. God forgive me I had almost broke the tenth commandment on her account. Her simplicity, sweetness, kind hospitality—in short, if I say one word more about her I shall be directly in love.

Feb. 5th. Ellisland.   *To Mrs. MacLehose.*

Madam—When you in so many words tell a man that you look on his letters with a smile of contempt, in what language can he answer ?   R. B.

Feb. 9th. Ellisland. That damned mare is dead. She has vexed me beyond description. I fed her up for Dumfries Fair and then she was seized with an unaccountable disorder in the sinews or somewhere in the bones of her neck and a weakness—a total want of power—in her fillets. In short the whole vertebrae of her spine seemed to be unhinged. Everything was done for her that could be done, but in eight and forty hours, in spite of the two best farriers in the country, she died and be damned to her !

The theatrical company leaves Dumfries in a week. Their merit is indeed very great, both on the stage and in private life ; and their encouragement has been accordingly. Their usual run is from eighteen to twenty pounds a night.

I have made a very considerable acquisition in the acquaintance of their manager Mr. Sutherland, a worthier and cleverer fellow I have rarely met. I gave him a Prologue which he spouted to the audience with great applause. I have also written a Prologue for Mrs. Sutherland's benefit night.

I Begin as a Farmer

My little Bobby and Frank are charmingly well and healthy. A man's individual self is a good deal, but the welfare of those who are very dear—helpless little innocents . . .

> Three times crowdie in a day!
> Gin ye crowdie any mair,
> Ye'll crowdie all my meal away!

What a chaos of hurry, chance & change is this world, when one sits soberly down to reflect on it. The thought fills me with dread for my sons. I may die a poor man.

> Oh that I had ne'er been married!
> I would never had nae care.
> Now I've gotten wife and bairns
> And they cry crowdie evermair.

Dull, listless, teased, dejected and depressed, I am just in a vortex.

> But how capricious are mankind
>   How loathing, how desirous.
> We married men, how oft we find
>   The *best* of things will tire us.

Feb. 10th. Ellisland.   *To William.*

My Dear William—One or two things let me particularise to you. London swarms with worthless wretches who prey on their fellow creatures' inexperience. Be cautious. You cannot be too shy of letting anybody know you farther than as a Sadler. Another caution—Bad Women. I give you great credit with respect to the universal vice. It is an impulse the hardest to be restrained.

If ever you be—as perhaps you may be already—in a strait for a little ready cash, you know I shall not see you beat while you fight like a man. Farewell. God bless you.   R. B.

Sunday Feb. 14th. Ellisland.

All my fears are of *this* world. If there is another, an honest enquirer after truth has nothing to fear. Every fair, unprejudiced enquirer must in some degree be a sceptic. The universal beliefs of mankind have ever had extremely little weight with me. It is not that there are any very stag-

gering arguments *against* the immortality of man, but that the subject is so involved in darkness that we lack data.

Feb. 14th. Ellisland.   *To Mr. Alexander Cunningham.*
My Dear Cunningham—where are you? What are you doing? Can *you* be of those who take up a friendship as they take up a fashion? Or are you like some others, the worthiest fellows in the world, the victim of indolence? Farewell. Whatsoever things are lovely, whatsoever things are gentle, whatsoever things are kind, think on these and think on

Robt Burns.

Saturday morn. Ellisland.   *To Mr. Alex^r. Findlater.*
Mrs. B. like a true, good wife, looking on my taste as a standard & knowing that she cannot give me anything *eatable* more agreable than a new laid egg, begs your acceptance of a few. They are all of them not thirty hours out.   R. B.

March 2nd. Ellisland. I want second-handed or any way cheap copies of Otway's Dramatic Works, Ben Jonson's, Dryden's, Congreve's, Wycherley, Vanburgh's, Cibber's or any of the more Moderns—Maclin, Garrick, Foote, Colman or Sheridan. Moliere in French I much want, as well as Racine Corneille & Voltaire.

March. Ellisland. I was born a poor dog and I know that a poor dog I must die. At Martinmass 1791 my rent rises to £20 per annum & then

I Begin as a Farmer

I am determined to give up this farm. And even then I shall think myself well quit if I am no more than a hundred pounds out of pocket. So much for farming.

The Excise, notwithstanding all my objections to it, pleases me tolerably well. It is indeed my sole dependance.

[Professor Gillespie saw him on a Fair day at Thornhill village. A poor woman, Kate Watson, had for this one day taken up the trade of publican—without a licence. ' I saw Burns enter her door and anticipated ' a seizure of the barrels containing precisely the contraband commodities ' of which he was in quest. A significant movement of his forefinger ' brought Kate to the doorway and I was near enough to hear " Kate, are ' " you mad ? Don't you know that the Supervisor and I will be in upon ' " you in the course of forty minutes ? Good-by t'ye at present." He ' was in the street and in the midst of the crowd in an instant.

' The hint was not neglected. It saved a poor widow from a fine of ' several pounds.']

My fingers are so wore to the bone holding the noses of his Majesty's liege subjects to the grindstone of Excise, that I am totally unfit for wielding a pen. Besides I have galloped over *ten parishes* these four days untill my poor jackass skeleton of a horse has let me down. I am just this moment returned. The miserable devil has been on his knees half a score of times within the last twenty miles. In short I have broke my horse's wind & have almost broke my own neck, besides some injuries in a part that shall be nameless.

Measles introduced into the house. I shall be very uneasy untill we get them over.

What hidden trap-doors of disaster beset our paths. Men are benevolent creatures, but amid so much poverty we are under a damning necessity of studying selfishness.

> The westlin wind blaws loud and shrill,
>   The night's baith mirk and rainy O,
> But I'll get my plaid and out I'll steal,
>   And owre the hill to Nanie O.

I had a pint of wine yesterday [served by Anna the barmaid at the Globe Tavern, Dumfries, Jean being away on a visit to her parents. 'Anna', says Allan Cunningham, 'was accounted beautiful by the 'customers at the inn.']

Yestreen I had a pint o' wine
  A place where body saw na.
Yestreen lay on this breast o' mine
  The gowden locks of Anna.

Ye monarchs, take the East and West
  Frae Indus to Savannah—
Gie me within my straining grasp
  The melting form of Anna.

There I'll despise imperial charms
  Of Empress or Sultana
While rapt, encircled in her arms,
  I'll speechless gaze on Anna.

The Kirk and State may join and tell
  To do sic things I maunna,
The Kirk and State may gae to hell
  And I'll gae to my Anna.

(Not quite a lady's song. R. B.)

[Jean's remark to a gossiping neighbour on her return was—'Oor 'Robin should hae had twa wives.' She brought up Anna's child with her own children.]

The smiling spring comes in rejoicing
  And surly winter grimly flies.
Now crystal clear are the falling waters
  And bonie blue are the sunny skies.

[More from William: '*March 21st London.* Dear Brother—I have 'been here three weeks come Tuesday. We were ten days on our passage. 'The weather being calm I was not sick except one day when it blew 'pretty hard.

I Begin as a Farmer

' I have got work in a shop in the Strand. Wages here are very low in
' proportion to the expense of living. I wish you would send me all my
' best linen shirts. Some of them are too little. Don't send any but what
' are good and I wish one of my sisters could find time to trim them at
' the breast, for there is no such thing to be seen here as a plain shirt. I am
' going to write to Gilbert to send me an Ayrshire cheese. I will have a
' pride in eating Ayrshire cheese in London. Remember me to my sisters
' and all the family. I shall give you my observations on London in my
' next, when I shall have seen more of it. I am, dear brother, yours &c
' WB.']

Early June. Ellisland.

> On ilka hand the burnies trot
> And meet below my theekit cot
> The scented birk and hawthorn white
> Across the pool their arms unite
> Alike to screen the birdie's nest
> And little fishes' caller rest.
>
> The craik amang the claver hay,
> The paitrick whirrin o'er the ley,
> The swallow jinkin round my shiel—
> Blest wi' content and milk and meal
> Oh wha wad leave this humble state
> For a' the pride of a' the great ?

June 7th. Ellisland.   *To William.*

My Dear William—I have scarce time to write a line, but I just
write you that line. I duely received your two letters and am exceedingly
happy to hear of your welfare. You may do miracles by persevering.
I have indeed been very throng. I shall write you again soon & get your
shirts forwarded to you. All here are well and beg to be remembered to
you. I am ever yours   R. B.

July 16th. Ellisland.   *To Mr. John Murdoch.*[1]

My Dear Sir—My brother William, a journeyman Saddler, has been
for some time in London, No. 181 Strand. If you can find a spare half
minute, please let him know by a card where & when he will find you &

[1] [*Whose pupils at a very early age Robert and Gilbert had been.*]

the poor fellow will joyfully wait on you and pay his respects to his *father's friend*. My kindest compliments. I am ever your oblidged friend

Robt Burns.

[Two distinguished visitors now, Ramsay of Auchtertyre and Stewart of Luss. The former in a letter to Dr. Currie says—' I proceeded to the ' house, being curious to see his Jean. I was much pleased with her ' and the modest mansion. In the evening, having ridden home fast after ' receiving my note, he suddenly *bounded* in upon us. We fell into conver-' sation directly. He told me that he had now gotten a story for a drama.']

Captain Mathew Henderson of Tannoch, he's gone, he's gone. O Death, thou tyrant, fell and bloody ! The Elegy that I have written is a tribute to the memory of a man I loved much. Of all the men I ever knew he was one of the first for a nice sense of honor and a generous contempt for adventitious distinctions. Mathew was a true, a rare and a kind man. This Elegy has pleased me beyond any of my late efforts. Perhaps 'tis the memory of joys that are past that biasses me. But whether Poems can be of any real service to our friends after they have passed that bourne beyond which all other kindnesses cease to be of any avail is, I fear, very problematical.

> Mourn, ilka grove the cushat kens,
> Ye hazly shaws and briery dens,
> Ye burnies, whimplin down your glens . . .
>
> Mourn, little harebells o'er the lea,
> Ye stately foxgloves, fair to see,
> Ye woodbines hanging bonilie . . .
>
> Mourn, ye wee songsters o' the wood
> Ye grouse that crap the heather bud
> Ye curlews calling thro' a cloud . . .
>
> Mourn, sooty coots and speckled teals
> Ye fisher herons watching eels
> Ye duck and drake wi' airy wheels
>   Circling the lake,
> Ye bitterns, till the quagmire reels,
>   Rowte for his sake.

I Begin as a Farmer

Mourn him, thou sun, great source of light,
Mourn, empress of the silent night,
And you, ye twinkling starnies bright,
  My Mathew mourn,
For through your orbs he's taen his flight
  Ne'er to return.

EPITAPH

An honest man lies here at rest . . .
If there's another world, he lives in bliss.
If there is none, he made the best of this.

July 30th. Ellisland. A letter from London acquainting me with the death of William [quite suddenly on July 24th from some kind of fever]. He was just twenty-three. I am not collected enough to write more.

TO A MOUNTAIN DAISY
turned down with the plough

Stern Ruin's plough-share drives elate
  Full on thy bloom
Till, crushed beneath the furrow's weight . . .

Aug. 8th. Ellisland. A long day's toil, plague and care.

Aug. 29th. Ellisland. I am in a hurry, a damned hurry.

Sept. Ellisland. REPORT TO THE EXCISE OFFICE
by R. Burns.
on the case against Mr. Thos. Johnston accused of illicit
distilling.

When Mr. Burns came to the kiln, a servant belonging to Mr. Johnston was ploughing *at a considerable distance*, who left his plough & three horses in the middle of the moor and came into the kiln—which Mr. B. thought rather a suspicious circumstance. On being repeatedly questioned by Mr. B., the lad seemed determined to be entirely ignorant, until bye and bye Mr. Johnston's son came in. Mr. Johnston Junr., on being questioned referred me to the said ploughman, who, he said, would know. The lad *then* recollected all about it. I told the son & the servant-lad the nature of the premunire they had incurred. They pleaded for mercy keenly. . . . It was put to Mr. Johnston in open Court after a full investigation of the case ' Was he willing to swear that he meant no fraud in the matter ? ' The Justices told him that if he swore to that, he should not be fined. Mr. Johnston, after ten minutes consideration, found his conscience unequal to the task and declined the Oath.

Now he says he *is* willing to swear. He has been exercising his conscience in private & will perhaps stretch a point . . .

Sept. 4th 1790. Ellisland. I have taken, I fancy, rather a new way with my cases of Fraud. I record every Defaulter. But at the Court I myself beg off every poor body that is unable to pay. Which candour gives me implicit credit with the Bench.

[A letter of recommendation for still another young friend in search of a job. The letter is to an Edinburgh acquaintance, a lawyer in the Cowgate, Mr. John Somerville, who will surely not mind. Indeed . . .] . . . Mr. Somerville is such an honest, contented, happy man that I know not *what* can annoy him.

I Begin as a Farmer

Sept. 11th. Ellisland.   *To Mr. John Somerville. W.S.*

My Dear Sir—Mr. Wilson from Ayr-shire is a particular friend of mine. He comes to your good city to see for a job as clerk copyist or so, for which whoever employs him will find him eminently qualified. If you can be of any service to him it will truly oblige your humble serv^t Robt Burns. My best compliments to Mrs. Somerville, little Harry and all the cherubs.

Oct. 5th. Ellisland. Some days ago I was seized with a slow, illformed fever. I am just risen out of bed, a weary sickness. I have likewise had a most malignant squinancy which had me very near the precincts of the grave. I am now got greatly better, though by no means in a confirmed state of health.

Oct. 8th. Ellisland.   *To Messrs. Crombies & Co. Merch^ts Dumfries.*
Please send me by the bearer a bar of shoeing iron, which place to the acc^t of your humble serv^t   Robert Burns.

Oct. 15th. Ellisland.   *To Crauford Tait Esqre Junr Edinburgh.*
Allow me to introduce the bearer, Mr. William Duncan, whom I have long known & loved.

I am the worst hand in the world at asking a favor. But, my dear Mr. Tait, the young lad is of your own profession and a gentleman of much modesty & great worth. Perhaps it may be in your power to assist him.
R. B.

Here is a piece I did lately.

> On a bank of flowers in a summer day,
>   For summer lightly drest,
> The youthful, blooming Nelly lay
>   With love and sleep opprest
> When Willie wand'ring thro' the wood
> Who for her favour oft had sued—
>   He gaz'd, he wish'd
>   He fear'd, he blush'd
> And trembled where he stood.

As flies the partridge from the brake
    On fear-inspired wings
So Nelly, starting, half-awake,
    Away affrighted springs.
But Willie follow'd—as he should.
He overtook her in the wood,
    He vow'd, he pray'd
    He found the maid
Forgiving all and good.

Oct. 15th. Kirn Night (End of Harvest). This is the merry night we get the corn in and ploughmen gather. My punch bowl has been brought from its dusty corner in honor of the occasion.

The lads and lassies, blythely bent
    To mind baith soul and body,
Sit round the table weel content
    And steer about the toddy.
On this one's dress and that one's look
    They're makin observations
While some are cozie in the nook
    And formin assignations. . . .

[Robert Ainslie, arrived from Edinburgh in time to join in the celebrations, writes a letter the following morning. ' There were Robert ' and Jean and Jean's sister and three male and female cousins who were ' assisting in the harvest work, as well as a few homely neighbours. We ' spent the evening in a way common on such occasions, dancing—and ' kissing the lasses at the end of every dance. Robert is as ingenious as ever ' and seems happy.'
The letter was addressed to Mrs. MacLehose.]

[One other evening this autumn would remain long in Jean's memory. ' He had spent most of the day on his favourite walk by the river. In the ' afternoon I joined him with some of the children. He was busily croon-' ing to himself, so I loitered behind with the little ones among the broom.

'He had written very little that year. He presently began reciting as if
'agonised with joy. He was reciting very loud with the tears rolling down
'his cheeks' a poem which he had only begun that morning, a poem to be
called 'Tam o' Shanter'.]

Among the many witch stories that I know, relating to Alloway Kirk
(the TAM O' SHANTER Kirk), this is one—

Upon a stormy night, amid whistling squalls of wind and bitter blasts
of hail, in short on such a night as the Devil would chuse to take the air
in, a farmer's servant was plodding and plashing homewards with his plough
irons on his shoulder, having been getting some repairs on them at a neighbouring smithy. His way lay by the Kirk and he was struck aghast by
discovering through the storm a light which plainly shewed itself from the
haunted edifice.

Whether he had got drunk at the smithy or not I will not pretend
to determine, but so it was that he ventured to go up to—nay into—the
very kirk. As good luck would have it the members of the infernal junto
were all out on some midnight business or other and he saw nothing but
a kind of caldron depending from the roof over a fire, simmering some
heads of unchristened children &c. So without ceremony the honest
ploughman unhooked the caldron and, pouring out the damnable ingre-
dients, inverted it on his head and carried it fairly home, where it remained
long in the family, a living evidence of the truth of the story.

And I know two others which I can prove to be equally authentic.

One of these, though equally true, is not so well identified with regard
to the scene, but the best authorities give it for Alloway—

On a summer's evening a shepherd boy belonging to a farmer in the
neighbourhood, had just folded his charge and was returning home. As
he passed the Kirk he fell in with some men and women who were busy
pulling ragwort. He observed that as each person pulled a ragwort he or
she got astride of it and called out 'Up horsie!' on which the ragwort
flew off through the air with its rider. The foolish boy likewise pulled his
ragwort and cried with the rest 'Up horsie!' and strange to tell, away he

flew with the company.   The first stage at which the cavalcade stopt was
a wine cellar in Bourdeaux where they quaffed away—untill morning
frightened them from their carousals.

The poor shepherd lad had heedlessly got himself drunk; and when
the rest took horse, he had fallen asleep and was found so next day.   Somebody that understood Scotch asked him what he was.   He said he was a
herd in Alloway.

By some means or other he got home again and lived long to tell the
wondrous tale.

[Mr. James Tennant's version is that ' once when Robert was a boy of
' perhaps eight or ten, a Highland bullock went amissing from one or
' other of the neighbouring pastures, strayed into the Kirkyard and passed
' into the Kirk itself.   A day or so after, some woman-body passing the
' Kirk, looked in and was saluted with a fearful roar.   Seeing a pair of
' horns projecting above the seats (the old high pews) in which the animal,
' half mad with hunger, had become entangled, she fled in terror and raised
' the alarm that the Deil was in the Kirk.
' In extricating the missing bullock, one of his horns was knock off.
' It was long used for giving medicine to cattle.   Robert remembered the
' story and afterwards wove it into his poem TAM O' SHANTER.']

> . . . Winter howls in gusty storms
> The lang dark night . . .
> Hark how the cry grows on the wind . . .
> Nae star blinks thro' the driving sleet . . .

Books.   I want more books, but those vampyre booksellers, they drain
me to the heart.

[The Edinburgh earnings were by now all but exhausted.]

1791

Jan. 17th.   *To Peter Hill, Bookseller. Edin^r.*
Take these three guineas & place them over against that damned account
of yours, which has gagged my mouth these five or six months.   I can

as little write apologies to the man I owe money to as . . . . O Poverty, thou half-sister of Death, cousin-german of Hell . . .

The Divines may say what they please, but I maintain that after a hearty blast of execration I feel myself easier. I can now go on. You will be so good as to send by the first Dumfries carrier—Joseph Andrews, Don Quixote, The Idler, Arabian Nights, Roderick Random & the 5th Volume of the Observer.

Feb. 7th. Ellisland. This is the first effort that my hand has made since the last disaster that my evil genius had in store for me. My black mare came down with me and broke my right arm.

[Janet Little, dairywoman and minor poetess, now arrived on a visit,

speaks of her 'painful alarm when the news of the accident came' and 'my sympathy for the tears of his affectionate Jean'.]

Feb. 28th. Ellisland. Whether it is that the story of our Mary Queen of Scots has a peculiar effect on me or whether in a Lament that I have just finished I have succeeded beyond any late effort of mine I know not, but it pleases me. Lovely, hapless Scottish Queen—she fell to glut the vengeance of a rival woman, a woman as able and as cruel as the Devil. What a rocky-hearted perfidious succubus was that Elizabeth. Judas Iscariot was a sad dog to be sure, but his demerits shrink to insignificance compared with the doings of the infernal Bess Tudor. He, poor wretch, was a man of nothing at all per annum & in consequence thirty pieces of silver was a very serious temptation.

I have had an immense loss in the death of the Earl of Glencairn, to whom I owe more than to any man on earth, the patron from whom all my good fortune took its rise. I have endeavored to express my sense of his goodness in a Poem to his memory.

March. Ellisland. I have been this week plagued with an indigestion. Indigestion is the devil. It besets a man in every one of his senses. I prescribe cheese, patience and a bit of fine old ewe-milk cheese.

Sunday. Ellisland. Our parish priest, who is one vast constellation of dullness, rays out stupidity at his weekly zenith to the no small edification of his gaping admirers. They are stupid, patient, quiet and without any idea beyond their circle.

I am in perpetual warfare with the doctrine of our reverend priesthood that we are born bondslaves of iniquity. I believe that the case is quite contrary; but they are so accustomed to soaring the wild-goose heights of Calvinistic theology . . .

March. By the side of a fire in a little country inn. While here I sit sad & solitary drying my wet clothes, in pops a poor fellow of a sodger & tells me he is going to Ayr. By heavens, I say to myself on a tide of good spirits which the magic of that sound conjures up—Ayr [on the River Doon] . . . And this evening I sketch out a song—to be sung to a

Strathspey reel of which I am very fond called Ballendalloch's reel. It takes three stanzas of four lines each to go through the whole tune, thus—

> Ye flowery banks of bonie Doon
> How can ye bloom sae fair ?
> How can ye chant, ye little birds
> And I sae full o' care ?

> Thou'll break my heart, thou bonie bird
> That sings upon the bough,
> Thou minds me o' the happy days
> When my false love was true.

> Wi' lightsome heart I pulled a rose
> Frae aff its thorny tree,
> And my false lover stole my rose
> But left the thorn wi' me.

Stephen Clarke by the way says that you only have to keep to the black keys and preserve some kind of rythm and you will infallibly compose a Scots air. Ritson has the same story of the black keys.

April 11th. Ellisland. Amid my poverty I am as independant & much more happy than a monarch of the world. I can look on a worthless fellow of a Duke with unqualified contempt & can regard an honest scavenger with sincere respect.

Life is chequered, joy & sorrow. Jean has made me a present of another fine boy, rather stouter than little Frank but not so handsome.

May. Ellisland. Looking over MacDonald's collection of Highland Airs recently with a musical friend, I was struck with one, a Skye tune, called ' Oran an Aoig '—the Song of Death—to the measure of which I have composed some stanzas. I have also composed two or three other little pieces which (ere yon full orbed moon, whose broad impudent face now stares at old Mother Earth all night, shall have shrunk into a crescent just peeping forth at dewy dawn,) I hope I shall find an hour to transcribe.

I have many other songs on the stocks.

I was so lucky lately as to pick up a copy of Oswald's Scots Music and I think I shall make glorious work out of it. I also want much Anderson's collection of Strathspeys.

I Begin as a Farmer

Early summer. Ellisland. I am just five shillings rich at present, tho' I was considerably richer three days ago when I was obliged to pay twenty pounds for a man who took me in, to save a rotten credit. I heedlessly gave him my name on the back of a bill wherein I had no concern & he —gave me the bill to pay. It is not in my power now to give any assistance even to my dearest friends.

I know that a poor dog I must live & die. But I induldge the flattering faith that my Poetry will outlive my Poverty.

June 11th. Ellisland.   *To Mr. Alex^r Cunningham.*
Let me interest you, my dear Cunningham, in behalf of the gentleman who gives you this. He is a Mr. Clarke, a schoolmaster and at present suffering severely under the persecution of his malicious but powerful patron Lord Hoptoun. Clarke is accused of harshness to some perverse dunces that were placed under his care. God help the teacher when a blockhead father presents him his booby son & insists on having the rays of science lighted up in a head impervious & inaccessible by any other way than a positive fracture with a cudgel. I know the merits of the case thouroughly & long much to hear from you.   R. B.

June 16th. Ellisland. A very pressing occasion, no less than Gilbert's wedding, calls me to Ayr-shire.

Blythsome Bridal. This song refers to a favourite kind of dramatic interlude sometimes acted at country weddings here in the south-west. A young fellow is dressed up like an old beggar. A peruke, commonly made of carded tow, represents the hoary locks. He wears a ragged plaid, an old bonnet, a pair of old shoes with straw ropes twisted round the ancles as is done by shepherds in snowy weather. His face they disguise. He is brought into the wedding-house, frequently to the astonishment of strangers who are not in the secret. He is asked to drink and by and by to dance, which, after some uncouth excuses, he is prevailed on to do, the fiddler playing the tune.

Ellisland. Drank tea at Craigieburn Wood with the charming Miss Lorimer. Craigieburn Wood a beautiful house.

July. Ellisland.   *To Mrs. MacLehose.*

I have rec^d both your letters, Madam, but how can you expect a correspondent should write you when you declare that you mean to preserve his letters for derision ?   R. B.

Lovely Davies ! [Miss Deborah Duff Davies, a relative of the Riddells of Friar's Carse.] Bonie wee thing ! By heavens, though I had lived threescore years a married man, my imagination would hallow the idea of her. When I meet with a person after my own heart I positively feel what an orthodox Protestant would call a ' species of idolatry '—which acts on my mind like inspiration & I can no more resist rhyming on the impulse than an Eolian harp can refuse its tones to the streaming air.

Sept. 1st. Ellisland. I sold my crop on this day se'ennight past & sold it very well, a guinea an acre, on an average, above value. But such a scene of drunkenness ! After the roup [the sale] was over, about thirty people became engaged in a battle, every man his own hand, & fought it out for three hours. Nor was the scene much better inside the house.

No fighting indeed, but folks lying on the floor & both my dogs so drunk that they could not stand. I enjoyed it.

Sept. Ellisland.   *To John Ballantine Esq.*

Sir—Inclosed you will receive a draught on the *Paisley* bank for the thirty two pounds I discounted in a bill at *your* bank. I would have sent you the cash, but I did not like to send money so far. But I suppose (for I am miserably ignorant in the business) that this draught will do quite as well. The banker in Dumfries assured me that you banking-folks hold draughts on one another as equal to cash.

Robt Burns.

Sept. Ellisland. A very oblidging neighbour of mine Captain Robert Riddell of Glenriddell has set on foot a species of circulating library on a plan so simple as to be practicable in any corner of the country and so useful as to deserve the notice of every country gentleman who thinks the improvement of the humble peasant and artisan a matter worthy of his attention.

Captain Riddell has got a number of his own tenants and farming neighbours to form themselves into a society. Each member at his entry pays 5/-. With this entry money and credit on the faith of their future funds, a tolerable stock of books has been laid in. They have made me factotum in the business. What authors are to be purchased will always be decided by the majority. Members have their choice of the volumes in rotation. Eventually the books are to be sold by auction, but only among the members themselves.

To store the minds of the lower classes with useful knowledge is certainly of very great consequence, both to them as individuals and to society at large. Giving them a turn for reading and reflection is giving them a source of innocent and laudable amusement; and besides, raises them to a more dignified degree in the scale of rationality. A peasant who can read and enjoy good books is certainly a much superior being to his neighbour who perhaps stalks beside his team very little removed except in shape from the brutes he drives.

> While larks with little wing
> Fann'd the pure air . . .
> Forth I did fare.

In each bird's careless song
Glad I did share . . .
Chance led me there.

Sept. 24th. Ellisland. Introduced to the Duke of Queensberry. I spent the evening with him. He treated me with the most distinguished politeness, affability & marked attention. Though I am afraid his Grace's *character* is very equivocal, yet he certainly is a nobleman of the first *taste* and a gentleman of the first *manners*. [But later the Duke is referred to as 'that reptile'.]

Down in a shady grove
Doves cooing there,
I marked the cruel hawk
Caught in a snare.
So kind may fortune be,
Such make his destiny,
He who would injure thee . . .

[and later again—]
Miss Burnet [the 'heavenly Miss Eliza Burnet', Lord Monboddo's daughter] is not more dear to her Guardian Angel than his Grace of Queensberry to the Powers of Darkness.

Oct. Ellisland. I am giving up my farm. My landlord is offering the lands to sale.

The Excise, after all has been said against it, is the business for me. I find no difficulty in being an honest man in it. The work itself is easy. And managing matters when I care not a damn whether the money is paid or not is a devilish different affair from the long faces made to a haughty laird or still more haughty factor when rents are demanded & money, alas, is not to be had.

I'll count my health my greatest wealth
Sae lang as I'll enjoy it.
I'll fear nae scant, I'll bode nae want
As lang's I get employment.

Oct. Ellisland. I was never more unfit for writing—a poor devil late crippled of an arm, nailed now to an elbow chair, writing in anguish with a bruised leg laid out on a stool before me.   If my unlucky limb would give me a little ease. . . .

I am thinking to flit Monday or Tuesday.

Oct. Ellisland.   Creech, my Publisher, has written me a fine fair letter telling me he is going to print a Third Edition.   As he has ' a brother's ' care for my fame ', he wishes to add every new thing I have written since the Second Edition.   And he says I shall be amply rewarded with—a copy or two to present to my friends !   All my friends know that I do not value money, but . . .   I lay down my goose-feather.

IV

I GIVE UP FARMING

Oct. 26th. The Wee Vennel, Dumfries. I have taken a house here in town & have furnished it. [The 'house' in the Wee Vennel consisted of three rooms on the first floor, the central room, hardly more than a cupboard, being used as a study.]

['Nothing', says Allan Cunningham, 'was left at Ellisland save a 'putting-stone with which he loved to exercise his strength.' Jean says, 'We did not come empty-handed to Dumfries. The Ellisland sale was 'a very good one and was well attended. One cow in her first calf brought 'eighteen guineas and the purchaser never rued his bargain. Two other 'cows also—they had been presented to Robert by Mrs. Dunlop—brought 'good prices. We brought with us a nice little braw cow, but this had 'to be sold, as no proper grazing could be got for her.']

Nov. Dumfries. Leaving Ellisland & settling in here have so engrossed my time & attention that except letters of indispensible business I have not lately put pen to paper on any subject. I am now getting deeply engaged in the Excise business. I have got into the routine. I have far less occupation than at Ellisland & upon the whole I shall be more confortable for the change. Indeed a change was become a matter of necessity. Ruin awaited me as a farmer.

I am today so completely nettled with the fumes of wine that I cannot write. Headache, nausea, and all the horrors of penitence that beset a poor wretch who has been guilty of the sin of drunkenness . . .

I Give up Farming

In this gloomy month of November anything is better than one's own thoughts. I have tried everything, *miserable perdu* that I am, everything that used to amuse me, but in vain. Even bawdry has lost its power to please. Here must I sit, a monument of the vengeance laid up in store for the wicked, slowly counting every chick of the clock as it slowly slowly numbers over these lazy scoundrels of hours, and there is none to pity me. My wife scolds me, my business torments me.

My conscience too, hackneyed & weather-beaten as it is, has contrived to blame & punish me sufficiently.

A girl Jenny Clow, who had the misfortune [in Edinburgh] to make me a father contrary to the laws of our holy Presbyterian hierarchy—with contrition I own it—is in distress. I shall be in Edinburgh on Tuesday first for certain. I shall see the poor girl and try what is to be done for her relief. I would have taken her boy from her long ago, but she would never consent.

It is one thing to know one's error & another & much more difficult affair to amend that error.

Nov. Dumfries.   To Mrs. MacLehose.
It is extremely difficult, my dear Madam, for me to deny a lady *anything* and I shall do myself the very great pleasure to call for you when I come to town. Your most obedient   Robert Burns.

Dec. Dumfries.   To Mrs. MacLehose.
My dearest Nancy, ever dearest of women—This is the sixth letter that I have written to you since I left you in Edinburgh [those few days ago]. Misfortune seems to take a peculiar pleasure in darting her arrows against honest men & bony lasses. Of this you are too too just a proof. May your future fate be a bright exception. Adieu. Remember me. [She had resolved to accept an invitation from her husband and join him in Jamaica.]   R. B.

Dec. 27th. Dumfries.   To Mrs. MacLehose.
I have yours, my dearest Nancy this moment. Ten minutes before the Post goes & these ten I shall employ in sending you some songs I have just been composing to different tunes.

The boat rocks at the pier o' Leith
   Full loud the wind blows at the Ferry
    The ship rides by the Berwick Law . . .

Endless and deep shall be my grief
   Alang the solitary shore
    Where fleeting sea-fowl round me cry . . .

Jan. 10th. Dumfries. I sup with Capt Robert Riddell in town to-night.

1791–2

Maria Riddell [the wife of Captain Robert Riddell's brother Walter] a girl of eighteen and in the first ranks of fashion, is a character both as naturalist & philosopher. The lady too is a votary of the Muses. Her verses, always correct and often elegant, are very much beyond the common run of the lady poetesses of the day. To be impartial however, she has one unlucky failing and she seems rather pleased with indulging it. Where she dislikes or despises, she is apt to make no more secret of it than where she esteems & respects. She is just going to pay her first visit to our Caledonian Capital.

[' None', writes Maria, ' could outshine him in the charms—the ' sorcery I would almost call it—of fascinating conversation. His form' she considers ' manly, his action energy itself devoid however of those ' graces and that polish acquired only in society.' And she harps on ' the ' irresistible power of attraction that encircled him. I remember I pressed ' him to tell me why he never took pains to acquire Latin. He replied ' with a smile, " I already know all the Latin I desire and that is ' Omnia ' " ' vincit amor '. " "]

[Mrs. MacLehose, ' agitated, hurried to death ', departs for Jamaica at the beginning of February. And her ' ever-dear dear friend ' as she calls him writes:]

    . . . Naething could resist my Nancy.
    But to see her was to love her
    Love but her and love for ever.

I Give up Farming

[and then]

> Had we never lov'd sae kindly,
> Had we never lov'd sae blindly,
> Never met—or never parted—
> We had ne'er been broken hearted.

I have been all along a miserable dupe to love and have been led into a thousand weaknesses and follies by it.

1792

Feb. 5th 1792. Dumfries. I owe £5-10 for erecting the memorial over poor Fergusson's grave. The man was *two years* in erecting it after I commissioned him for it & I have been two years paying him after he sent me his account. So he & I are quits. He has now had the *hardiesse* to ask me interest on the sum. But considering that the money was due by one poet for putting a tombstone over another, he may with grateful surprise thank heaven that ever he saw a farthing of it.

Feb. 5th. Dumfries.   *To Mr. Alex Cunningham W.S. Edinburgh.*
My Ever Dear Cunningham—You remember Mr. Clarke, Master of the Grammar School, whom I recommended to your good offices? The crisis of his fate is just at hand. Several gentlemen who know him intimately are straining every nerve to serve him, but alas, poor Clarke's foes are mighty. Lord Hoptoun, irritated that any son of a plebian should dare to oppose his Lordship's high & mighty will, has sworn his destruction. What you know I would do for a friend of *yours* I ask you to do for a much-esteemed friend of *mine*. Get the Principal's interest in his favour. Be not denied. You shall hear from me again soon. God bless you.   R. B.

The air for my composition ' The Posie' was taken down from Jean's voice. It is well known in the West, but the old words are trash. Two more songs finished—one of them is already set to the ' Lament for Abercairny', the other is to be set to an old Highland air, ' Ha a Chaillich air ' mo dheith' [' Tha a Chailleach air mo dheith ',—' The Old Woman ' is after me '.] I have got one most beautiful air that sings to the measure of ' Lochaber no more ' [' Cumhadh a' Bhard ']. I shall try to give it my very best words.

[' On Feb. 27th '—this is from Lockhart—' a suspicious-looking brig ' had been discovered in the Solway Firth. Burns was one of the party ' to watch her motions. She got into shallow water. Her crew seemed ' numerous and well armed, so a request was sent to Dumfries for a guard ' of dragoons. When the dragoons arrived, Burns, putting himself at their ' head, waded sword in hand to the brig and was the first to board her. ' The crew lost heart and submitted, though their numbers were greater. ' The vessel was condemned and, with all her arms and stores, sold next ' day at Dumfries.

' Burns thought fit to purchase four carronades by way of trophy. ' These four guns (which cost him £3) he dispatched to France in aid of ' the Revolution. They were intercepted by the Customs at Dover.']

Late Feb. Dumfries.   *To Maria, Mrs. Riddell.*
My Dearest Friend—Yours was the welcomest letter I ever received. God grant that now, when your health is re-established, you may take a little, little more care of a life so invaluable to your friends.

I am happy to inform you that I have just got an appointment which adds to my salary. My Excise income is now £70 a year. My perquisites I hope to make worth 15 or £20 more.

Apropos—has little Mademoiselle been inoculated with the small-pox yet ?   Robᵗ Burns.

[Mrs. Riddell notes—' *March 7th 1792 Woodley Park.* Robie Burns ' dined with us the other day. He is in good health and spirits.']

August 22nd. I am in love, souse ! over head and ears, with a charming Ayr-shire girl, most beautiful & elegant, Miss Lesley Bailie [daughter of Mr. Bailie of Mayfield, a neighbour of Mrs. Dunlop]. Mr. Bailie with his two daughters were passing through Dumfries a few days ago on their way to England. They did me the honor of calling on me. On which (tho' God knows I could ill spare the time) I took horse and convoyed

them fourteen or fifteen miles & dined with them. 'Twas about nine,
I think when I left them. While riding home I composed a ballad
beginning

> Oh saw ye bonie Lesley
>   As she gaed o'er the Border?
> She's gaen like Alexander
>   To spread her conquests further!

> To see her is to love her
>   And love but her for ever . . .

This world of ours, notwithstanding it has many good things in it,
yet ever has had this curse—that two people who would be the happier
the oftener they met together, are almost without exception so placed as
never to meet but once or twice a year.

I hope & believe with a kind of conviction (though not with absolute
certainty) that there is a state of existance beyond the grave where we renew
our former intimacies—with this endearing addition that we meet to part
no more. But the damned dogmas of reasoning philosophy still throw
their doubts.

I have just set a nipperkin of toddy by me just by way of spell to keep
away the meikle horned Deil or any of his subaltern imps who may be
on their nightly rounds.

Next morning. I believe that last night the Devil, taking advantage
of my being in drink (he well knows he has no chance with me in my
sober hours) tempted me to be a little turbulent.

Sept. 10th. Dumfries. Of all nonsense religious nonsense is the most
nonsensical. Enough and more than enough of it. Why has a religious
turn of mind always a tendency to narrow & illiberalize the heart? Your
children of sanctity, they are orderly, they may be just, nay, I have known
them merciful. But still they move among their fellow-creatures with that
conceited dignity which your titled Scots lordlings of seven centuries
standing display when they accidentally mix among the aproned sons of
mechanical life. I remember in my ploughboy days I could not conceive

it possible that a noble lord could be a fool or a godly man a knave. How ignorant are ploughboys !

Sept. 16th. Dumfries.   *To Mr. George Thomson. Edinburgh.*
Sir—I have just this moment got your letter.

As to any remuneration, you may think my songs either *above* or *below* price. They shall absolutely be the one or the other. I rhyme for fun.
Your humble serv[t]   Rob[t] Burns.

Oct. Dumfries. I am now at work correcting a new edition (the Third) of my Poems. This, with my ordinary business, keeps me in full employment.

Nov. 8th. Dumfries. There is a peculiar rythmus in many of our airs and a necessity for adapting syllables to the emphasis or what I would call the feature notes of the tune. I take up one or another of my songs just as the bee of the moment buzzes in my bonnet-lug.

We have had a brilliant theatre here this season. One of the actresses, a Miss Fontenelle . . .

Nov. 20th. Dumfries.   *To Miss Louisa Fontenelle.*
Madam—What an enviable creature you are, there in an overflowing house to be calling laughter forth this gloomy day ! But your charms would insure applause to the most indifferent actress.

Were I a man of fashion, fluttering on the foreground of life, this letter to a lovely young girl might be construed to be one of the doings of All-powerful Love. It is not Love, but just an honest compliment to your amiable manners & gentle heart from, God knows, a powerless individual too proud to flatter & too poor to be of any consequence.
Your most devoted humble serv[t]   Rob[t] Burns.

The date fixed for Mr. Grant's benefit night is Friday first. I have the pleasure to know Mr. Grant. He has genius. But he is a modest and a *poor* man. The play is an interesting one, 'The way to keep him'. Yet a Scottish audience would be better pleased with performances of *native* growth than with these two and three act pieces exhibiting manners which to by far the greatest number of them can only be second hand.

Liberty—to me with my National prejudices how dear that theme is. Liberty is *invaluable* and never too dearly bought. I sit and muse on those fields where Caledonia's Bloody Lion was born through broken ranks to victory and fame. And then later, alas, the trajic scenes of our fate. An ancient Nation that for many ages had gallantly maintained the unequal struggle for Independance with her much more powerful neighbour, at last agrees to a Union which should ever after make them one people. But what are all the boasted advantages which my country reaps from the Union that can counterbalance the annihilation of Independance ?

. . . English gold has been our bane
We're bought and sold for English gold.

I Give up Farming

An unequal struggle. We with all that was near and dear to us were sacrificed to Political Expediency. In our misery—for Scotland and me's in great affliction—in our misery are involved the most numerous part of the community—all those who immediately depend on the cultivation of the soil . . .

I remember even in my boyish days

> The rough burr-thistle spreading wide
> Among the bearded bear,
> I turned the weeder-clips aside
> And spared the symbol dear.

And while I was yet simple and rough at the rustic plough

> Ev'n then a wish (I mind its power)
> A wish that to my latest hour
> Shall strongly heave my breast
> That I for poor auld Scotland's sake
> Some useful Plan or Book could make
> Or sing a sang at least

Flowers of Edinburgh. I suspect that there was once an older set of words to this song, of which the title is all that remains. By the bye, it is singular enough that the Scottish Muses were all Jacobites. I have paid more attention to every description of Scots songs than any body living and I do not recollect one single stanza or even the title of the most trifling Scots air which has the least panegyrical reference to the families of Nassau and Brunswick, while there are hundreds satirizing them.

At a period when the science of government was but just emerging from ages of ignorance and barbarism the Stuarts only contended for prerogatives which they knew their predecessors enjoyed and which they saw their contemporaries enjoying. These prerogatives however were inimical to the happiness of the nation and the rights of subjects. In the contest between Prince and People, luckily with us the monarch failed. But the kingly power was only shifted into another branch of the family ! And now America beyond the Atlantic has had its Revolution for the very same maladministration & legislative misdemeanours in the family of Hanover as was complained of in the house of Stuart. Let every Scotsman who ever looked with pity on the dotage of a parent, cast a veil over the fatal mistakes of the kings of his forefathers.

Dec. 1st. Dumfries. Once more I hail thee, gloomy December.

I have been reading the Lounger—a very high luxury—and the Mirror. I often read the Spectator and other periodical papers such as the Rambler, the World &c., but they are all so thoroughly and entirely *English.*

I am disposed to be melancholy. Our country has been deeply wounded, but I can do nothing for a cause that is nearly no more. I find myself powerless, a poor powerless devil, impotent as a child to the ardor of my wishes. Why this disparity between our wishes and our powers ? Statecraft is a horrid mass of corruption and Politics—I care not two skips of a cur-dog for Politics. I have avoided taking a side. I scorn to belong to *either* party. Out upon the world, says I, that its affairs are administered so ill. They talk of Reform. My God what a reform would I make ! Down immediately should go fools from the high places where chance has perked than up. When fellow partakers of the same nature have the same benevolence, the same detestation of everything dishonest and the same scorn at everything unworthy, in the name of common sense are they not Equals ? So much for the fools in high places. As for the knaves, I should be at a loss to know what to do with them. Had I a world of my own there should not be a knave in it.

While Europe's eye is fixed on the fate of empires and the fall of kings, we too in this part of the kingdom are a good deal in commotion, with many alarms about the spread of the Republican spirit.

In our theatre here ' God save the King' has met with some groans and hisses, while ' Ca ira ' [the French Republican song] has been repeatedly called for.

> Then let us pray that come it may
> As come it will for a' that,
> That man to man the world o'er
> Shall brothers be for a' that !

[Possibly. But meanwhile, with so many Officers and Tories in the town it is surely imprudent to have aroused further hostility by giving at

a recent dinner this toast—] 'Here's to the Last Verse of the Last Chapter
'of the Last Book of Kings!'

[And at another dinner—at which again there were some Officers—
a still more obnoxious toast gave still greater offence . . .]
  But what after all *was* the obnoxious toast ? 'May our success in the
'present war be equal to the justice of our cause'—a toast that, I should
have thought, the most outrageous frenzy of loyalty could not object to.
'God save the King' a cuckoo sang . . .

On reading the Laureate's Birthday Ode in the public papers of June
4th (1786) I was no sooner dropt asleep than I imagined myself transported
to the Birthday Levee.

> Guid mornin to your Majesty
>   May heaven augment your blisses !
> My bardship here at your Levee
>   On sic a day as this is
> Is sure an uncouth sight to see
>   Amang thae birthday dresses.
>
> For me—before a Monarch's face
>   Ev'n there I winna flatter.
> For neither pension, post nor place
>   Am I your humble debtor;
> So nae reflection on your Grace
>   Your Kingship to bespatter.
>
> Far be't frae me that I aspire
>   To blame your legislation
> Or say ye wisdom want or fire
>   To rule this mighty nation,
> But faith, I muckle doubt, my sire . . .

Dec. 6th. Dumfries. Again last night at the playhouse 'Ca ira' was
called for.
  I was in the middle of the pit & it was from the pit that the clamour
arose. But I neither joined in nor ever openened my lips to hiss or huzza
to any political tune whatever. Politics is dangerous ground for me [as
a Government Servant in the Excise] to tread on. Besides I looked on

myself as far too obscure a man to have any weight in *quelling a riot*. What
my private sentiments were . . .

[A different account of this scene at the theatre is given by a boy Charles
Kirkpatrick Sharpe. ' Many members of the Caledonian Hunt were
' there ', says Charles, ' to see Miss Fontenelle as Rosalind. When " God
' " save the King " was sung we all stood up uncovered. But Burns sat
' still in the middle of the pit with his hat on. There was a great tumult,
' with shouts of " Shame ! " " Turn him out ! " This continued a good
' while.']

A few days later. A letter just received from my worthy friend Willie
Nicol of the High School, Edinburgh.
  ' Dear Christless Bobbie—But what concerns it *thee* whether the lousy
' Dumfriesian fiddlers play " Ca ira " or " God save the King " ? Suppose
' you *had* an aversion to the King, you could not as a gentleman wish
' him worse. The infliction of idiocy is no sign of love on God's part.
' There are reports of your imprudence. . . .
  ' But enough of politics. What is become of Mrs. Burns and the dear
' bairns ? My best wishes. Thine sincerely, Willm Nicol.'

Dear, kind, honest-hearted, wise and witty Willie, poets are perhaps
not famous for their prudence, but I never uttered *any* invectives against
the King. *I never even opened my lips !*

Alas, the Millenium, spotless with Monarchical Innocence and Despotic
Purity, the Golden Age of sweet chords & concords seems by no means
near. War . . . ruin to thousands . . .

Just now I am Revolution-mad, but my madness is no mere tarantula-
frenzy. It is rather the madness of an enraged scorpion shut up in a phial.

Dec. 31st. Dumfries. I have been surprised, confounded and distracted
by Mr. Mitchel the Collector telling me just now that he has received
an order from the Excise to enquire into my political heresies & blaming

me as a person disaffected to the Government. Because some malicious devil has raised a demur on my political principles the Board have made me the subject of their animadversions. I am accused of being a Republican and on that account am very near being turned adrift to all the horrors of Want.

I could brave misfortune for myself alone, but to see my so much loved wife & helpless prattling little ones left almost without support . . . Good God, how these ties ennerve courage & wither resolution.

It has been said, it seems, that I not only belong to but *head* a disaffected party in this place. I know of no party. I have never corresponded with or had the least connection with any political association whatever. As to France, I was her enthusiastic votary in the beginning of the business, but when she came to annexing Savoy &c and invading the right of Holland, I altered my sentiments. War I deprecate—misery & ruin . . . but I have set henceforth a seal on my lips.

1792

Accused before the Board. But for the exertions of Mr. Graham of Fintry, I would have been turned adrift, without so much as a hearing. All, however, is set to rights now in that quarter. I am still in the Service, but I understand that all hopes of my getting officially forwarded are blasted.

Well——

> Sing on sweet thrush upon the leafless bough
> Sing on sweet bird, I listen to thy strain . . .

It is probable that this may be read when the hand that now writes it is mouldering in the dust.

Everybody who is in the least acquainted with the character of a poet knows that there is nothing in the world on which he sets so much value as his verse. Don't be afraid. I'll be more respected a hundred years after I am dead than I am at present.

I have wrote a poem to Mr. Graham of Fintry. God help a poor devil who carries a load of gratitude of which he can never hope to ease his shoulders. The poem is, *like most of my poems*, connected with my own story.

Jan. 2nd. Dumfries. I love social pleasures in moderation, but here I am *impressed* into the service of Bacchus. Against this I have again and again bent my resolution and have greatly succeeded. Taverns I have totally abandoned. It is the family parties among the hard drinking Gentlemen of this country that does me the mischief—but even this I have more than half given over.

My political sins seem to be forgiven.

Feb. 28th. Dumfries.   *To Mr. Creech, Publisher, Edinburgh.*
Sir—I understand that my new book is soon to be published. I beg that you will send me twenty copies. I mean to present them among a few Great Folks whom I respect and a few Little Folks whom I love.

            Robt. Burns.

March 18th. Dumfries. I have just made my appearance [Third Edition] in two volumes.

[On March 5th 'The Committee of the Subscription Library, Dum-
'fries, resolved to offer to Mr. Robert Burns a share in the Library free
'of any admission money (10/6d.) or quarterly contributions (2/6d.) to
'this date, out of respect and esteem for his abilities as a literary man.'
 And a few months later 'Mr. Robert Burns appointed a Member of
'the Committee.']

March 21st. Dumfries.   *To Miss Anna Dorothea Benson.*
Madam—I beg leave to send you the inclosed sonnet, though, to tell the truth, the sonnet is a mere pretence, that I may have the opportunity of declaring with how much respectful esteem I have the honour to be . . .

I Give up Farming

[And here is Miss Benson's account of the party: 'He was witty,
'drank as others drank and was long in coming to the tea-table. I was
'working a flower. He sat down beside me and put his hand so near
'the work that I said "Well take it and do a bit yourself." "O ho!"
'he said, "You think my hand is unsteady with wine?" He pulled
'the thread out of the needle and re-threaded it in a moment. "Can a
'"tipsy man", he asked "do that?"

'He talked to me of his children, more particularly of his eldest and
'called him a promising boy.'

Later Miss Benson describes R. B. as 'the most royally courteous of
'mankind'.]

Late March. Dumfries.   *To Mrs. MacLehose.*
I congratulate your friends, Madam, on your return.

[The reunion in Jamaica with her husband had been a complete
failure.]

I suppose by neglecting to inform me of your arrival in Europe—a
circumstance that could not be indifferent to me—you meant me to gather
that a correspondence I once had the felicity to enjoy is to be no more.
Or shall I hear from you? But first hear *me*. No cold language.
Mind! If you send me a mere page of sanctimonious produce, by
heaven and hell I will tear it into atoms. May all good things attend
you.   R. B.

April. Dumfries. Damn the frigid soul of criticism and these canker-
toothed caterpillar critics for ever and ever—cut-throats in the path of fame
—bloody dissectors—

> Th' envenom'd wasp, victorious, guards his cell.
> The cit and polecat stink and are secure.

A thousand times have I trembled in anticipation at the idea of all the
degrading epithets that Misrepresentation may affix to my name. However inferiour I may rank as a poet, the causeless, wanton malice of the
critics and their blasting degradations are not *fair* statements. Those savage

paragraphs, slanderous, heavy malice—though I grant that the periods are often very well turned.

[A stray thought on the subject of eggs.] A fresh egg is a very good thing, but when thrown at a man in the Pillory, it does not at all improve his figure—not to mention the irreparable loss of the egg.

My verses to ' Cauld Kail' I will suppress, as also those to ' Laddie 'lie near me'. They are neither of them worthy of my name. I still have several Scots airs by me, which I have pickt up mostly from the singing of country lasses. They please me vastly. Learned lugs would be displeased with the very feature for which I like them. I call them simple. They would pronounce them silly.

Let any poet if he chuses take up the idea of another and work it into a piece of his own, but let him mend it as the Highlander mended his gun: he gave it a new stock, a new lock and a new barrel.

April. Dumfries. I have often told my dear friend Mrs. Maria Riddell that she has a spice of caprice; and she has as often disavowed it, even while at the very moment proving it. Most accomplished of women, to-morrow I shall have the honor of waiting on her—with all her little caprices.

Could *anything* ever estrange me from such a friend ?

June. Dumfries. The following is an epigram which I made the other day on a stupid money-loving dunderpate of a Galloway laird—Maxwell of Cardoness—

> Bless Jesus Christ, O Cardoness,
>   With grateful lifted eyes,
> Who taught that not the *soul alone*
>   But *body too* shall rise
> For had he said ' The soul alone
>   From death I will deliver'
> Alas, alas, O Cardoness,
>   Then hadst thou lain forever !

I Give up Farming

Happy is the man Madam who ever has it in his power to contribute to your enjoyments. Ah, quelle enviable sorte!

NB. If this is not French, it ought to be. Should the inclosed song give you any entertainment, it more than repays me for composing it. R. B.

Miss Deborah is positively the least creature I ever saw, but indeed uncommonly handsome & beautiful. Only compare her with Mrs. S——, that huge, bony, masculine, horse-godmother, he-termagant of a six-feet figure, who might have been bride to Og, king of Bashan!

After balancing myself for a musing five minutes on the hind legs of my elbow-chair, I have produced yet another poem ' O were my love ' yon lilack fair'.

1793

Fraser the hautboy player from Edin^r is here instructing the Band of a Fencible Corps quartered in this country. Among many of his airs that please me there is one which I remember a grand-aunt of mine used to sing by the name of ' Liggeram cosh, my bonie wee lass——' Mr. Fraser plays it slow and with an expression that quite charms me. I got such an enthusiast in it that I have made a song for it.

Another favourite air of mine when sung slow with expression is ' The muckin' of Geordie's lyre'.

[Archie Lowrie, who, as a student at Edinburgh University, had been so intimate with Robert, is now twenty-five and inclined to be patronizing. While visiting Dumfries, he writes from the King's Arms to a friend—
' I sent for Burns the poet yesterday. He came soon after I sent for him.
' I was supping with a number of strangers. He said he could *not* sup
' with me, but sat down and was there till 3 next morning. I left them
' about 12 midnight and had a most confounded extravagant bill to pay
' this morning. After breakfast I called on Burns and found him at home.

'Took a plateful of broth with him and afterwards a walk thro the town
'and along the banks of the Nith, extremely pleasant. We returned to his
'house where I spent the day and dined. After dinner we had some
'charming music from a Mr. Fraser, master of a Band of Soldiers. Having
'drunk tea, we went to a wood upon the banks of the river. Mr. Fraser
'took out his hautboy and played a few tunes most delightfully, which
'had a very pleasing effect in the wood. We then left this rural retire-
'ment and walked back.

'*June 21st.* Rested my mare one day more. I could not withstand
'the temptation of Burns's company.']

July. Dumfries.   *To Mr. George Thomson.*
I assure you, my dear Sir, that you truly hurt me with your pecuniary
parcel. [A dislike of receiving money in payment of each song as it was
produced had led gradually to this final refusal of any payment at all.
Poetry should be written ' for fun '.]

To return it [the pecuniary parcel] would savour of bombast. But
as to any more traffic of that D^r & C^r kind, I swear by the upright statue
of Robt Burns's integrity, that on the least notion of it I commence entire
stranger to you. Yours   R. B.

July. Dumfries.   *To Miss Jean MacMurdo.*
[daughter of the Factor to the Duke of Queensberry,] inclosing a ballad
that I had composed on her—

Madam—In these frivolous times may you escape frivolity. The mob
of fashionable female youth, they prattle, laugh, sing, dance & turn over the
pages of a fashionable novel; but are their minds stored with any reason or
with generous sentiments ? I would call them butterflies, remarkable only
for the idle variety of their gaudy glare, sillily straying from one blossoming
weed to another, without a meaning, without an aim, the idiot prey of
every pirate of the skies & speedily by wintry time swept to that oblivion
whence they might as well never have appeared. Amid this crowd of
Nothings may *you* be Something.

                                                        R. B.

[Another tour, this time through Galloway with a friend John Syme of Ryedale, who writes—

'*July 27th*. I got Robert a grey Highland shelty to ride on. The first
'day at Glendenwyne's—a beautiful situation on the banks of the Dee.
'But we had resolved to reach Kenmure that night. We arrived as
'Mr. and Mrs. Gordon were sitting down to supper.
'*July 28th*. This old castle stands on a large moat. On the north
'the aspect is wild and I may say tremendous. Robert thinks highly of
'it. We spent three days with Mr. Gordon whose polished hospitality
'is of an original and endearing kind. Mrs. Gordon's lapdog Echo
'was dead. She would have an epitaph for him. Robert disliked the
'subject, but to please the lady he produced two verses.']

[A Mr. Carson and an old Mr. Gillespie, the Minister of the parish,
were the only other guests at Kenmure. Mr. Carson says—'The evening
'preceding the departure of Burns and Mr. Syme, all the gentlemen (the
'weather proving propitious) sailed down Loch Ken on the Earl's barge.
'The barge however unfortunately grounded before reaching the landing
'place at the foot of the loch. Mr. Gordon with the assistance of an oar,
'vaulted from the prow of the little vessel to the beach. He was soon
'followed by Mr. Syme and myself. But when the Minister, Mr. Gillespie,
'being too feeble to jump, said he would remain on board till the others
'returned, Burns instantly slipped into the water, which came up to his
'knees, and succeeded in getting the Minister on to his shoulders. On
'observing which, Mr. Syme laughed immoderately and exclaimed,
'"Well, Burns, of all men you are the last I should have expected to see
'"priest-ridden!"
'We laughed also, but Burns did not seem to enjoy the joke. He
'made no reply, but carried his load silently through the reeds to land.']

[*July 31st*. 'Left Kenmure'—Mr. Syme's diary now continues—'for
'Gatehouse, taking the moor road, where savage and desolate regions
'extended wide around. The sky was lowering. Lightnings gleamed,
'the thunder rolled. He enjoyed the awful scene. It began to rain.

'For three hours rain poured in floods upon us. We were utterly wet.
'Robert insisted on our getting drunk at the Inn at Gatehouse.

'*Aug. 1st.* But the new Wellington boots with white tops which he
'had got for the journey had now been twice soaked through. And,
'after being dried [no doubt too close to the inn kitchen fire] it was not

'possible to get them on again. A whiffling vexation of this sort is more
'trying to the temper than a serious calamity. The brawny poet tried

'force and the boots were torn to shreds. He was forlorn at the sight of
'his ruined boots—quite accablé. Nothing could reinstate him. I tried
'various expedients and at last hit on one that succeeded. I showed him,
'across the bay, the Earl of Galloway's house. Against the Earl he
'expectorated his spleen and regained a most agreeable temper!']

> Bright ran thy line, O Galloway
>   Thro' many a far-famed sire.
> So ran the far-famed Roman Way
>   And ended in a mire.

[And—at a later date this—on hearing that the Earl threatened to take
action—]

> Spare me thy vengeance, Galloway,
>   In quiet let me live.
> I ask no kindness at thy hand
>   For thou hast none to, give.

['Well we went on to Kircudbright, he without boots and I carrying
'the torn ruins across my saddle. I had promised that we should dine
'with one of the first men in our country, John Dalzell of Barncroch. But
'Robert, in an obstreperous humour swore he would not dine where he
'should be under the smallest restraint. We prevailed therefore on Mr.
'Dalzell to dine with us at the Inn and had a very agreeable party. In
'the evening we set out for St. Mary's Isle, the seat of the Earl of Selkirk
'(father of friendly young Lord Daer). We arrived about eight o'clock as
'the family were at tea and coffee. We found all the ladies of the family
'at home (and all beautiful). We had the song of "Lord Gregory"
'which I asked for in order to have an opportunity of calling on Robert
'to recite his ballad to that tune. He did recite it; and such was the
'effect that a dead silence ensued.
   'It was a most happy evening.
   '*Aug. 2nd*. We returned. And Lord Selkirk, who insisted that the
'boots were worth mending, carried them to Dumfries in his coach.']

Aug. 13. Dumfries. I was yesternight in a composing humour. That
crinkum-crankum tune 'Robin Adair' had been running so in my head
that I tried my hand on it. But it is such a damned, cramp, out-of-the-

16   229

way measure that I succeeded ill. I have during this morning's walk ventured one essay more.

A musical Highlander in Breadalbane's Fencibles, now quartered here, assures me that he well remembers his mother's singing Gaelic words to 'Robin Adair'. This man comes from the vicinity of Inverness. I shrewdly suspect that wandering minstrels, harpers or pipers, used to go frequently errant through the wilds of both Scotland and Ireland and so some favorite airs might be common to both. Case in point—they have lately in Ireland published an air called 'Caun du delish' [Ceann dubh dileas—Faithful dark head]—an Irish air as they say. But the fact is that in a publication of Corri's a great while ago you find the same air—called a Highland air—with a Gaelic song 'Oran Gaoil' [Oran Ghaoil—Song of Love] set to it.

Aug. 19th. Evening.

> The hunter now has left the moor
> The scattered coveys meet secure.

Autumn is my propitious season. I make more verses in it than in all the year else.

My pretensions to musical taste are merely instincts, untaught. For this reason many musical compositions, particularly where much of the merit lies in counterpoint, however they may ravish the ears of connoisseurs, affect my simple lug no otherwise than as Medodious Din. On the other hand I am delighted with many little melodies which the learned musician despises. The old air 'Hey tutti taitie' on Fraser's hautboy has often filled my eyes with tears. There is a tradition which I have met with in many places of Scotland that it was Bruce's March at Bannockburn. This thought in my yester evening walk warmed me to a pitch of enthusiasm on the theme of Liberty which I threw into a kind of Scots Ode, fitted to the air.

> Scots, wha hae wi' Wallace bled . . .

Aug. 28th. Dumfries. 'Dainty Davie.' The words 'Dainty Davie' glide so sweetly in the air that I have composed yet another song to the old tune (which first appears in Playford's Collection, 1657). In the Scots'

Musical Museum they have drawled out the tune to twelve lines of poetry, which is damned nonsense. Four lines of song & four of chorus is the way —the chorus to the low part of the tune.

Sept. 12th. Dumfries. George Thomson says that 'Dainty Davie' must be sung *two* stanzas together and then the chorus. I have heard 'Dainty Davie' sung nineteen thousand nine hundred & ninety-nine times & *always* with the chorus to the low part of the tune. Nothing, since a Highland wench in the Cowgate once bore me three bastards at a birth, has surprised me so much as George Thomson's opinion on this subject.

Sept. Dumfries. Untill I am compleat master of a tune in my own singing (such as it is) I never can compose for it. My way is—I consider my idea of the musical expression; then I chuse my theme; begin on one stanza; when that is composed, which is generally the most difficult part of the business, I walk out & sit down now and then, humming the air with the verses. When I feel my Muse beginning to jade, I retire to the solitary fire-side of my study & there commit my effusions to paper, swinging at intervals on the hind legs of my elbow-chair. This, at home, is almost invariably my way. What damn'd egotism !

['When the verses are finished', Allan Cunningham says, 'he passes 'them through the ordeal of Mrs. Burns's voice, listens attentively while 'she sings and if she finds any word difficult to sing he will change it. But 'he never, save at the resolute entreaty of a scientific musician, sacrifices 'sense to sound. Twilight is his favourite hour of study.']

[William Nicol and another friend to dine at the Globe Tavern. By mistake no dinner ordered. Nothing to be had but a share of the kitchen dinner—a sheep's head. Nicol, in spite of hunger, asked for 'something new as a grace'. Whereupon Robert with folded hands said—]

> Oh Lord, when hunger pinches sore
> Do thou stand us in stead
> And send us from thy bounteous store
> A tup or wether head. Amen.

Oct. 25th. Dumfries. From my late hours last night & the dripping fogs & damn'd east wind of this stupid day, I have as little soul as an oyster. My head achs miserably.

[This autumn Miss Anna Dorothea Benson (now married) saw Robert again. ' It was at the Hunt Ball. I had just stood up to dance with a ' young officer when a whisper ran " There's Burns." I looked round ' and there he was—his dark bright eyes full upon me. I shall never forget ' that look. I saw him again next day in the street. He would have ' passed me, but I spoke. I said " Come, you must see me home " and ' took his arm. He said he would gladly see me home, but not along the ' pavement " lest I have to share your company with some of those ' " epauletted Puppies ".']

[The accomplished and vivacious Maria, Walter Riddell's wife, now nineteen, she too, being ' in the first ranks of fashion ', is surrounded by Officers.]

Nov. Dumfries.   *To Mrs. Walter Riddell.*
Dr Madam—I meant to have called on you yesternight, but as I edged up to your box door at the play, the first object which greeted my view was one of those lobster-coated Puppies sitting like another Dragon, guarding the Hesperian fruit. On Sunday I shall have the pleasure of assuring you in propria persona, how sincerely I am yours   R. B.

Nov. Dumfries.
Here I sit, altogether Novemberish & melancholy, my soul fluttering round her tenement like a wild finch in a cage. *If* I am in love as, God forgive me, I sometimes am . . .
The passion of love, where it takes thorough possession of a man almost unfits him for anything else.

Sunday. Sunday closes a period of our cursed Revenue business which may probably keep me employed with my pen untill noon.

I Give up Farming

Nov. Dumfries.   *To Maria, Mrs. Walter Riddell.*

On the conditions you so obligingly make I shall *certainly* make my plain, weather-beaten, rustic phiz a part of your box furniture at the theatre.   R. B.

Dec. Dumfries.   *To Mr. John MacMurdo.*

Sir—We take the greatest liberties with our greatest friends. I have owed you money longer than ever I owed it to any man. Here are the six guineas.   R. B.

> The forests are leafless, the meadows are brown
> And all the gay foppery of summer is flown.
> How quick time is flying . . .

Dec. 3ʳᵈ. Dumfries.   *To Major William Robertson of Lude.*

Sir—Heated as I was with wine yesternight, I was perhaps rather seemingly impertinent in my anxious wish to be honoured with your acquaintance. You will forgive me. It was the impulse of heartfelt respect for a patriot to whom the rights of his country are sacred. I had a woman's longing to take the father of Scotch Country Reform by the hand and say to him ' Sir I honor you.' Your very humble servᵗ Robᵗ Burns.

Many of my trifles in verse are local, some of them puerile and silly and unfit for the public eye. Some are ill-natured and so in unison with my present feelings. [This for example.]

ON JOHN RANKINE

> One day as Death, that gruesome carl,
> Was driving to the t'ither warl'
> A mixtie-maxtie motley squad
> And monie a guilt-bespotted lad,
> Black gowns of each denomination
> And thieves of every rank and station
> ' Lord God' quoth he, ' I have it now—
> *There's* just the man I want, i' faith ! '
> And quickly stoppit Rankine's breath.

[or these lines written—and not found till a good while afterwards—on the fly-leaf of a magnificently bound but obviously unread Shakespeare in a certain nobleman's library.]

> Through and through th'inspired leaves
> Ye maggots make your windings,
> But Oh respect his Lordship's taste
> And spare the golden bindings.

Dec. 15th. Dumfries.   *To Mrs. Dunlop.*

My Dear Friend—I am in a compleat Decemberish humour, gloomy, sullen, stupid. My sweet little youngest child has been so ill that every day has been threatening to terminate her existence. I cannot describe to you the anxious, sleepless hours. If I am nipt off at the command of Fate, even in all the vigour of manhood (and such things happen every day), what would become of my little flock? 'Tis here I envy your people of fortune. But, my God, I shall run distracted if I think any longer on the subject.   Robt Burns.

1793-4

Jan. 7th. Dumfries.   *To Robert Graham of Fintry.*

Sir— . . . Let me recommend to your humanity and justice the present officer of the 2nd Division, John MacQuaker, 43 years of age, 7 of a family, 13 years in the service and burdened with some debts of early days which crush him to the ground. He is a very good Excise officer.

Your much indebted and ever grateful humble servant,

           Robt Burns.

Feb. Dumfries.   *To James Johnson, Edinburgh.*

My Dear Sir—I have got an old Highland durk for which I have a great veneration. I have some thoughts of sending it to your care, to get it mounted anew. Our friend Clarke owes me an account, somewhere about one pound, which would go a good way in paying the expense of remounting the dirk. I remember you once settled an account in this way

before and as you will still have money matters to settle with him, you might accommodate us both. I beg you will not hint this to Clarke. If we do it at all, I will break it to him myself. Yours   R. B.

1794

[A dinner towards the end of the season with the Bushbys, well-to-do people, at Tinwald Downs. This is what happened. 'The pudding

' was too hot. But Mr. Bushby having burnt his tongue, remarked to his
' wife that in future the food must really not be brought in so *cold.* Burns,
' engaged in conversation, took some. His agony in swallowing the
' scalding mouthful delighted Mr. Bushby and his son Maitland, who led
' the laughter.' Our Robert never liked being laughed at.]

[And then worse, far worse at another dinner party, given by the
Walter Riddells at Woodley Park. 'After the withdrawal of the ladies,
' too much wine was drunk. And when the talk turned to the Rape of
' the Sabines, the gentlemen, urged on by their tottering host, trooped away
' into the drawing room. Robert made straight for Mrs. Riddell.' Maria
was furious.

On the following day she got this letter.]

Madam—I daresay this is the first epistle you ever received from Hell.
I write you from the nether world amid the horrors of the damned. The
time and manner of my leaving your earth I do not exactly know, as it
was in a fever of intoxication at your too hospitable mansion. But on my
arrival here in Hell I was fairly tried and sentenced to endure purgatorial
tortures on account of the impropriety of my conduct.

Madam, if I could in any measure be reinstated in the good opinion
of the fair circle whom my conduct last night so much injured, I think it
would be an alleviation to my torments. To the men of the company I
will make no apology. Your husband, who insisted on my drinking more
than I chose, has no right to blame me. But your good opinion I valued
as one of my greatest acquisitions on earth and I was truly a beast to forfeit it.

To all the other ladies present please present my humblest contrition.
My errors though great were involuntary. It is not in my nature to be brutal
to anyone. To be rude to a woman, when in my senses, *that* is impossible,
but . . .

Regret. Remorse. Shame. Forgive the offence.   R. B.

Later. Dumfries. And yet if it is true that offences come only from
the heart I am guiltless. It is not in my nature to be brutal to anyone. To
be rude to a woman, *that* is impossible——

Later still. Dumfries. *To Samuel Clarke, Junr. [aged twenty-five].*
I recollect something of a drunken promise yesternight to breakfast
with you this morning. I am very sorry that this is impossible. I remember
too that you very oblidgingly mentioned your intimacy with our Supervisor
General. Some of our folks about the Excise Office have conceived a
prejudice against me as a drunken dissipated character. *You* know that
I am an honest fellow and nothing of all that. In your own way let him
[the Supervisor General] know that I am not unworthy of subscribing
myself, my dear Clarke, your friend, R. B.

Early Jan. 1794. Dumfries. I have seen Mrs. Riddell once since. Her
reception of me froze the very life-blood of my heart.

Jan. 12th. Dumfries. Where I used to meet kind, friendly confidence,
now to find cold neglect and contemptuous scorn I can ill bear. And
De-haut-en-bas has a tendency to rouse a stubborn something in me. I
have been prodigiously disappointed. But I hate this theme and never
more shall write or speak of it.

Feb. 25th. Dumfries. Just of late a number of domestic vexations
(and some pecuniary losses—my share in the ruin of these damned times—
losses which, though trifling, were yet what I could ill afford) have so
irritated me that I have exhausted every topic of comfort. A mind at ease
would have been charmed with my reasonings, but I am like Judas
Iscariot preaching the Gospel. He might melt and mould the hearts of
those around him, but his own kept its native incorrigibility.

Pert, affected, vain coquette ! She has steered so far to the north of my
good opinion that I have made her the theme of several ill-natured things.
So, Maria,

> Prepare for Burn's venom when
> He dips in gall unmixed his eager pen.

238

I Give up Farming

MONODY

ON THE [IMAGINARY] DEATH OF A LADY FAMED FOR HER
CAPRICE, A WOMAN OF FASHION IN THIS COUNTRY WITH
WHOM AT ONE PERIOD I WAS WELL ACQUAINTED.

We'll search through the garden for each silly flower
　　We'll roam through the forest for each idle weed,
But chiefly the nettle, so typical, shower
　　For none e'er approached her but rued the rash deed.

Here lies now, a prey to insulting neglect
　　Who once was a butterfly, gay in life's beam.
Want only of wisdom denied her respect,
　　Want only of goodness denied her esteem.

How pale is that cheek where the rouge lately glistened !
　　Thou diest unwept as thou livedst unloved . . .

Late Feb. Dumfries. I have all this winter been plagued with low
spirits and blue devils.

March 3rd. Dumfries. Thank heaven I feel my spirits buoying upwards
with the renovating year.

I have gotten a Highland pebble which I fancy could be made into
a very decent seal with my armorial bearings cut on it. I will be Chief
of my name and, by the courtesy of Scotland, will likewise be entitled to
Supporters. These however I do not intend having on my seal. I am a
bit of a Herald.

My arms—On a field azure a holly-bush, seeded, proper. In base a
shepherd's pipe and crook Saltire-wise, also proper, in chief. For Crest—
on a wreath of the colours a wood-lark perching on a sprig of bay-tree,
proper. Two mottoes—round the top of the crest ' Wood-notes wild '—
at the bottom of the shield, ' Better a wee bush than nae bield [shelter] '.

By the shepherd's pipe I mean a stock-and-horn such as one sees in
David Allan the artist's quarto edition of the Gentle Shepherd.

That David Allan must be a man of very great genius. Why is he

239

not more known ? I am highly delighted with his etchings. His *grouping* is *beyond praise.*

I am sure that we only want the trifling circumstance of being known to one another to be the best friends on earth. Has he no Patrons ? If I were rich as the sun, I would be generous as the day. A friend of mine who is positively the ablest judge on the subject I have met with is quite charmed with David Allan's manner. He pronounces him a most original artist of great excellence.

April 21st. Dumfries. This morning's loss I have severely felt. Poor Glenriddell [Maria's brother-in-law]. Alas, he too is now gone, a friend, a man I loved. The many many happy hours I have spent at the fireside of Himself and his Lady ! I have enjoyed more pleasant evenings there than at all the houses of fashionable people in this country put together. Such cordiality, kindness and warmth of friendship. I shall send a small heart-felt tribute to his memory to some newspaper. But in the present hurry of Europe, nothing but politics will be regarded.

For all that, against the days of Peace, which heaven send soon, I have it in my head to try my hand in the way of little Prose Essays which I might send into the world through the newspapers.

May. Dumfries. Now for six or seven months I shall be quite in song I have at last gotten a stock-and-horn. It is a very rude instrument, composed of three parts, the stock, which is the thigh bone of a sheep ; the horn, which is a common Highland cow's horn cut off at the smaller end; and lastly an oaten reed exactly cut and notched like that which you see every shepherd boy have when the corn stems are green.

[New friends, Willie Stewart, Factor of the Closeburn estate, and his daughter Polly.]

Willie Stewart is a man whose head is a credit and whose heart is an honour to the works of God. He is now my intimate friend.

> You're welcome, Willie Stewart,
>   You're welcome, Willie Stewart,
> There's ne'er a flower that blooms in May
> That's half sae welcome's thou art.

And O lovely, charming Polly ! I have seen the day—but that is a tale of other years.

Thanksgiving Services throughout the country for a national Victory [off Ushant, June 1st]. Hypocrites ! Murder men and give God thanks ? God won't accept your thanks for murder.

A truce with bloody armaments. Anger, resentment and envy eat up the immortal part of man.

> Dangers, eagle-pinioned, bold
> Soar around each cliffy hold,
> While cheerful Peace with linnet song
> Chants the lowly dells among.

June 21st. Dumfries.   *To David MacCullogh Esqre. of Ardwell.*

Syme will meet us about the dish-of-tea hour at Kiroughtree and let me remind you of your kind promise to accompany me there also. I will need all the friends I can muster, for I am indeed ill at ease whenever I approach your Honorables and Right Honorables.

Another letter from Miss Peacock. There is a fatality attends Miss Peacock's correspondence. Her last, which came while I was in Ayrshire, was unfortunately mislaid and only found about ten days ago on removing a chest of drawers.

June 25th. Dumfries. I have been in poor health. My medical friends threaten me with a flying gout. I trust they are mistaken.

Fame does not blow her trumpet at my approach now. Yet I am as proud as ever. When I am laid in my grave I wish to be stretched at my full length, that I may occupy every inch of the ground I have a right to.

Late June. Dumfries.   *To Mrs. MacLehose.*

Before you ask me why I have not written, first let me be informed *how* I shall write. In friendship, you say. I have many times taken up my pen to try. But it will not do. Recollection ruins me.

My friend Ainslie has indeed been kind to you. Tell him that I envy him the power of serving you.   R. B.

Late June. Dumfries. I had a letter from him [Robert Ainslie] a while ago, but it was so dry, so distant that I could scarce bear to read it and have not yet answered it. He *can* write a friendly letter as a whole sheaf of them that I have by me will witness. When he first honored me with his friendship. . . .

July. Dumfries.   *To Captn. John Hamilton.*

Sir—You are the only person in Dumfries, or in the world, to whom I have run in debt. I will settle with you soon. I assure you, Sir, it is with infinite pain that I have transgressed on your goodness. God forbid that anything should ever distress you as much as writing this has distressed me. Your very humble servant   Robt Burns.

I am so poorly this morning as to be scarce able to hold my pen and so deplorably stupid as to be totally unable to hold it to any purpose. A fine constitution is of immense consequence to happiness.

I Give up Farming

The other day Mrs. Burns presented me with my fourth son, whom I have christened James.

October 19th. Dumfries.   *To Mr. George Thomson.*

My Dear Friend—The lady on whom the songs ' CRAIGIEBURN WOOD ' and ' LASSIE WI' THE LINT-WHITE LOCKS ' were made [Jeanie Lorimer, aged 16, daughter of a farmer] is in the guileless simplicity of Platonic love, my mistress—or what you will.   Now don't put any of your squinting construction on this or have any clishmaclaiver about it among your acquaintances.   No, no !

Whenever I want to be more than ordinary in song, do you imagine that I fast and pray ?   *Tout au contraire,* I put myself on to a regimen of admiring a fine woman.

Some years ago perhaps, when I was by no means the saint I am now . . .   R. B.

> Lassie wi' the lint-white locks . . .
> The primrose bank, the simpling burn,
> The cuckoo on the milkwhite thorn,
> The wanton lambs at early morn
> Shall welcome thee my dearie O.

Oct. 29th. Dumfries.   We have had the Caledonian Hunt here for this bypast fortnight and of course we have had a roar of dissipation.

One of the Corps, the Honble. Mr. Ramsay Maule of Panmure, provoked my ire the other day, conceited gowk on his high phaeton ; I suppose the doting mother of a parcel of these rakehelly prodigals must continually put her hand in her pocket and pay whatever scores the young dogs think it proper to contract.   Profligacy and outrage *sometimes* accompany superiour understanding and brilliant wit, but most of our fashionable young men are without talent, fools.

> For all their colleges and schools,
> At operas and plays parading,
> Mortgaging, gambling, masquerading.

They not only deafen us with their equipage and dazzle us with their pomp, but they must also be dictatorial. But I hate an ungenerous sarcasm. Though I may be sometimes guilty myself, I cannot endure it in others.

TO THE EARL OF BREADALBANE

[Known to be having trouble with his Highland tenants]

Long life, my lord, and health be yours
Unskaithed by hunger's Highland boors !
They, and be damned, what right hae they . . .
Poor dunghill sons of dirt and mire,
To meat or sleep or light o' day
Far less to riches, power or freedom
But what your lordship likes to gie them ?

Late Oct. Dumfries.   *To Mr. Peter Hill.*
My Dear Hill—By carrier of yesterday I sent you a kippered salmon. If you have the confidence to say that there is anything of the kind in all your great city superior in true kipper relish and flavor, I will be revenged —by not sending you another next season. Ever yours   R. B.

Nov. 19th. Dumfries. This morning in my walk before breakfast, through a keen blowing frost, I finished my Duet 'O PHILLY, HAPPY BE THAT DAY'. Nelly and Sally, the only other names that will suit, have to my ear a vulgarity about them which unfits them for anything but burlesque.

I have been appointed to act as Supervisor. The appointment is only temporary but I look forward to an early period when I shall be appointed in full form. My political sins do seem to be forgiven.

Dec. 20th. Dumfries. What a transient business is life. Very lately I was a boy. But t'other day I was a young man. And I already begin to feel [at 35] the rigid fibre and stiffening joints of old age coming fast o'er my frame.

> . . . I'm grown sae cursed douce
> I pray and ponder butt the house,
> My shins my lane I there sit roastin'
> Perusing Bunyan. . . .

For I too shall tread the shadowy path to that dark unknown world. Fate is relentless and severe.

[There had been a reconciliation with Maria, but letters are now mostly about literature, rather formal.]

Jan. Dumfries.   *To Mrs. Walter Riddell.*
Mr. Burns' compliments to Mrs. Riddell—is much obliged to her for her polite attention in sending the book. When the other book which Mrs. R. mentioned comes to hand, Mr. B. will thank her for a reading of it, as it is a book he has never seen and he wishes to have a longer perusal of it than the regulations of the library allow.

Jan. 15th. Dumfries.   *To Mr. William Stewart, Factor.*
This is a painful, disagreeable letter. I am in serious distress for three or four guineas. Can you, my dear Sir, accommodate me ? These accursed times, by stopping up importation, have for this year at least, lopt off a full third part of my income—and with my large family, you would indeed truly oblige me.   R. B.

[*Jan. 16th. Closeburn Castle.* This day forwarded to Mr. Burns £3 3s. for which I hold no security in writing.   WILLIAM STEWART.]

Jan. 29th. Dumfries.   *To Capt. John Hamilton.*
SIR—I enclose three guineas and shall soon settle all with you. It is needless to attempt any apology for my remissness to you in money matters. My conduct is beyond all excuse. Literally, Sir, I have it not. I shall

not mention your goodness to me nor my feelings at not being able to pay you as I ought. Your deeply obliged humble serv^t Robt Burns.

> Th' unwary sailor thus aghast
> The wheeling torrent viewing
> 'Mid circling horrors sinks at last
> In overwhelming ruin.

1795

April 23rd. Dumfries. In these days of volunteering I have come forward with my services to the Royal Dumfries Volunteers.

[' War ', he had written, ' I deprecate—misery and ruin to thousands . . .'

Cunningham says: ' I remember well their appearance—their white ' breeches and waistcoat, short blue coat faced with red, and round hat ' surmounted with a bearskin like the helmets of the Horse Guards. And ' I remember Burns, his large dark eyes and his indifferent dexterity in the ' handling of arms.']

March 8th. Dumfries.   *To Patrick Miller, Junr.*

. . . When you return to the country, you will find us all *Sogers*. I have not a moment more than just to say—God bless you. R. B.

May 3rd. Dumfries.   *To Mr. George Thomson.*

How did you like my ' Sweet warbling woodlark on the trembling spray . . .'? Johnie Cope is an air would do it very well. Still, whether it be the association of ideas I cannot say, but there is a squalidity, an absence of elegance in that air that does not altogether suit the spirit and delicacy I have endeavoured to transpire into the song.

Feb. 7th. Ecclefechan. In the course of my duty as Supervisor I came yesternight to this unfortunate, wicked little village.

Snows of ten feet deep have impeded my progress. To add to my misfortune, since dinner a Scraper has been torturing cutgut in sounds that would have insulted the dying agonies of a sow under the hands of a butcher. I have been in a dilemma—either to get drunk to forget these miseries or to hang myself to forget these miseries. Like a prudent man I have chosen the least of two evils and I am *very* drunk. I am just going to bed.

March. Dumfries. I am sitting to Reid in this town for a miniature and I think he has hit off by far the best likeness of me ever was taken. Several people think that Allan's likeness of me is more striking than Nasmith's. I sat to Nasmith half a dozen times.

Later. In my opinion Reid has now spoilt the likeness.

Later in May. Dumfries. I am so ill as to be scarce able to hold this miserable pen to this miserable paper.

V

WHERE ARE THE JOYS . . .

Where are the joys I hae met in the morning
    That danced to the lark's early sang ?
Where is the peace that awaited my wand'ring
    At evening the wild-woods amang ?

June. Dumfries. Health is I think flown from me forever. I have not been able to leave my bed today till an hour ago.

Aug. Dumfries. I have been a grievous sinner against etiquette in not writing to Mrs. Riddell long ere now. But 'tis ten o'clock—too late to detain her poor fellow of a servant untill I hawk up an apology.

August. Dumfries.   *To Mr. Wm. Lorimer, Farmer.*
My Dear Sir—I want you to dine with me to-day. I have two honest Midlothian farmers with me. I promise you a pleasant party, a plateful of hotch-potch and a bottle of sound port. Mrs. Burns desires me to beg Jeanie [the lassie wi' the lint-white locks] to come too. Dinner at three. If you can both come I shall take it very kind. Yours   R. B.

[This month an old acquaintance, a Mr. Pattison of Kelvin Grove, passed through Dumfries with his son John and a groom.
   'At dinner,' says John, 'I sat opposite him. I can never forget the 'animation and glorious intelligence of his countenance, the deep, rich 'tones of his musical voice and those matchless eyes which absolutely 'seemed to flash fire and stream forth rays of light.']

[Not very long after this Josiah Walker came to Dumfries. 'I called
' on him early in the forenoon and found him in a small house sitting on a
' window seat reading, but with the doors open and the family arrangements
' going on in his presence and altogether without that snugness which a
' student requires.']

Jessy [the sister of John Lewars, a brother Exciseman] is the one seraph
left on earth.   Lovely Jessy !

1795–6

   O wert thou in the cauld blast,
    On yonder lea, on yonder lea,
   My plaidie to the angry airt
    I'd shelter thee, I'd shelter thee.

   O were I in the blackest waste,
    Sae black and bare, sae black and bare,
   The desert were a paradise
    If thou wert there, if thou wert there . . .

[Sometimes Jessy, at present helping Jean in the house, must be teased
about her matrimonial prospects. . . .] ' Now there's Bob Spalding.'
[Jessy herself reports the conversation.] ' But he hasn't as much brains as
a midge could lean its elbow on.   He won't do.   I foretell that James
Thomson will be the man.'   [' He was,' says Jessy.]
 And Jessy remembers well that ' his (Burns's) habits were generally
' simple and temperate.   If he chanced to come home and find dinner not
' ready, he was never in the least irritated.   There was usually abundance
' of good cheese sent by Ayr-shire friends.   He would sit down to bread
' and cheese with his book by his side and seem as happy as at a feast of
' kings.   He was always anxious that his wife should be well and neatly
' dressed and did his utmost to counteract any tendency to carelessness, not
' only by remonstrance but by buying for her the best clothes he could
' afford.']

1796

Jan. 31st. Dumfries.   *To Mrs. Dunlop.*
Alas, Madam, you have not written lately and ill can I afford to be
deprived of any small remnant of my pleasure. The autumn robbed me
of my only daughter and darling child. I had scarcely begun to recover
from that shock when I became the victim of a most severe rheumatic fever
and long the die spun doubtful. I am now beginning to crawl across my
room and once indeed have been before my door in the street.

I know not how things are in Ayr-shire, but here we have actual famine
and that too in the midst of plenty. Many days my family and hundreds of
other families are absolutely without one grain of meal, as money cannot
purchase it. How long the Swinish Multitude will be quiet, I cannot tell.
May all good things attend you.   R. B.

April. Dumfries. I have been counting time by the repercussions of
pain. Rheumatism, cold and fever have formed a terrible Trinity in Unity
which makes me close my eyes in misery and open them without hope.

May. Dumfries. I have now reason to believe that my complaint is a
flying gout, a damnable business. I am still very poorly (but not too
poorly to write this, playfully, of Jessy Lewars).

> Talk not to me of savages
> From Afric's burning plain
> No savage e'er could rend my heart
> As Jessy, thou hast done.

June 1st. Dumfries. This slow consuming illness will, I doubt, arrest
my sun before he has reached his middle career. I endeavour to cherish
hope as well as I can.

> In vain to me the cowslips blaw
> In vain to me the violets spring
> In vain to me in glen or shaw
> The mavis and the lintwhite sing.

251

Early June.   Dumfries.   *To Maria Mrs. Riddell.*

[On receipt of an invitation to attend the Birthday Assembly ' to show your loyalty '.]

I am in such miserable health as to be utterly incapable of ' shewing ' my loyalty' in any way.   Rackt with rheumatisms I only say Curse that east wind.   Write a love song ?   No !   If I must write, let it be sedition or blasphemy.   R. B.

> When disappointment snaps the clue of hope
> And thro' disastrous night they darkling grope
> With deaf endurance sluggishly. . . .

June 26th.   Dumfries.   *To James Clarke, Schoolmaster.*

My Dear Clarke—Were you to see the emaciated figure who now holds the pen to you, you would not know your old friend.   Whether I shall ever get about again is only known to the Great Unknown, whose creature I am.   Alas, I begin to fear the worst.   But enough of this. Adieu dear Clarke.   That I shall ever see you again is, I am afraid, highly improbable.   R. Burns.

July 4th.   Brow.   My health being so precarious, I am here, as a last effort, sea-bathing [by doctor's orders].   Besides my rheumatism, my appetite is quite gone.   I am so emaciated as to be scarce able to support

myself on my own legs. Alas, is this a time to woo the Muses ? I am still anxiously willing and will if possible try.

> But lately seen in gladsome green
>   The woods rejoiced the day,
> Thro' gentle showers the laughing flowers
>   In double pride were gay.
> But now our joys are fled
>   On winter blasts awa'
> Yet maiden May in rich array
>   Again shall bring them a'.

> But now . . . the weary days
>   And nights o' sleepless pain—
> Thou golden time o' youthful prime
>   Why comes thou not again ?

July 7th. Brow.   *To Mr. Alexr Cunningham.*

Mr Dear Cunningham—In these eight or ten months I have been ailing, sometimes bedfast and sometimes not. But these last three months I have been tortured with an excruciating rheumatism which has reduced me to nearly the last stage. You actually would not know me—pale, and so feeble as occasionally to need help out of my chair. My spirits are fled, fled.

The deuce of the matter is this—when an Exciseman is off duty, his salary is reduced to £35 instead of £50. What way, in the name of thrift, shall I maintain myself with a wife and four children on £35 ? I beg your utmost interest to move our Commissioners to grant me the full salary.

Mrs. Burns threatens in a week or two to add one more, a fifth, to my paternal charge. Farewel.   R. B.

[An invitation to dinner from Maria, Mrs. Riddell, now on a visit not far from Brow ; and with the invitation her carriage. ' I was struck with ' his appearance on entering the room,' she says in a letter to a friend. ' He seemed already touching the brink of eternity. His first salutation

' was, " Well, Madam, have you any commands for the other world ? "
' At table he ate little or nothing. His anxiety for his family seemed to
' hang heavy upon him. He showed great concern about the care of his
' literary fame and particularly about the publication of posthumous works.
' He lamented that he had written epigrams on persons whose characters he
' should be sorry to wound. He deeply regretted having deferred arranging
' his papers, as he was now incapable of exertion. The conversation was
' kept up with great evenness and animation on his side. I seldom saw his
' mind greater or more collected. We parted at sunset. The next day I
' saw him again and we parted—to meet no more.')

> Thus wasted are the ranks of men
> Youth, health and beauty fall
> The ruthless ruin spreads around
> And overwhelms us all.

Time cannot aid me. My griefs are wounds which Time can never cure. Sleep I can get none.

July 10th. Brow. I have now been a week at salt water and though I think I have got some good of it, I have secret fears that this sea-bathing [as a remedy for rheumatic fever] is dangerous.

> Me, nae cheerful twinkle lights me
> Dark despair around benights me.

July 10th. Brow.   *To Gilbert.*

Dear Brother—It will be no very pleasing news for you that I am ill and not likely to get better. An inveterate rheumatism has reduced me to such a state of debility that I can scarcely stand. My appetite is tottally gone. I have been here a week at sea-bathing. God help my wife and children. They will be poor indeed. I have contracted one or two serious debts, partly from my illness these many months and partly from thought-lessness as to expenses in Dumfries. These debts will cut in on the little I leave them. Remember me to my mother. Yours   R. B.

> To heaven's gate the lark's shrill song ascends,
> But grovelling on the earth the carol ends.

June 12th. Brow.   *To Mr. James Burness, W. S. Montrose.*

My Dearest Cousin—When you offered me money-assistance, little did I think I should want it so soon. A haberdasher [of the firm of Brown & Williamson, Clothiers, Dumfries] to whom I owe a considerable bill [£7. 9. 0 for Volunteer Uniform] taking it into his head that I am dying has commenced a process [—it was only a solicitor's letter really, but still a menace] against me. They will infallibly put my emaciated body into Jail. Will you be so good as to accommodate me—and that by return of post—with ten pound ? O James, did you know the pride of my heart you would doubly feel for me. Alas, I am not used to beg. My physician assures me that melancholy and low spirits are half my disease. Guess then my horrors since this business began. If I had it settled I would be I think quite well in a manner. Do not disappoint me. Save me from the horrors of a Jail.   R. B.

Forgive me for once more mentioning *by return of post*

> Gentle night, do thou befriend me
> Downy sleep, the curtains draw
> Spirits kind, again attend me. . . .

July 12th. Brow.   *To Mr. George Thomson.*

After all my boasted independance, curst necessity compels me to implore you for five pounds. A cruel scoundrel of a haberdasher to whom I owe an account, taking it into his head that I am dying, has commenced a process and will infallibly put me in Jail. Do for God's sake send me that sum and *by return of post*. Forgive me this earnestness, but the horrors of a Jail have made me half distracted. Forgive me.   R. Burns.

> Sleep whence thou shalt ne'er awake
> Night where dawn shall never break. . . .

July 14th. Brow.   *To Jean.*

My Dearest Love—I delayed writing until I could tell you what effect sea-bathing was likely to produce. It has eased my pains and I think has strengthened me. But my appetite is still extremely bad. Porridge and milk are the only things I can taste. I am very happy to hear from

Jessy Lewars that you are all well. My very best and kindest compliments to her and to all the children. I will see you on Sunday. Your affectionate husband   R. B.

> When that grim foe of life below
> Comes in between to make us part,
> It breaks my bliss, it breaks my heart. . . .

July 16th. Brow.   *To John Clark Esq. of Locherwoods.*
My Dear Sir—I anxiously wish to return to town, as I have not heard any news of Mrs. Burns these two days. Dare I be so bold as to borrow your gig? Any time about three in the afternoon will suit me exactly. Yours most gratefully and sincerely   R. Burns.

> Now a' is done that men can do
> And a' is done in vain.
>
> Every hope is fled
> Every fear is terror
> Slumber ev'n I dread
> Every dream is horror.

July 18th. Dumfries.   *To Mr. James Armour, Builder, Mauchline.*
My Dear Sir—Do for heaven's sake send Mrs. Armour here immediately. Jean is hourly expecting to be put to bed, poor girl.
I returned from sea-bathing to-day and my medical friends would almost persuade me that I am better. But I think and feel that my strength is so gone that the disorder will prove fatal to me. Your son-in-law. R. B.

> Life is but a day at most
> Sprung from night—in darkness lost. . . .

[On the 21st the four boys were brought to see their father for the last time. They stood round the bed until there was no more breathing. Five days later Jean gave birth to yet another son. It was the day of the funeral.

The funeral is described by Dr. Currie who was present.

'The Gentlemen Volunteers of Dumfries determined to bury their
'illustrious associate with military honours and every preparation was made
'to render this last service solemn and impressive. The Fencible Infantry of
'Angusshire and a regiment of Cavalry at that time quartered in Dumfries
'offered their assistance. The principal inhabitants of the town and neigh-
'bourhood determined to walk in the funeral procession. A vast con-

' course of persons assembled, some of them from a considerable distance.
' On the evening of the 25th the remains of Burns were removed from his
' house in Mill Vennel to the Town Hall. The funeral took place the next
' day. A party of the Volunteers selected for duty in the churchyard were
' in front of the procession with arms reversed. The main body of the
' Corps surrounded and supported the coffin on which were placed the
' hat and sword of their friend. The numerous body of attendants came
' in the rear. The Fencible regiments and the Cavalry lined the streets
' from the Town Hall to the burial ground, a distance of more than half a
' mile. And the procession moved forward to the Dead March in Saul.']

<blockquote>
Now Robin lies in his last lair,
He'll gabble rhyme nor sing nae mair.
Cauld Poverty wi' hungry stare
   Nae mair shall fear him
Nor anxious Fear nor cankert Care
   E'er mair come near him.
</blockquote>

Printed in Great Britain by
Butler & Tanner Ltd.,
Frome and London